RED PRINCESS

RED PRINCESS

A REVOLUTIONARY LIFE

Sofka Zinovieff

PEGASUS BOOKS
NEW YORK

RED PRINCESS

Pegasus Books LLC
45 Wall Street, Suite 1021
New York, NY 10005

First Pegasus Books edition 2008

Library of Congress Cataloging-in-Publication Data is available.

ISBN: 978-1-60598-009-6

10 9 8 7 6 5 4 3 2 1

Printed in the United States of America
Distributed by W. W. Norton & Company, Inc.

To my mother and father
Victoria and Peter

CONTENTS

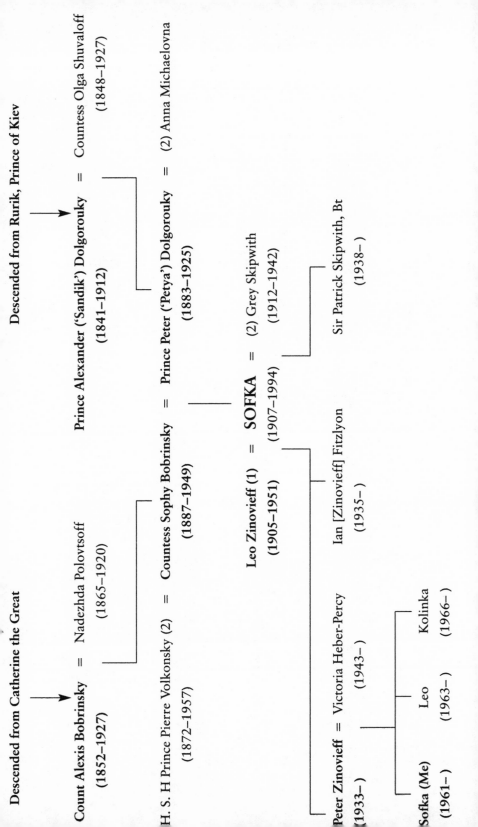

Descended from Catherine the Great

Descended from Rurik, Prince of Kiev

Count Alexis Bobrinsky = Nadezhda Polovtsoff
(1852–1927)   (1865–1920)

Prince Alexander ('Sandik') Dolgorouky = Countess Olga Shuvaloff
(1841–1912)   (1848–1927)

H. S. H Prince Pierre Volkonsky (2) = Countess Sophy Bobrinsky = Prince Peter ('Petya') Dolgorouky = (2) Anna Michaelovna
(1872–1957)   (1887–1949)   (1883–1925)

Leo Zinovieff (1) = SOFKA = (2) Grey Skipwith
(1905–1951)   (1907–1994)   (1912–1942)

Ian [Zinovieff] Fitzlyon   Sir Patrick Skipwith, Bt
(1935–)   (1938–)

Peter Zinovieff = Victoria Heber-Percy
(1933–)   (1943–)

Sofka (Me)   Leo   Kolinka
(1961–)   (1963–)   (1966–)

'Oh Granny dear when you were young
Did many men kiss you?'
I paid my debts with all my songs
But claimed rings as my due.

No night of mine was spent in vain
In paradise I stayed . . .
'But Granny how will you appear
'Fore God on Judgement Day?'

The birds in trees are twittering
And look, the spring is green.
I'll say: 'Dear Lord, a sinner, but
A merry one I've been.'

And you who bone are of my bone
When dead and gone I be,
A handful keep of my grave mould
And both take after me.

From *Grandmother* by Marina Tsvetaeva, 1919
Translated by Sofka Skipwith, 1941

RED PRINCESS

CHAPTER 1

THE DIARY

Beauty is mysterious as well as terrible.
God and devil are fighting there,
and the battlefield is the heart of man.
— Fyodor Dostoevsky

My grandmother Sofka didn't tell me why she gave me her diary. She just handed over a surprisingly heavy book, covered in dark, curlicued brass and soft, moss-green velvet. She explained that it had been made for my great-great-great grandmother. I was sixteen at the time and pleased with my present, but I didn't really care about the content. It just looked old. I flicked through it, then put it away in a drawer.

It was only recently that I decided to read the diary properly, on a gloomy January day. Ten years had passed since Sofka's death and Jack, her partner for the last three decades of her life, was dying in an old people's home. Their isolated stone cottage in Cornwall was already on the market and my father and his brother were arguing doggedly about what should happen to their mother's remaining papers. It seemed as though the threads connecting me to my grandmother were breaking and I hoped that reading the diary would bring something of her back to me.

The book looks both fragile and strong. Despite the sturdy metal frame, the spine is shredding away to reveal the secret craft of the Russian bookbinder who sewed and glued it some 150 years ago. On the edge, a cherub-faced clasp opens on to watered-silk endpapers and thick, creamy, gold-edged pages that are filled with a rapid, curvaceous script in blue ink. Here and there, brittle, yellowing newspaper clippings and letters slip, leaving ghostly imprints of where they have lain for years. These pages were designed to contain the feminine musings of a privileged St Petersburg lady: drives in a carriage along Nevsky Prospekt; love secrets; intrigues at society teas and palace balls; mushroom-picking in birch woods; family scandals; journeys to foreign spas; and maybe even the occasional duel. This was the sort of life that Sofka was born into in 1907, as Princess Sophy Dolgorouky. But by the time she used the book as a diary in 1940, both she and her circumstances had changed dramatically: she was Mrs Sofka Skipwith, a British citizen, and the world was at war.

Sofka began writing in the diary in Paris. Perhaps she sensed that 1940 would be a turning point in her life; it's the kind of book you'd wait to use at the right time, for the right purpose. She was thirty-two. Photographs show a lovely, expressive face set on a strong, sculpted neck. High Slavic cheekbones, a finely chiselled nose, and a slightly pouting upper lip which can't help appearing flirtatious. Her long black hair has a neat centre parting, and is pulled into a sleek bun or coiled into 'earphones'. Large, dark eyes look out boldly, as if challenging someone: 'I am not afraid!' But there is also a feminine softness tinged with sadness in her beauty. Sometimes, her eyes seem to say, 'I have been afraid.'

Sofka was in France visiting her mother. It was utterly characteristic that she should have overcome the practical difficulties of being a lone female civilian travelling abroad during wartime; a friend in the Foreign Office helped with the paperwork and she managed to cross the English Channel on a British troopship. It was still the 'phoney war' and nobody knew what was going to happen. Sofka hoped to slip across (and then back again), to take some money to help her mother and stepfather. Like many of the older White Russian refugees, they were finding it hard to establish a new life, and their Parisian exile was grimly restricted and filled with regrets. They had come to rely on Sofka for financial support, and although she was far from flush with funds, she'd learned to get by. Sofka had intended to take what money she had in England and then stay in Paris for a couple of months – long enough to find a temporary job, translating or as a secretary – and pay off six months' advance rent for her mother's apartment.

I already knew the story from Sofka's 1968 autobiography. Her adored second husband, Grey Skipwith, had recently joined the RAF. They had only been married for three years, and their eighteen-month-old son, Patrick, was staying temporarily in England with 'the milkman's mother-in-law'. Sofka's two older sons, Peter (my father) and Ian, from her first marriage to Leo Zinovieff, were living in London with their paternal grandparents.

I also knew what was to come: how Sofka's existence would be violently dislocated by world events for the second time in her life; how she wouldn't see her children for another four years; and how this war would bring her tragedy and leave her changed in ways she couldn't imagine. She always spoke about the war as being the greatest catalyst in her life: it seared her soul, she confessed. But reading this diary, it was different. I could watch events unfold as they happened, before she could analyse them or apply the irony which came later, with the benefit of hindsight. As an old woman, she could be cynical and self-mocking and her own writing tends towards a wry detachment. Here, on the other hand, I was meeting her as an emotional, contradictory, troubled young woman, whose responses were immediate. She wasn't my grandmother then. Nothing was inevitable about how her life would work out.

The diary begins about a month after her arrival in Paris. The Nazis had already invaded France and the French Army had scattered in a quick, humiliating retreat. Many people panicked and some (including her fellow émigré, Vladimir Nabokov) managed to leave. Sofka imagined that her planned return to England would probably be delayed, but at first she sounds quite chirpy.

21 May

Evacuation of Paris continues – banks, businesses etc all moving although the Germans have apparently announced that Paris is not to be bombed . . .

Today newspapers are one sheet only on account of paper shortage. All music has ceased on all French wireless transmissions . . . dancing is forbidden.

There is hardly anyone in the streets of the residential quarters and one has the impression of a new Pompeii, undamaged but uninhabited.

3 June

Today Paris was bombed for the first time . . . Alarm ignored . . . within a few minutes, however, the shooting became frantic, the roar of engines deafening and we began to hear the whistle of falling bombs and violent explosions. The air was making the windows rattle, and we decided to go down into the cellar.

10 June

The town to-day is empty and void. There is not a taxi to be found anywhere – either they are all mobilized or busy evacuating. Streams of cars with mattresses on the roofs pelting out of Paris . . . and the whole town loading its bedding onto cars and handcarts . . .

Children, dropping to sleep on the pavements where their families with bundles are gathered on street corners waiting for tram or car. Intermittent and fierce firing and drone of aeroplanes – and blazing hot sun.

11 June

The British Consulate, whom I phoned this morning, says that there are no orders about evacuation and that British Subjects will be informed through the medium of the press. Presume we will be told how and when to get out if we so wish. Everyone says they'll probably heave us all out on lorries when it's necessary and that any individual attempt at leaving is sheer madness . . .

Montparnasse – people of all ages sitting on streets, backs against walls of houses, filling doorways. Round the station itself they are about 10–15 rows thick, all with their bundles and suitcases. A soldier was handing out wafers from a huge basket. The station is closed with iron gates and police cordons to keep the crowd from storming them. People fainting, people ill, children screaming, women sobbing, girls giggling, others reading, sleeping, eating, just staring. People, people, people . . . the stench defies description . . .

Here again there is no one to tell them where to go, how long they will have to wait, to see about any food for them. Nothing. The Red Cross left yesterday.

Wednesday 12 June

... The evacuation in a state of fever, rushing from one station to another, making off on foot ... The road of evacuation is now called *La Route du Sang*. The cars and lorries rush headlong not caring who or what is in their way – handcarts, bicycles, prams – all are upset into the ditch or run over and the bodies left to be run over by the cars that follow. Bodies lie on the side of the road ... There is no food to be found and a glass of water costs ten francs. Panic is terrible ...

Apparently a terrifying quantity of children has perished during the evacuations. Corpses mingle with rifles, equipment, machine guns etc ...

When at 1 o clock, I opened the window and shutters, the silence was deeper than any in the country. There was no street lighting at all in Paris tonight, not a footfall could be heard, not a car was moving. Absolute silence and darkness ...

Thursday 13 June

At about 4.30 a heavy, pitch black 'thunder-cloud' covered the sky from the north, growing more and more ominous. Shortly after, it began to rain soot. One felt it falling on hands and face like rain drops – all became covered – pavements, skin, clothes ... it is the oil supplies all round Paris being burned. The fire was terrific – a huge column of smoke some 300 yards wide going up into the sky ... the base of the column torn by great flashes of flame. As it grew dark the red glow illuminated the whole sky.

Friday 14 June

Hitler promised to be in Paris on the 15th. This morning at
7.30 the German officers were on the Concorde. At about
10 I went out to buy potatoes and heard it from the
épicière . . .

The German soldiers are young and strong and stern.
Dirty but not despondent or worn out as our men. Some
people smiled at them (they were throwing kisses) but most
of the people stood watching them, silent and unsmiling.
Here and there a woman was in tears . . .

In the Champs Elysées they are already walking up and
down as though the place belonged to them, sitting in the
two or three open cafes, picking up girls . . . The red flag
with a swastika is on the Eiffel Tower, on the Arc de
Triomphe, on the admiralty and the Crillon.

Yesterday's 'black rain' has left its mark on the town.
Every flat space is covered with a thin layer of 'soot', like
black snow in which footmarks are seen.

As Nazi rule strengthened, Sofka became increasingly panic-
stricken by the realization that she might be trapped. Her
pessimism was undoubtedly exacerbated by reading Kafka's *The
Trial*, with its forebodings of a dark world where innocent
people can be arrested and swallowed by dehumanizing
bureaucracy. A rash of blisters erupted on her chin – a nervous
reaction she dubbed 'leprosy', which later recurred in other
times of crisis. At this point, Sofka's writing becomes more
personal and revealing; the bewilderment and suffering of her
daily life are channelled into what becomes a series of letters,
addressed to Grey, or Puppa as she calls him.

At first sight, Grey was not an obvious choice for the great
love of her life. A slim, delicately built man, four years her

junior, his springy hair was neatly oiled and parted, and a small moustache over his full lips added dash to a sensitive, boyish face.

The eldest son of a baronet, Grey's background was solidly establishment: Harrow, Cambridge and hopes of entering the Foreign Office. Few could have predicted that he would fall in love with an older, married Russian émigrée and then plunge even deeper into scandal by acting as co-respondent in her divorce and marrying her.

Sofka was staying with her mother and stepfather in their apartment at 2 Boulevard de la République – a tired old building in a street running down to the river near Porte de St Cloud. Many of the thousands of Russians who flooded into Paris after the 1917 Revolution lived dreary, demeaned lives in these peripheral districts. Sofka's mother, Princess Sophy Volkonsky, had been among the exceptional Russian women of her generation – a surgeon and one of the first female pilots. In France, she was reduced to working as a night taxi driver, and at piecemeal secretarial jobs. Her once brilliant, polyglot diplomat husband, Prince Pierre Volkonsky, had become a gloomy, diminished figure, whose genealogical expertise and old-fashioned finesse were now practically redundant. In the 1920s and '30s, it seemed that every other waiter surviving on tips had some glorious past in imperial Russia. A joke did the rounds at the time:

Two men sit in a Parisian restaurant.

'You see that waiter over there? He was a count in St Petersburg. And you know the chef in the kitchens? He was a Grand Duke back in Russia.'

'Well,' replies the other, 'you see that little poodle sitting by the door? In Russia he used to be a Great Dane.'

Sofka never explained why she gave me her old Russian diary.
Later, after her death, I finally read it and was pulled into her life
in ways I couldn't have imagined.

There were many White Russians in Paris who were not displeased to see the Germans, hoping they might provide a route to finishing off the Bolsheviks' twenty-three-year reign. Others were simply content to find work with the occupiers. When Sofka's stepfather got a job as an interpreter in a German office, she realized that staying on in their apartment would compromise him as harbouring an 'enemy alien'. Glad to move away from her coldly severe mother and dithering stepfather, she moved up to a room on the seventh floor of the same building – a dirty attic looking out over the dark roof slates. Days were spent disinfecting, delousing and decorating, and Russian friends helped her paint the walls 'bright yellow and Nile green'. They'd stop for *café national*, the horrible mix of acorns and chickpeas which had replaced real coffee in France. Out on the landing was a Turkish-type lavatory, a cold tap and 'landlord's lights', which turned off after thirty seconds. It sounded quite like George Orwell's *Down and Out in Paris and London*; the squalid yet prosaic and deeply boring nature of poverty. Orwell's rooms, too, had walls 'covered with layer after layer of pink paper which had come loose and housed innumerable bugs. Near the ceiling long lines of bugs marched all day like columns of soldiers, and at night came down ravenously hungry.'

9 August

Englishmen are being interned but women so far go free . . .

Horror stories abound. The plight of many Russians is becoming desperate – 'soupe populaire' [soup kitchens] and German left-overs.

23 August

English women have to go daily to the Commissariat to sign a book. Tiresome but inevitable. The war goes on and England is still un-invaded . . .

A series of Jewish shops on the Champs Elysées have had their windows broken . . .

9 September

It is impossible to try and keep an objective and impersonal chronicle when every second of the day and night is brimful of personal feeling.

Puppa, my love, if you only could guess how lonely and miserable I am. Suddenly in the midst of anything I think of you or them [the children], and tears begin to pour. Morning and evening I always speak to you darling – and I know that during the last 3 nights or so we've been together. I saw you very vividly last night . . . You came in dressed in a sort of leather short jacket and greyish trousers and tousled hair. You were very thin and sunburnt and grown up and you rushed in . . .

Good night my dearest love – all my thoughts are yours and yours only. Please to meet soon.

Friday 13 September

To-day is our day, Littlest. I wonder where you are and have you realized it?

Sunday 22 September

My own, my little one . . .

God, if only I could get some news. But love, I do so believe that all will be well and that we'll be together again. You're so close to me all the time, my dearest.

13 October

Oh, my Littles, things are no better . . . Downstairs [with her parents] tears my nerves to shreds . . .

Moppy [her name for her mother] seems to dislike the very sight of me. U.P. [her stepfather] is weak and dithery.

16 October

There's a new decree that anyone harbouring a British Subject must declare his presence by the 20th, or else be shot.

. . . Please, I love you so much and am in such agony of pain for you and Baba [Patrick, their son].

Wednesday 30 October

Darlingest, am in the 7th heaven since Monday, cos then I sent off a letter to my Puppadog. 25 words via Red Cross and hopes of an answer. Darling, do you understand!!! So am leaping about the world like a goat gone mad.

> Tuesday 19 November

... Have learned that for the sum of 15,000 [francs] can get across to you – will hope for some miracle – please, Little God!

> 26 November

A red-letter day, my precious – news from you through the Geneva Red Cross – letter here as historical document. It's from 20th September, but of you, darling, of you. Rushed into the street and howled for joy.

The telegram, in French, is still inside a pale blue Red Cross envelope, stamped with a swastika on the back. It is hardly a love letter: THE INTERNATIONAL COMMITTEE OF THE RED CROSS HAS RECEIVED A TELEGRAPHIC COMMUNICATION CONCERNING YOU, FROM GREY SKIPWITH AND SONS, WHO SEND YOU THEIR AFFECTIONATE MESSAGES. WE HOPE THIS COMMUNICATION FINDS YOU AT YOUR OLD ADDRESS AND THAT YOU ARE IN EXCELLENT HEALTH.

> 1 December

For the last 2 days have stayed in bed with a horrible chill and cough, not reporting to police or anything, so I'll probably catch it when I do go ...

... There can't be another parent like mine in the world: I've just realised that she's never yet been up to this room and although I've been laid up only U.P. has come to enquire. Wonder why she dislikes me and whether my inordinate feeling for Pips [Peter] and Crust [Patrick] isn't a subconscious reaction.

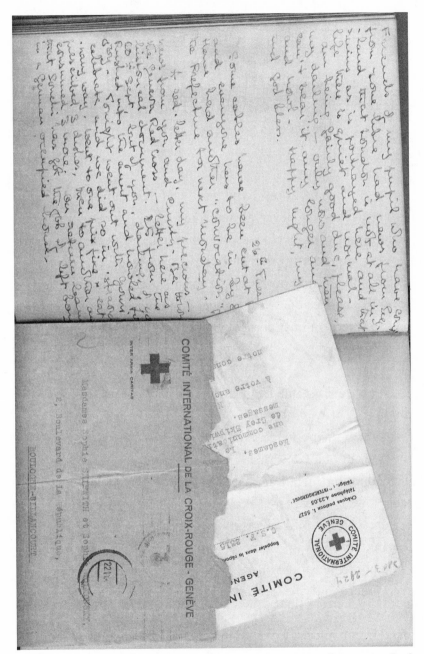

The 1940 Red Cross telegram was the first news Sofka received of Grey for months – it was almost as good as a love letter and she was ecstatic.

By the time my father sent me an email with a macabre photograph of Jack on his deathbed – skeletal, skin like yellow parchment, lying open-mouthed and only just alive – I had already decided to write about Sofka. I'd often thought about it before, but now I was convinced. The diary had pulled me into her life and I wanted to go deeper: to see the places where she had lived, to meet people who knew her, but also to identify her legacies – the patterns, details and characteristics that filter down through the generations, whether by DNA, example or even by absence. She was never a family matriarch, but her influence went deep with her sons and grandchildren. Her incessant moving around until she was middle-aged and her struggles to feel at home were now far easier for me to understand. It didn't seem like chance that with refugee grandparents, I should often have felt like an outsider growing up in England, or that I had ended up leaving the country of my birth and making my life elsewhere.

I flew to England from my home in Greece and travelled down to Cornwall for Jack's funeral. On the way, I went for a last look at their cottage. Someone once said that Sofka lived 'at the bottom of a God-forsaken lane on Bodmin Moor', and she liked quoting that. But that day, it looked enticing; the high mossy walls edging the road were primrose-strewn and the granite cottage looked pretty beside the fast-running brook. Peering through the windows to the empty sitting room, I remembered evenings there by the fire. There had been books everywhere and cheap 1950s armchairs and sofas covered in rugs and sleeping dogs.

I'd begun my visits to Moppy (we used the same nickname for Sofka that she'd had for her mother) when I was old enough to take the train from London to Bodmin, aged about ten. At that time, Sofka was approaching seventy. She had put on weight, and would sit, huge, comfortable, overflowing, in her chair. Her eyes were hawkish and questioning, and her features still strong and attractive. She wore her hair in a loose, haphazard bun, though occasionally, early in the morning, I'd see it hanging down her back, shockingly long and grey, like a witch's. She dressed with an exceptional lack of consideration for anything beyond practicality; thinking about clothes was a waste of time that could be spent reading, writing or talking.

On one trip, when I was eleven, Sofka asked me about my parents' recent separation. I remember her initial look of bafflement as I burst into huge, heaving sobs; wailing children were not her speciality. It was the first time I had spoken to someone about my shattered world since my mother moved out, and I was shocked too. However, as hot tears gave way to conversation and eventually laughter, I realized for the first time that Sofka had lined up as my ally. She knew all about broken families; they ran like a fault-line through the generations. She was proof that you survive.

Sofka's manner was a characteristic mix of knowing and curious, opinionated and open-minded, with a good dose of devil-may-care. Having seen so much and suffered so badly in her life, it was now time to be quiet, but her appreciation of independent thought and dark humour was revealed in the many commonplace books she filled with extracts from a lifetime's favourite quotes and aphorisms. These were regularly copied into small notebooks and handed out as presents to favoured friends and relations. (All the epigraphs in this book are from her collections.) She gave advice readily; anything from reading-lists (long, varied, inspiring) and recipes (informal, Russian, delicious) to drugs ('Never touch them; I've seen what they can do') and adolescent love ('It doesn't matter how many lovers you have . . . Just don't have more than one at the same time'). She was haughtily dismissive about death ('I don't care what happens to me when I die; you can bury me in a cardboard box') and she still enjoyed surprising people. She recommended sitting down on the pavement in crowded streets for its persuasive powers on boyfriends who don't agree on something. 'I always found it an efficient method of getting my own way,' she said wickedly.

As the years passed and I grew older, I'd be offered Jack's smelly but potent elderflower or gorse wine, and maybe a stale Gitanes, long left over from some London party or previous visitor. We'd eat Russian food on trays. And then, if Sofka didn't get out her photograph albums, I'd ask her to. It was part of the ritual of going to stay. 'Here's Grandfather Dolgorouky,' she would say, pointing to a dauntingly severe, bearded man in a long brocade robe. Her deep, imperious voice was half-mocking, half-proud, swooping up to an unexpected soprano squeak and back down to a vibrato growl. Her speech betrayed her formative experiences: the richly rolled Rs of a Russian, the slightly nasal tones of the English upper class, and the perfect French interpolations of her generation of European exiles.

'And here I am when I used to play with the Tsarevich,' Sofka would say, grimacing at how ridiculous it all was, yet pleased at the name-dropping. A pretty, mischievous-looking child in white muslin, with long, dark plaits and large, shrewd, almond eyes gazed out. We'd pass through the Revolution, the escape to England, the marriages, working for Laurence Olivier and the Old Vic, the war, the Communist Party, right up to Jack and their gaggle of whippets out on the moor. A dash across the twentieth century and a life like a seismograph of its great events and political movements.

Jack's funeral was at Bodmin Crematorium, where we'd all gathered for Sofka's ten years previously. The humanist (brought in to respect Communist sensibilities) was friendly and sensible, but made me nostalgic for a little 'opium of the people', which can soothe these desolate moments so skilfully. Afterwards, in the car park, my Uncle Ian handed me two large cardboard boxes – there had finally been an agreement that I could take Sofka's papers. But before I took my treasure back to Athens I contacted various people who had known Sofka. First call in London was my Great-uncle Kyril. Aged ninety-four, he is the younger brother of my Zinovieff grandfather, who died before I was born, and is friend, confidant and substitute grandfather to me all at once. Uncle Kyril is one of the few Russian émigrés still around who remember Russia before the Revolution ('From Rasputin to Putin,' as he quips), and who knew Sofka when she was young.

Tall, thin and still handsome, with a long face and aquiline nose, Uncle Kyril is always well dressed, favouring a jacket and tie even at home. With his many languages, daunting intellect and phenomenal memory, there are enough clues to suggest that he worked in intelligence for his adopted country. But he won't talk about that, merely saying that he joined the Ministry of Defence after the war. Until recently, he resolutely ignored his advanced age, but his blue eyes have gradually lost their sight, and by the time I went to see him, he was only distinguishing between dark and light. I wanted to ask his advice on writing about Sofka, even though I knew that he didn't have the best of opinions about his former sister-in-law. I was not prepared, however, for what emerged.

'I liked her very much when I first met her,' he began cautiously, trying to be fair. 'We recited poetry to each other. I thought she had an original mind. But she should never have married my brother. She and Leo were completely unsuited.'

'Sofka liked to *épater les bourgeois*,' he continued. 'She enjoyed shocking people. And she was *very* promiscuous. When

I say promiscuous, I mean the sleeping-with-the-window-cleaner-and-postman-sort-of-promiscuous.' I laughed, but Kyril persisted, using words like 'needs' and 'nymphomania' with an ominous air.

'Kinsey said the only definition of a nymphomaniac is someone who has more sex than you do,' I retorted, trying to find some defence for Sofka, and Uncle Kyril laughed too.

'Her mother also had many lovers,' said Uncle Kyril. 'And don't forget, her family, the Bobrinskys, have a direct line right back to Catherine the Great. It was in the blood.' I felt the uncomfortable implication of this biological determinism lurking, but I didn't say anything.

'I suppose I must have been very influenced by the aura surrounding your grandmother,' Uncle Kyril admitted. 'It was a very unfavourable one, I must say.' I could sense Kyril's generous nature losing the battle. He is one of the wittiest conversationalists I know, but that day he seemed tense. A seventy-year-old resentment against the person who made his brother unhappy and who broke ranks with her fellow Russians could not be suppressed. I had never seen him quite like this.

'I was speaking with some Russians the other day,' he went on. 'And Sofka's name cropped up. "Filth!" That's what they said about her. You must understand what all the Russian refugees felt about Sofka's Communism. She was at best extremely naïve to believe in Communism during the Stalinist period, or to think that there is any distinction between the two doctrines of Nazism and Communism. They are the same thing. Becoming a Communist when you are a Russian refugee is like a Jew from Germany becoming a Nazi. There's no difference. And after the war, people said, "Look, she had no sense of morals anyway, and she's just the kind of person who joins the Communist Party!"

'But my sister could never forgive her for what she did with the children,' said Uncle Kyril. 'She behaved monstrously. She just left Ian as a baby of three weeks with my parents and went off with her lover. But apparently she didn't make Grey happy either. Becoming a rear-gunner in the RAF was practically a form of suicide. We all believed that he didn't want to go on living.'

If I was a little shocked by the onslaught, I was also fascinated. If true, Uncle Kyril's annihilation left Sofka with little integrity. I found some things hard to believe, but I was still left with many questions. It seemed impossible to me that Sofka hadn't really loved Grey, but could their relationship have been more complicated than I imagined? And did she really abandon such a young baby? Could she have been as wilfully selfish and destructive as her in-laws claimed? I wondered too about the Communism. What were her motives? And did she care about how other exiled Russians felt about her?

'She may have changed, later . . . that I don't know,' Kyril said as he kissed me goodbye – three times, Russian-style. His advice was to think again about writing a book about Sofka: 'Her life isn't interesting enough – there isn't enough material.' But I was becoming steadily more ensnared by my quest to understand Sofka.

Back home in Athens, I unpacked Sofka's documents. In addition to the boxes, I'd acquired several packages of letters and memorabilia from my uncles, my father and some old friends. I sat surrounded by piles of papers: pre-Revolutionary Russian certificates, love letters to Jack, notebooks filled with quotations and poems, telegrams, appointment diaries, loose envelopes filled with photos, essays on Shakespeare's plays, drafts of memoirs, passports, photograph albums. They smelled musty and old. Sometimes I thought I got a whiff of the cottage (dogs, woodsmoke, melted butter and damp bathroom), but then it just seemed like dust. They were an opening to Sofka's life but also a confirmation of her death.

I was now full of questions; there seemed to be certain discrepancies and gaps in Sofka's own portrayal of her life. What really went on with Grey? During Sofka's lifetime he had seemed an almost sacred subject – too painful and significant to talk about. Even his son, Patrick, claimed to know almost nothing about his father. I wanted to find out what sort of person he really was. Uncle Kyril's warnings of unreliability and promiscuity haunted me. The idea that Sofka might have betrayed the supposed love of her life spurred me on to find out more about what her priorities were. I wanted to get to know her well enough to understand her motives as well as her actions. And what about Leo, my grandfather? What was his story? All I knew were the stiff 1930s photographs of a severe if interesting-looking man, with round spectacles and sparse hair. Nobody spoke about how he lived.

My solution was to begin at the beginning and to look at the extraordinary intertwining of fate and character which produced such extremes in Sofka's life. She always felt herself to be firstly a Russian, claiming jokily that 'All Russians are crazy!' And her own definition of the Russian character was based on its contrariness: 'a paradox, a series of conflicting elements . . . mysticism and realism, apathy and achievement, thirst for knowledge and abysmal ignorance, idealism and greed . . .'.

Sofka's story wasn't just the familiar one of a princess who loses her privileges, or an exile who loses her homeland. She was a refugee from Communism who embraced the philosophy of her supposed enemy. Here was a strongly emotional person who could show remarkable detachment, a mother who placed other priorities – romantic love, literature, work and travel – before her children. Sofka behaved as many men have always done, but if this is still provocative and unusual, in her era it was far more shocking.

The deeper I dug, the more fascinating these oppositions appeared: the principled, practical person who extolled the pleasures of drinking, party-going and *far niente*, and the sensitive woman who longed for security yet lived a life which practically ensured that she remained broke and peripatetic.

> *Because I seek for roots who am a leaf*
> *Whirled blind upon a gale,*
> *Because I strive for stillness through the storm,*
> *Because I long for peace . . .*

she wrote in her forties, when stillness and peace were still years away.

Before going back to Sofka's origins, I finished reading the diary. It was one of her many Russian admirers in Paris who offered her a way out. Nikolai evidently had connections in the right place, and promised that he could raise the fifteen thousand francs necessary to smuggle Sofka out of the country through unoccupied France and then Spain. The agreement was that the lenders would be paid back double after the war.

On 5 December, there is a pencil scrawl:

Just back from seeing Nikolai – he has fixed for me to leave on 10th. Not a word to anyone, specially not parents. No luggage. He got money from all round . . . Hardly dare even think, can't wait, can't wait.

Monday 8 December

Darling. I do love you. It's agony cold today – a black frost. Bloody. G'night, beloved – please not to forget me.

The writing in the diary ends there. The planned escape was only two days away. Early the next morning, there was a loud knocking on the door. Sofka opened it to find a French gendarme. He was not unpleasant, but firm. She must go with him, he told her, and bring things for twenty-four hours.

CHAPTER 2

THE PRINCESS

Fear not for the future,
Weep not for the past.

           – Percy Bysshe Shelley

I arrived in St Petersburg on the 'Red Arrow'. It had looked full
of promise at midnight the night before, in Moscow's busy
Leningrad Station: painted a smart shade of rusting burgundy,
with its name streaking along the sides. I liked it being red – the
colour of blood, freedom, love and magic, as well as the
Bolsheviks' flag, and, in Russian, linked to the word for 'beauty'.
The right colour for Sofka and for my journey. Standing stiffly
outside each carriage were smart, uniformed female attendants,
with hats and white gloves. They looked ready to salute. Or
execute. Amidst the bustle of last-minute goodbyes, it was
impossible not to fantasize about other Russian train journeys:
the legendary Trans-Siberian Express; countless departures to
exile, war and gulags; the joyous returns; the Romanovs' one-
way trip to the Urals; Lenin's arrival from Finland. And of
course, this was Anna Karenina's ride.

I also had my own memories. I lived in Moscow for over a
year in my twenties, having fallen in love with Vassilis, a Greek,

who worked there. Sofka found all that very amusing and demanded written updates. By the time Vassilis and I left Russia for London, Communism had fallen and I was six months pregnant. Before that, we made several short trips to Leningrad (before it made its third name change in a century and reverted to the original). We'd seen the summer 'White Nights', walking with crowds at 2 a.m., ghostly in a milky glow, and winter white days, trudging distances past frozen canals and snowy parks. Was it possible that I remembered trains with samovars? Or was that from some novel? Certainly tea was served in tall glasses with metal glass-holders bearing designs of heroic Soviet engines.

Then there were Sofka's journeys. When she was a child, her grandmother took her by rail to their far-off country estates, and to take the waters in Germany or Switzerland. And on their many visits to France they would surely have ridden the luxury train linking St Petersburg with Nice, nicknamed 'le train des grands-ducs'. They occupied an entire coach, with well-equipped bedroom, dressing room, sitting room and dining room leading to compartments for Sofka and her nurse, more for the maids and others for the male servants.

One of the intimidating serge-encased attendants showed me to my compartment, and the sight of my three prospective travelling companions banished all fantasy, and brought me firmly back to the early twenty-first century. Sitting on the lower bunk, with *my* number, was a vast woman with tiny eyes and flaming orange hair. Opposite her was a sad, curvaceous, young Japanese woman, who spoke only Japanese and kept surreptitiously wiping away tears, and a cunning-faced, gold-toothed man of about forty, drinking beer from a bottle. The two Russians introduced themselves, all smiles and evidently ready to make a party out of the situation: Alexei was going to visit his student son in Petersburg, while Natasha had been away on holiday and was returning home to her job in a computer company. The air was hot and reeked of alcohol, old sweat, engines and rancid butter. I was reminded again of how foreign I had felt when I lived in Russia. Having been brought up with a Russian name, religion, literature (albeit in translation) and my father's insistence that I was 'half Russian', I had somehow expected to feel at home there, even though I didn't know the language. It was a shock to realize that most of what I had ever known were half-remembered, second-generation hand-me-downs of an internalized, pre-Revolutionary Russia. My father had organized Russian-style mushroom hunts, tried to persuade me and my two brothers that the bowl of disgusting soured milk in the airing cupboard was actually delicious *prostokvasha*, and once spent ages constructing a pyramid-shaped, wooden mould so we could make authentic, sweet, creamy *paskha* to go with the *koulitch* Easter cake. But this hadn't brought me closer to Soviet Russia any more than reading Turgenev enabled me to understand its political structure.

Natasha took charge, even ushering everyone out of the compartment so I could change into my nightclothes, and persuading the Japanese woman to exchange beds (fortunately, as it would have surely been impossible for her to reach the upper berth). Eventually we all climbed into our bunks but it was hard to sleep: Alexei's arm hung out precariously in the dark above me and Natasha smelled more strongly than anyone I've ever encountered and snored like a bull all night.

St Petersburg's outskirts were wet and grey as we drew near in the morning, although it was still late summer. Natasha had woken me somewhat severely, claiming quite wrongly that we were almost there, and was quickly relishing the garlic-flavoured salami, dry bread roll and Kit-Kat from the unappetizing pre-packed breakfast boxes. The Japanese woman was still wiping tears. I felt nauseously tired and pessimistic enough to weep too. The journey suddenly felt like a waste of time. Gogol's existential questioning, 'Russia, what do you want from me? What inexplicable tie binds you and me?' had become 'Russia, what do *I* want from *you*?' I knew that there was nobody left with connections to Sofka – any contemporaries would be pushing one hundred now, but they had nearly all fled after the Revolution anyway. The few who remained were imprisoned or executed, or changed their names and ended up somewhere else as someone else. This gloom lifted somewhat, however, when my prior arrangement with the attendant succeeded and (paid in kopeks) she brought me tea with lemon. And it still came in a tall glass, with water from an electric samovar in the corridor.

At the station, I was willingly fleeced by a young taxi driver, who insisted on foreign currency, and drove me through a quiet, early-morning city, playing growling Russian rap. The last time I'd seen this country, the Soviet Union had just been dismantled. Russians were preparing to forget about breadlines, delayed salaries, empty shelves, drab clothes, communal flats and Lenin's dried-out cadaver, still lingering in Red Square. They were ready to pluck the marvellous fruits promised by democracy and capitalism. Now, it seemed that yet another dream had soured and Russia still had to face more transformation and pain. True, I'd heard that Moscow had become filled with Europe's most expensive hotels, restaurants, boutiques and luxury cars. Its élite was busy building ever more ostentatious villas, and best-selling books revealed the fabulous excesses of the *nouveaux riches*, with their plastic surgery, foreign holidays, resident masseurs and designer clothes. But large numbers were living in poverty and there was talk of an AIDS epidemic contributing to Russians' plummeting average age of death. St Petersburg, however, had lagged behind the capital's excesses; a friend told me that some film-makers recently found it was the only European city that could serve unaltered as a location for post-war Berlin.

I had arranged to rent a room on Bolshaya Morskaya, or Greater Maritime Street, and we arrived at a pretty, pale-ochre façade, masking a grim, dirty inner courtyard filled with muddy potholes and weeds. A bald poodle sniffed about pessimistically, and someone inside was shushing a crying baby. From the first floor an old man with a long, Tolstoyan beard looked down at me, framed by the window like a nineteenth-century portrait. Pushing open a metal door, I entered a dank stone stairwell with slime-green walls, feeling like an interloper in a Dostoevsky novel.

Irina Sergeyevna, my landlady, was a compact woman in her sixties, with short blond hair, manicured nails and a warm manner. She ushered me into her large, dark, tall-ceilinged apartment, decorated with a variety of ageing, patterned wallpapers. We proceeded down a narrow corridor, emerging at the front of the building in a room looking out on the Moika canal and the vast extravagance of the canary-coloured Yusupov Palace. This was the St Petersburg of dreams: 'the brother of water and sky', as Osip Mandelstam put it, with its glamorous waterfront mansions and gleaming churches. Here were Peter the Great's colossal abstractions turned to stone – bridges leading back to an early-eighteenth-century firework display of enlightenment. From this viewpoint, I could imagine that the gigantic upheaval of Communism was just one phase in many that this 'beauty and marvel' of the north (known familiarly as Peter) had experienced, an extraordinary twentieth-century experiment, which was becoming a part of history. But when my landlady started to talk, I realized that this hadn't happened yet.

'Renting out rooms to tourists is the only way we can possibly survive,' explained Irina Sergeyevna, who had worked as a scientist but now charged foreigners a modest rate for bed and breakfast. She was already taking on the role of my St Petersburg mother as she soothed and settled me into my room, and I quickly realized I'd been lucky to find her. Later, she would nurse me when I was ill, go in search of the best *kefir* (buttermilk) for my breakfast and help me with my search for Sofka's roots. She was one of the archetypal strong, determined Russian women, whose suffering only increases their capacity for bravery and survival. 'It's very hard now,' she continued. 'At least in Soviet times they'd care for things – they painted the stairs every three years. You'd get free medicines, and if something went wrong, they'd come to fix it.' She spoke to me in Russian up to the point where my frail grip on the language gave way, followed by careful, slow English, and then reverted to Russian. It worked surprisingly well.

'Don't misunderstand me – I hated the Communists,' said Irina Sergeyevna. 'When Gorbachev first came here, we went to throw flowers on the road for him. But now we hate him. Foreigners can't understand that. Now we don't have enough work, there's crime, there's war in Chechnya, Nazi youths are on the streets in Latvia and pensions are only a hundred roubles. I see old ladies counting out kopeks to see how many eggs they can afford. It's impossible . . .'

In the kitchen, Irina Sergeyevna sat me down at a round table, already laid with pretty crockery, berry jam in a cut-glass bowl and a vase of brightly coloured garden flowers. She fried pancakes and made coffee while a Pekinese pottered about, sweeping the floor with its plumed tail. 'Yana, Yanushka, my darling . . .' she cooed, picking up the placid creature and kissing it with emotion. Looking across the courtyard, I could see old Tolstoy's window.

'All the people across the courtyard there used to work in the

Maryinsky Theatre. They're still living in communal apartments,' explained Irina Sergeyevna. 'What's really hard is that they don't even have a bathroom – only a toilet. They have to go to the *banya*, the public baths, once a week. But the restaurant out there in the front part of the building . . . there are Russians who pay a hundred euros each to eat there.'

After breakfast I headed out into the city, light-headed from lack of sleep, but more hopeful. There might not be people who remembered Sofka, but here, in her city, I could walk in her footsteps, see the places she'd seen, and find some sort of communication with her across the decades. I made straight for the English Embankment, where Sofka was born. The day had become bright and sunny and by the time I arrived at the banks of the Neva a refreshing, salty breeze was coming off the broad blue river. In Sofka's youth, the quays were a fashionable place to stroll: elegant officers in colourful uniforms; young women out with their chaperones; families taking the air. For a winter treat, people would hire a *troika* here. Pulled by three horses, bells ringing, they'd glide along the snowy roads and over the frozen river to the islands.

It is still a romantic place. Renamed Embankment of the Red Fleet when this was Lenin's city, it has reverted to being 'English'. Young couples ambled by, the girls clutching bouquets brought by their admirers. One of Sofka's favourite sayings was 'If you have money for two loaves, buy one and some flowers,' and this was evidently practised in Petersburg. Every other person carries flowers. Some sailors passed, broad black ribbons fluttering from their white caps, heading in the direction of the battleship *Aurora*, which fired the first, blank shots at the Winter Palace in 1917. The whole scene can't have looked very different when Sofka took her first walks here, with her *niania*, one of the village women traditionally hired as nannies. You often see them in old photographs, sometimes dressed in pretty peasant costumes with headdresses and clutching plump, titled babies. Sofka remembered her *niania* as having a broad, flat face and being 'unlike all the nurses in Russian literature', as she 'seems to have told no stories and sung no songs'. Nevertheless, they'd stroll along to the Bronze Horseman, Falconet's statue of Peter the Great, always believed to be bound up with the city's fate. I thought of Sofka, looking out at the boats, from elegant imperial yachts to heavy, dark barges. On the opposite bank of the Neva, on the Vasiliyevskiy Island where Peter began his 'holy city', the same graceful façades with stage-set beauty stared back.

Near the far end of the English Embankment, I found number 70, where Sofka's parents lived after they married in 1907 – a handsome, three-storey, caramel-coloured building, with fancy white mouldings. The newlyweds' top-floor apartment – a gift from the groom's parents – was intended as a *pied à terre* until they found somewhere larger and more permanent. Both sets of parents were pleased that the young couple had only moved around the corner from their respective homes in Galernaya Street.

Countess Sophy Bobrinsky had been little more than a girl when, at eighteen, she became the wife of Prince Peter Dolgorouky (or Petya, as he was known). He had apparently asked for her hand fifty times, at the various dances, picnics, sleigh rides and 'at-homes' where their families met, until she finally agreed. According to Sophy, even then their youthful enthusiasm and their shared interests in poetry, music, riding, skating and tennis were not enough to bridge the gap caused by their fundamental differences. These oppositions in outlook and aspiration reflected the families they came from, but also their own natures, and some of Sofka's apparent contradictions almost certainly had their roots in her parents' diversity.

From her father, Sofka must have taken her fun-loving gregariousness, her romantic dreams and a fondness for drinking and parties. Petya was handsome, affectionate and what was then called gay – a natural charmer, always ready for games or adventure. In a photograph of him in his parents' formal drawing room, his lazy-lidded gaze comes sideways at the camera, part sullen, part sensual. He is perched uneasily on an armchair and his body language suggests a boy who wants to go out and play. At twenty-one, he had just finished the Military Academy and a perky moustache complements a buttoned-up army coat. He was now entitled to wear the fantastically glamorous white tunic, gold breastplates and eagle-topped helmet of the Horse Guards parade uniform. Petya's preoccupations and desires were a continuation of countless earlier St Petersburg generations. As the youngest of six children (born in 1883, the year of Alexander III's coronation), Petya had always been the pampered darling of his older sisters. His parents had tried to bring up their offspring in the 'English way' with 'backbone' and formal reserve, but the two Dolgorouky sons turned out to enjoy thoroughly Russian pleasures and intrigues. Sergei, the oldest (also in the Horse Guards), was the long-term favourite of the Tsar's married sister, Grand-Duchess Xenia, while Petya loved nothing better than parties, *troika* rides and, above all, going to hear the gypsies sing.

Going to the gypsies was an exciting opportunity to dabble in romance, potential danger and exotic love affairs. Petya's sister, Varvara, wrote of these nocturnal trips to the *tsiganes* in her memoirs: 'It meant a Bohemian mood, to feel one's heart, moving, softening and stirring. *Tsiganes* and some champagne, something too wonderful for words! Reborn, forgetting all around, listening until the early morning hours and yearning for more and more!'

Petya, Sofka's father, followed his forebears into the glamorous Horse Guards regiment, but his passion was going to the Gypsies.

The young Dolgoroukys were not alone in this almost addictive passion; Maurice Paléologue, France's last ambassador to the Russian Court, wrote: 'Thomas de Quincey, the author of *Confessions of an English Opium Eater*, tells us that the drug often gave him the illusion of music. Conversely, the Russians go to music for the effect of opium.'

Though Sophy too was daring, she was altogether different. Deeply serious about living her life usefully and improving herself and the world, she wanted to stretch her mind to its limits. Sofka's restlessness, boundless curiosity, love of books and a ruthlessness mixed with sensitivity were probably inherited from her mother. Sophy and her siblings had been brought up by somewhat 'alternative' parents, who frequently eschewed Petersburg in favour of a simpler existence on their country estate. Despite their progressive outlook, however, Sophy's parents rejected her request to attend university instead of marrying as too bold. But Sophy was formulating her own ambitious plans; marriage just had to become part of them. In photographs, she stares ahead uncompromisingly and almost hypnotically, her dark eyes and attractive, regular features set in determination.

According to Sofka, her parents' January wedding was considered the most brilliant of the 1907 season. Certainly, the Romanovs attended the service joining these two prominent families, which was held in a private church in the Winter Palace, and afterwards at the bride's home, the Bobrinsky Palace. Petya chose well in his wedding gift to his bride: as Sophy came out into the large, icy courtyard after the reception, there was a brand new automobile with a chauffeur waiting to crank it up. No pictures remain, but if it was anything like what other grandees were going around in, it was probably open-sided, with capacious, armchair-like leather seats, a long cylinder engine in

*Sophy, Sofka's mother, was never going to be a conventional wife.
Even aged eighteen she was forging secret, ambitious plans.*

front, slim white tyres on spoked wheels and a black, bat-wing canopy reminiscent of the carriage that would now be relegated to the back of the stables. The groom knew what many of the guests would not have guessed – that the slim, serious, girlish bride, wrapped in furs over her gown, already knew how to drive. Sophy had learned in secret the previous year, as a seventeen-year-old, sneaking out at night on the country estate and borrowing her cousin's automobile. In front of the wedding party she would have to keep quiet; the next day she would drive her own car.

Sophy became pregnant immediately after the wedding, probably during the honeymoon to Paris and Monte Carlo, and her only child was born nine months later on 23 October. She was given the same saint's name as her mother, but with a fashionable diminutive ending; there was something light-hearted and jokey, and just very slightly contemptuous, in calling your baby 'Sofka'.

This was an extraordinary time. Russia was richer than ever before, trade was booming and the revolutionary terrorists had gone relatively quiet. People were already starting to forget the humiliating defeat in the war with Japan, and the carnage of 1905 with Bloody Sunday, when troops and police fired on a peaceful demonstration of workers. Liberals were still hopeful that the country could reform itself, while revolutionaries got depressed; Lenin (in exile) kept complaining that he'd never live to see the revolution. St Petersburg was witnessing the height of the cultural blossoming known as the Silver Age. Russia's painters, poets, writers, musicians and dancers were now leading European trends and it was hard to keep up with the latest movement; Symbolists, Modernists, Acmeists and Futurists competed for attention with dilettanti, rebels, revolutionaries, pamphleteers, pornographers, Bohemians . . . Court circles may not have taken much notice, but St Petersburg was in ferment; a last mad flowering before it was all swept away by war and revolution.

Sofka was born into the traditions of the conservative Petersburg nobility, but all around, life was shifting: people saw the first aeroplanes flying over the city and watched the earliest (hugely popular) motion pictures; some intrepid types installed telephones in their houses. When Sofka was a baby, Diaghilev had just taken his Ballets Russes to Paris, and her parents could have listened to the first concerts with music by Stravinsky and Prokofiev, seen Sarah Bernhardt acting on stage and heard the legendary bass Fyodor Chaliapin singing, and it's likely that they were tempted to witness Vaslav Nijinsky's scandalously erotic dancing at the Maryinsky.

Trying my luck, I rang the bell at number 70, and, entering a hall, explained my purpose to a woman behind a desk. She stopped eating soft white cheese out of a plastic bag, and rang through to 'the manager'. A polite man with a Trotsky beard appeared, and was delighted to hear about my grandmother. When I mentioned she'd been a Dolgorouky, he looked impressed enough to make me feel rather proud, in spite of myself. I knew that the Dolgoroukys were one of the great old Russian families: I had all sorts of papers and genealogies showing the line running back to the ninth-century Prince Rurik of Kiev. A Dolgorouky founded Moscow in 1154, and these 'Long Arms' (the first one had a notoriously vindictive long arm for his enemies) had been linked closely – politically and romantically – with the Romanovs. Still, I hadn't realized the effect it would have on the many modern Russians who are utterly enamoured with the romance of their tsarist past and now view these troubled, if picturesque, bygone days through thoroughly rose-tinted spectacles. Having seen the value of my grandmother's family name, I went on to use it shamelessly throughout my travels, in the hope of getting people to help me or talk to me. And it worked wonders. I remembered Uncle Kyril's warnings about pathetic émigré Russians who harp on about how grand or rich their families once were: 'It's nearly always those who have not made a success of their lives later. My father warned us never to talk about the glories of the past,' he said. But I couldn't keep up to his rigorous standards.

Trotsky explained that the building had been a scientific institute but was now under reconstruction – destined to be a trade centre, congress hall and hotel, incorporating a theatre and a café. They would decorate the whole place in pre-Revolutionary style, with antiques, he announced. Designers would adhere to historically correct rules.

'We'll give you the presidential suite after the renovations,' he joked. I asked who was funding this project; was it Russians or foreigners?

'Russians, Russians . . .' Trotsky laughed bitterly. 'They've stolen enough money, the Russians. Now they're all bandits. It might have been very strict in Soviet days, but everyone was sure about tomorrow.' Trotsky had the bizarre ability to idealize two eras of twentieth-century Russia generally seen as antithetical, but I could see that, given the chaotic metamorphosis of these days, both the rigid nannying of Soviet life and the elegant grandeur of the tsarist years had their appeal.

We climbed the broad stone staircase to the top floor and walked into 'Sofka's apartment'. I immediately recognized the pretty, pale blue room as having been the sitting room, with its three tall windows looking out to the embankment. There was the marble fireplace, broken now, in front of which Sofka had sprawled on a bear-rug, keeping quiet so she wouldn't be sent away. She remembered listening to 'a thin dark woman who would sit with my mother in front of the fire and recite magical poetry which entranced me and which I didn't understand in the least'. Years later, she learned it had been Anna Akhmatova.

Sophy had returned from her honeymoon to find her new home decorated in the smart, spindly, silk-covered, gilt-ridden style so beloved of her mother-in-law, and she quickly changed everything, preferring a more unconventional, almost masculine approach. In this drawing room, she placed a gigantic divan covered with Persian rugs and cushions, some dark-green leather armchairs, and a large, practical desk by the window. Glass-fronted bookshelves covered one wall and were filled with a growing collection of volumes, all bound in red or green leather with a gold D and coronet on the spines. Sophy rebelled in her appearance too, always dressing simply in a long, dark skirt and white silk blouse and wilfully side-stepping the society game by almost always wearing the same, plain dress to parties, shockingly 'naked' without jewels.

The young mother continued in radical style. Sophy didn't hire the customary wet-nurse, insisting on breast-feeding her infant; and she generated much gossip by refusing on principle to go to church and driving herself around in her own car. More dramatic still, she announced her decision to study medicine and gained a place at the city's teaching hospital. Presumably enjoying the provocation, Sophy placed a full-sized human skeleton in the drawing room and on an occasional table, instead of the expected Fabergé box or porcelain figurine, a ceramic model of a man showing the body's muscles and organs.

Sofka's mother was born the ultimate insider in her tribe, but her horizons lay far outside. Most of her friends and relations had some privileged role within the imperial family, marking out their ranks with uniforms, glittering brooches, ribbons and medals. Sophy, though, was utterly uninterested in court duties.

Her mother, mother-in-law, sisters, sisters-in-law and many friends were all maids of honour and ladies-in-waiting to the Empress, the Dowager Empress or some grand-duchess or other. Sophy's male relations and in-laws carried great lists of appointments: her father was Marshal of the Nobility, president of the Union of the Nobility of the Russian Provinces, Knight of the Order of St Alexander Nevsky, and did something called 'carrying the Crown of Astrakhan at the Coronation of the Emperor Nikolai II'.

Having dropped court life, Sophy wasn't going to bother with genteel 'at-homes' either. Life was too short to have her 'day' of the week when visitors would come by for tea between four and seven, or leave their visiting card (folded over if given in person). Quite apart from the gossip and chit-chat, there were all the hostess's preparations: the flowers ordered at 'Fleurs de Nice', imported from the south of France in straw-packed baskets; the minuscule *petits fours* and fancy gateaus; the latest dress ordered from Paris.

Petya didn't exactly approve of Sophy's metamorphosis, but he was busy with his regiment. And there were plenty of distractions for the evenings, if his wife was studying. I pictured Sophy in this room. Perhaps with Sofka, who had toddled in with Niania for a brief visit to Mama; or more likely sitting alone at her desk with her anatomy books. The inspiring view from the three tall windows was one that Sophy always yearned for after she lost it: the great swathe of the Neva, changing constantly (iced white breaking up into pale, fog-drenched thaw, then summery blue ripples); the greys, pinks, ochres and blues of the graceful buildings on the other side; and down below in the street, the traffic of the horse-drawn carriages (with battery lights at night) and new-fangled 'taximotors' trundling along the quay. Nothing could ever live up to all this.

Sophy always yearned for the view over the broad Neva, with its dramatic seasonal changes and its constant traffic of boats entering and leaving St Petersburg. Surprisingly little has changed since then.

Leaving the front of the apartment, we crossed the landing to the back wing. This had been the realm of the dining room, the kitchen (no cooking smells should reach the drawing room) and accommodation for what was considered a minimal staff: Maxim, the butler, who sat near the front door to welcome visitors; Simyon, the young footman attached to the nursery; Pyotr, Petya's batman; Sasha, a maid, whose parents had been Dolgorouky serfs; a chef and his helper; and a couple of other housemaids. Servants all used 'the black way' or back stairs, down into the stableyard past the winter woodpiles and coachman's quarters, now occupied by the chauffeur. I looked down to where construction materials were already being gathered for the make-over, getting the sense that, to everyone except me, Sofka's story was now almost as distant as if she had been born hundreds of years earlier; she had become history. Just where she was coming to life, she was also receding into the past. Anna Akhmatova wrote, 'And slowly the shades withdraw from us.' But I was only more determined to get closer.

Sofka's own view of her childhood was one of amazement that she had lived through such times: 'The world into which I was born in 1907 seems as unimaginable today, sixty years later, as the way of life on some distant planet. In fact it is far easier to envisage tourist traffic to outer space than a return to the conventions and prejudices, the strict rules of etiquette, the luxury and the misery, the culture and the ignorance of that age.'

Among Sofka's earliest memories was being put to bed one night by Niania, who was crying. The next morning she was not there. Sasha arrived, as always, bearing a jug of hot water and her clothes (combinations; long brown stockings and sailor suits in winter; and white, starched broderie-anglaise dresses, changed at least twice a day, in summer). But in Niania's place was a plain, po-faced, buttoned-up Englishwoman – Miss King, her new governess. English had become the fashionable language, as 'the young Empress', Alexandra, preferred it to French, which she spoke almost as badly as Russian. Consequently, Russia's most European city was now filled with English governesses and tutors.

In later life, Sofka recognized that though Miss King was not the most loveable creature, she must (like other single, middle-class women who left England's suburbs for the colonies) have had a hidden intrepid streak. This was not generally apparent, however. Miss King glorified anything English and insisted on Anglo-Saxon standards, even refusing to shut the little *fortochka* opening in the sealed windows on bitterly freezing winter nights, to provide 'fresh air'. In the mornings the Englishwoman gave Sofka lessons, though other teachers came for Russian subjects, French and drawing, and there were dancing classes with other children. Later, Miss King took Sofka out to play (often meeting young friends with their English governesses) or for walks – such a relief when spring arrived and you no longer had to wear clumsy felt *valenki* over your boots and the padded lining under your fur coat.

Sofka looked back with pleasurable cynicism on her privileged existence: 'As the Child was heiress to some of the greatest wealth in the country and as uncles, aunts, grandmothers and other relations had more money than they even knew about, toys were brought on every visit, to say nothing of the conventional times such as Christmas and Easter, birthdays and name days.' There were child-size talking dolls in porcelain, pony-skin horses drawing carts, electric trains, mechanical bears, hens and tigers, and every sort of ball, hoop, skipping rope, puzzle and board game. Typically, Sofka preferred reading inside an improvised wigwam.

When Sofka went to Zyametchina, the Dolgorouky estate in Ukraine, Miss King came too, warning her charge to avoid the village children who shouted and threw dust at her. 'They were savage and rude and hated us,' Miss King explained. It was Simyon, the young footman who saddled Sofka's pony and pushed her swing, who explained things better: 'If I were hungry and had no shoes and no nice home, wouldn't I hate those who made me work all my life and didn't pay me enough?' Sofka solemnly swore never to repeat anything he told her, though Sophy had already tried to instil some liberal priorities from early on, insisting that Sofka should always use the correct formal 'you' to address everyone except her contemporaries. In a country

Aged four, Sofka changed her broderie-anglaise dresses at least twice a day and was often overwhelmed with presents from her indulgent relations.

where most servants were addressed by their employers using the familiar 'you' and answered back in the formal plural, this was still unusual.

It's possible that Simyon and Sophy were sowing some tiny seeds of Sofka's later political beliefs, but even without them she wouldn't have been the first privileged Russian to notice her country's deep conflicts. Poets and novelists had been addressing the dangerous contradictions inherent in Russian society for much of the previous century. Even though serfdom (or 'tax-paying slavery', as it has been described) had been abolished, the vast majority of the population remained poor, illiterate and powerless. Lenin was far from being the first Russian to think of revolution: it had been in the air since December 1825, when the noble-minded, noble-blooded Decembrists tried to overthrow the government and the monarch, with the intention of creating a better, more just society.

It was naturally a scandal, though it can't have surprised many people, when Sofka's parents separated. In five years of marriage, Sophy had created a new world for herself. Now, in addition to being attractive, clever, independent and still only twenty-four, she was a successful surgeon, creating ripples through Petersburg. Once, the head of surgery at her hospital recommended to Countess Shuvaloff that an operation she needed should be carried out by Sophy Alexeyevna Dolgorouky. 'I can't have that,' Aunt Betsy said, horrified. 'She's my niece!'

Sophy was also versatile enough to contribute satirical poems to a fashionable journal (under the pseudonym Todaneto), and in 1912 to be the only woman driver in a motor rally, along rough, potholed roads from Petersburg to Kiev. She frequented the legendary Stray Dog, the cellar cabaret where regulars witnessed every new type of play, dance, lecture, poem and exhibition in an atmosphere of alcohol-fuelled intrigue and love affairs. She was also invited to the Tower. This was one of the city's most vital points of intellectual life – the salon of the leading symbolist poet Vyacheslav Ivanov and his exotic, literary wife, Lydia Zinovieff (a relation on the other side of my family). While 'Vyacheslav the Magnificent' astounded and inspired his visitors, expounding eloquently on any number of themes, Lydia wafted about by candle-light in long velvet robes. Their famous Wednesdays (midnight till dawn, plenty of red wine and all watches and clocks banned as distractions) saw all the famous philosophers, intellectuals and poets of the day.

Petya was still dressing up, as his forebears had, in military uniform for Horse Guards parades, gambling at the exclusive Yacht Club (nothing to do with sailing) and attending vodka-drenched stag parties at the newly opened Astoria Hotel. More compromising, however, was that one of his affairs was becoming serious. Petya was in love with a spectacularly beautiful gypsy singer called Anna. So it was probably with relief as well as trepidation that he left the marital apartment on the English Embankment and returned home in disgrace to his outraged parents.

* * *

I spent the next days walking around St Petersburg, tracking down documents and photographs and meeting people. Sometimes, sitting in the metro, I looked at faces, spotting something distantly familiar. Could they include the grandchildren of Sofka's playmates or the descendants of the household servants? Did we share some blood link somewhere through the centuries? The more I heard, the more remarkable it seemed that so much energy was being put into resurrecting whatever could be salvaged from its glory days as capital city; both in terms of architecture and artefacts, but also in terms of family and descent. I was one of many people attempting to unearth personal archaeology and piece together shattered remnants of the past.

There were times when I felt that I glimpsed an older Russia. It happened momentarily, when people asked for my father's name and then called me Sofia Petrovna; some forms of politeness were not wiped out under Communism. As a name, 'Sofka' was rejected as now being inappropriate, almost disrespectful. Then there were the people I met who spoke of ideas and philosophy in a grand, expansive, unembarrassed way, and of books as forces that can change lives and societies. 'The question of blood is the most complicated problem in the world,' said an elegant, serious young librarian in the dark bowels of the National Library. She was quoting Bulgakov's *The Master and Margarita*, in response to my telling her about my grandmother. 'The Communists hated that idea,' she said, 'but when you take away people's property and their old lives, blood is what remains.'

Blood was certainly what counted for the dozen or so nobility associations, which had sprung up since 1990 when *perestroika* allowed the dismantling of many old Soviet taboos. Without good reason, I felt instinctively prejudiced against these institutions, which combed through genealogies with the obsessive attention Sofka's grandparents gave to someone's 'quarterings' (how many of their great-great-grandparents – the *seize quartiers* – had been noble) and whether a woman could be considered 'born' according to her social standing ('*Elle n'est pas née*' was said seriously of an outsider). So when I went to visit (Prince) Andrei Gagarin, the president of the most serious assembly for the nobility, I imagined I would encounter some snobbish, anachronistic relic. In fact, Andrei Petrovich Gagarin turned out to be a handsome, tanned, upright seventy-year-old scientist, who shattered my prejudices. He told me how he had to hide his name and background and how his father was executed in 1937 for the crime of bearing his name. It wasn't until 1964 that Andrei Petrovich discovered his father's fate, after writing (very courageously) to the KGB. The authorities' belated apology for killing an innocent man and throwing him into an unmarked mass-grave brought only the bleak relief of knowing the truth. Gagarin occasionally stuttered as he spoke, as though these shocking things were literally unspeakable. Listening to him, I realized that whereas an aristocrats' club in another country might tend to the conservative and exclusive, here, the members have often been rebellious and daring as they traced back their blood lines.

Of course, it wasn't only the former nobility who had suffered in Leningrad. My daily breakfasts with my landlady were stretching out into long conversations that sometimes ended with us both crying. Each morning, Irina Sergeyevna would fill me in on the latest horrors she had witnessed on television: a bomb on Moscow's metro had killed seven people; Chechnyan terrorists had occupied a school in Ossetya, and children, parents and teachers were trapped inside without food or water. Three days later Beslan was known around the world and hundreds were dead. When my landlady retreated into a past which was equally awful, it felt as though Russia would never escape its own particular tragedy.

'I was born in 1939 – the seventh generation of a St Petersburg family. When the siege began on 8 September 1941, I was only two, but I remember a lot. That first winter was the worst ever. It was minus forty-five degrees outside, and we were always hungry. We just stayed in the kitchen to keep warm and thought of bread all the time. We burned furniture and books when we couldn't get logs, and drank "tea" which was really hot water without tea.

'You see that?' said Irina Sergeyevna, pointing to a small slice of dark rye bread on my plate. 'That's what we each had to eat every day. We'd divide it up into three parts, to have as three "meals". In the summer we ate weeds and grass from the yard, and in the end, although two-thirds of the people here died, we survived by eating furniture glue made from bones. We'd boil it up in water. I remember waiting for this "soup", and calling to my grandmother, "Babushka, when is the soup going to be ready?" After those nine hundred terrible days, we had sold everything for bread and glue – even the kitchen table was burned for warmth. In the end, we just had one bed and this icon,' she said, showing me a small jewel-encrusted Madonna.

'After the blockade even atheists became religious. Of course, the suffering didn't end there. We survivors have very weak health, as do our children born later. Many of my friends died in their forties and fifties, and nobody is really healthy.'

When Sofka visited Leningrad in the 1950s, the legacy of the Germans' brutal siege was still fresh. Only ten years had passed since Anna Akhmatova returned from evacuation to 'the terrible ghost that pretended to be my city'.

'By November 1941, all dogs and cats had been eaten,' wrote Sofka, describing the stories she heard.

'By December, people were chewing leather to relieve the pangs of hunger and corpses sat or lay, frozen, in the streets. There was no electricity, no newspapers, no contact with the outside world except for loudspeakers all round town which broadcast news bulletins, music and poetry. And when the people manning the radio became too weak to keep up a continuous service, they set up a metronome beside the microphone. By its regular heartbeat it told the people that their city was still alive.'

* * *

My next foray into Sofka's past was at Galernaya, the narrow road where her two sets of grandparents chanced to live directly opposite one another. On the south side of the street, backing on to the Moika canal, was Sophy's home, the Bobrinsky House (or Palace, as it is now known – many former 'Houses' have been upgraded). The original gilded cast-iron gates had gone, replaced by a botched job with planks. I peered through a gap to a beautiful but dilapidated building with classical proportions and four tall white columns topped with voluptuous sculpted figures. The courtyard was derelict, filled with rubble and rusting pieces of metal. Grass covered the patterns in the red-granite, eighteenth-century cobbles. The place looked abandoned, with broken windows, crumbling stucco and the two wings on either side of the courtyard in urgent need of repair.

I gingerly pushed open the wooden gate and walked across the deserted courtyard. The front door was ajar, and as I entered I came face to face with a wild-eyed witch-like woman with grey hair, dressed eccentrically in a tweed jacket over a black housecoat. It turned out that Larissa Ivanovna had been a caretaker here since the early 1960s, when it had been the university's Geography Department. Despite the air of abandonment, the building was now the functioning Department of Literature – apparently the students would soon be back. It didn't look like it. I enviously recalled Sofka's description of her first return visit here in the 1950s, when 'very little had been altered' from the days when she visited her grandparents.

We stood for a moment in the dark hallway, looking around at the damp, crumbling walls and the remnants of an elegant mosaic floor. On the wall at the first stretch of the curving, double staircase was a large, ornately framed mahogany mirror.

'Nearly everything has gone now,' moaned Larissa Ivanovna, 'but that mirror has stayed. Your grandmother would have

Sofka loved playing at her Bobrinsky grandparents' house as a child and found it surprisingly unchanged on her return in the 1950s. It has now fallen into disrepair.

looked at herself in there.' I glanced at my reflection, imagining a young Sofka running past, and feeling like someone in an Anna Akhmatova poem:

> *'I myself, from the very beginning,*
> *Seemed to myself, like someone's dreams or delirium,*
> *Or a reflection in someone else's mirror.'*

We walked through to the garden at the back of the house – an overgrown mass of tall maple and linden trees throwing shade on the expanse of uncut grass. Sofka often came to this child's paradise, describing the secret hiding-places, the dogs' cemetery and the icy toboggan run in the winter. 'Children used to come and play here,' said Larissa Ivanovna, referring to more recent times. 'There were little paths, and roses . . . but then the garden was closed and now it's too dangerous, with criminals, bandits and mafia men driving by and shooting.'

Sofka's Bobrinsky grandparents were both exceptional personalities. A handsome, long-nosed, bearded man, Alexei Bobrinsky had numerous court appointments but he was also a member of the Duma – Russia's first parliament, established in the hope of moderating the Tsar's autocratic powers. 'Grandpa (Oumpa, we called him) was the wittiest person imaginable,' Sofka wrote to my father in the 1950s, trying to pass on a bit of family history. 'He had a talent for versifying and illustrating with ridiculous sketches, rather like Lear. He was also a great archaeologist and wrote learned volumes and had a terrific collection of early Russian pottery etc, which is now in the Leningrad Museum. At the age of 68, he remarried a housekeeper and at 72 produced a son, who is 12 years younger than I.'

Alexei Bobrinsky's line went straight back to Catherine the Great's illegitimate son by her lover Gregory Orlov. The story goes that Catherine managed to keep her pregnancy secret from her hated, feeble-minded husband, Peter III, making sure he was lured away from the palace when she gave birth in April 1762. Knowing her husband's childlike delight in witnessing fires, she arranged for a wooden house outside the city to be set alight when she felt labour pains beginning. Sure enough, Peter rushed to the blaze. When he returned to the Winter Palace, the baby had been born and Catherine was up and dressed as if nothing had happened. The infant boy was smuggled out of the palace, according to romantics, wrapped in a beaver fur (*bobr* in Russian). His mother called him Alexei and came up with the surname Bobrinsky (complete with a coat-of-arms featuring a beaver). She also bestowed upon her son the title of Count. While the boy was brought up by friends, the dashing Orlov brothers helped get rid of Peter more permanently; he was too risky alive. Catherine managed her rule as Empress with as much flair, organization and originality as she had shown in the birth of her son, while he adopted as his family motto, something his mother might have said: 'Thanks to God, life to thee.' When he was older, he was given this charming little palace (built for Catherine's last lover, Zubov, by Luigi Rusca, one of the many Italian architects working in the city at the end of the eighteenth century), and it remained the home of each eldest Bobrinsky son (always Alexei or Alexander) for the next six generations. Until 1917.

'Everything is chaotic and nothing works or is cared for now,' said Larissa Ivanovna gloomily, as she led me back into the house and up the stairs. Gone were the old burgundy-coloured carpets, the chandeliers, the grandfather clock and the stuffed bears which Sofka had seen fifty years previously. 'And they took the gates away for "restoration" in the seventies,' said the caretaker, 'but they were never brought back.' We walked through a strange mix of glamour, decay and seediness: Italianate cherubs and gold stars looked down from ornate ceilings on to shoddy desks and blackboards, and walls covered in great sheets of ornamental marble still had bomb damage from the Second World War and were mushrooming strange excrescences. The rotunda boudoir-study of Sofia Alexandrovna Bobrinsky (the beautiful, intelligent wife of the first Count's oldest son and a friend of Pushkin) still contained her curved mahogany bookcases, but the floor was covered with packing cases. 'It won't get better, it'll only get worse,' groaned Larissa Ivanovna.

We climbed up high into the large cupola at the front of the house, which had been used as an observatory by Sophy's mother Nadezhda, another remarkable Bobrinsky wife. Sofka described 'Granny Bob' as 'a severe, exceptionally intelligent woman, who was rather terrifying to children. Her joy was astronomy, and she calculated when comets would appear, and wrote articles in astronomical journals. She'd spend days covering sheets and sheets with minute figures. She had three chow dogs, which she adored, and so it is said, a romance, among others, with her French chauffeur.'

* * *

On the other side of Galernaya Street from the Bobrinskys lived the Dolgoroukys – the epitome of the conservative court family. Despite the Bobrinskys' wealth and lineage, the Dolgoroukys always had doubts about their son's marriage to Sophy. And they certainly disapproved of the Duma and Count Bobrinsky's participation in this experiment in liberalism.

Number 72, the Dolgorouky Mansion, was still reddish in colour, as it had been in the old days, but I could hardly believe that this dull block had once been a luxurious place, with courtyard and fine drawing rooms. It had been divided up and converted into student bedsits, and was now tired and undistinguished. When Sofka's parents separated in 1912, Petya moved back here to his rooms on the top floor. Later that year his father, Sandik, died. The family kept vigil by the coffin in the ballroom, where nuns read out prayers through the night, and the Emperor joined mourners at the funeral, walking through the city to the Alexander Nevsky Cemetery behind a hearse drawn by four white horses.

Sandik had been 'a rather terrifying figure in early childhood'. Grand Marshal of the Imperial Court and Master of Ceremonies, he would leave every morning for the palace in the court carriage permanently at his disposal, with driver and footman in pale grey livery bordered by two red bands. He'd been an intimate friend of 'the bearded giant', Alexander III, and like him believed in giving children a taste of Spartan austerity. Where the Emperor made his son, the future Nicholas II, sleep on a camp-bed and rise at dawn, Sandik tried to impart modesty and restraint to his children by sending them second-class on trains or taking them to cheap restaurants in Paris (as well as the best). Sofka described her grandfather as 'an autocratic stickler for absolute etiquette', whose stern voice would ring out if she forgot to kiss her grandmother's hand.

I'd always been impressed by the photograph of 'Grandfather Dolgorouky' in Sofka's album: an imposing, stern figure with piercing eyes and extensive white facial hair, wearing heavy, elaborate robes and fur hat. I'd imagined that this was how he normally dressed – after all, I'd read accounts such as Maurice Paléologue's (the French Ambassador), who described the theatricality of court life:

> In the opulence of the uniforms, the extravagance of the dress of the ladies, the richness of the liveries, the sumptuousness of the costumes, the entire display of splendour and power, this spectacle is so magnificent, no court in the world can vie with it. I will long remember the dazzling brilliance of the jewels strewn over the ladies' shoulders. It was a fantastic river of diamonds, pearls, rubies, sapphires, emeralds, topazes, beryls: a river of light and fire.

Recently, however, I discovered that 'Grandfather' had been in costume (though his outrageous plumage of side-whiskers was always present), and he was normally in morning coat and trousers like everyone else. He'd been photographed along with many of the 2,500 guests who attended the last great ball at the Winter Palace, in January 1903, where everyone dressed in the style of their seventeenth-century ancestors.

Whenever I saw this picture of Grandfather Dolgorouky in Sofka's album, I imagined that he always dressed like that. It was much later that I discovered he was wearing his costume for the famous Winter Palace ball in 1903, where everyone dressed as their seventeenth-century forebears.

After Sandik's death Sofka's grandmother, Olga, wrapped herself permanently in black widow's weeds and thick crape veils. She also decided to instil some of the backbone she considered her poor granddaughter was not acquiring from her gad-about father and horribly independent mother. Sophy didn't protest (her daughter could always come home for visits) and the five-year-old moved into an utterly different world: a step back into the nineteenth century, already experienced at Olga's stifling lunches in the gloomy dining room. 'Back straight, fingertips on the table.' Behind each dark-green leather chair, embossed with the Dolgorouky arms, stood a footman.

Each morning Sofka was woken by Sasha, the nursery maid. The tiled, ceiling-high stove was stoked, heavy curtains opened and hot water poured into the wash-stand basin. After Simyon had brought breakfast for Sofka and Miss King in the day nursery, 'the Child' was fetched to visit her grandmother as she took her breakfast in bed. Sofka used this title for herself in her memoirs, suggesting both the isolation and the pampering of an only child. I imagine it as an imperious order from Olga to a servant: 'Take the Child away now!' Sofka never said she was lonely, but the emotion is implied; there were no other children in the house.

Sofka enjoyed watching her grandmother – the unchanging rituals of this small woman with the haughty expression, proud nose, heavy eyelids and a mouth which twisted up into a one-sided, wry smile. Olga indulged her new charge with a lump of sugar dipped in coffee, and told stories of her youth: dresses measured up at Maison Worth in Paris; the flowers and ribbons distributed by men to their dancing partners at balls; the vast candelabras burning with hundreds of candles . . . Those were wonderful days. As *dame d'honneur* (they all spoke French then) and close friend to Marie, the beautiful, gregarious Empress,

Olga had witnessed balls and receptions as elaborate and glittering as any in Romanov history. Everybody remembered the now celebrated Bal Noir, where the death of some minor European royalty hadn't prevented the planned ball, but rather made it far more chic, as everyone was ordered to dress in black. Now Dowager Empress, Marie was well aware of the tension that existed between her and her son Nicholas's awkward, stern wife, Alexandra, whose interest in dubious 'holy men' was to lead to such trouble.

Olga's Latvian maid, Louise, busied around in the dressing room, preparing the bathwater and clothes for the day. She had been engaged over forty years previously, when Olga and Sandik married, and now had her own maid and footman. Without this woman, Princess Dolgorouky would have been helpless: Louise helped her down the steps into her sunken, grey marble bath; she was ready afterwards with the warmed towel, violet talcum powder and scent; and she laced up her corset and cambric underclothes. Finally, she smoothed fine silk stockings along Olga's legs, and deftly buttoned up the soft, pointed, high-heeled boots with a silver hook, something her mistress didn't know how to do by herself. In a moment of honesty, Olga once admitted to Sofka that she wouldn't know where to begin. And to the end of her life she never learned, revolutions notwithstanding.

Mornings were for practical issues: Monsieur Ducroix, the head chef, sent up menus for approval, letters and invitations were written and sent out with a liveried footman, Sofka had lessons, and by the time Olga left her suite all the rooms were freshly polished by 'floor rubbers', who hopped and slid over the gleaming parquet with a pad attached to one foot. In the afternoon, Olga and Sofka might go out in the carriage for visits (veiled hat, white kid gloves washed and smoothed by Louise each time), or on Sundays to one of her friends' private chapels (the Vorontsoffs, the Cheremetyeffs, the Shuvaloffs or the palace). Sofka remembered dreading her trips to play with the Tsarevich; the delicate, haemophiliac boy was forbidden to play at anything where he might fall, though sometimes the Emperor would lift him or Sofka on his back for a 'horse-ride' or play his favourite board game of halma. Apparently, the Empress would lurk in the doorway, watching.

'Later in life Granny told me that it had been decided that the next Empress had better not be a foreigner and the Child was among the suitable candidates and was to be groomed for the post,' Sofka wrote in her memoirs. Uncle Kyril, however, threw cold water on this picturesque notion: 'Sofka was *so* odd,' he remarked one day when we spoke on the phone. 'That idea couldn't *possibly* have been true. They'd have had to change the constitution; the Tsarevich had to marry the daughter of an actual monarch sitting on the throne.' Sometimes it seemed that little in Sofka's life would be left standing if I gave credence to everything Kyril said, though I prefer to believe that this story reflects the lost hope of Sofka's wistful grandmother rather than pure invention. Sofka herself was proud enough to mention it, and sceptical enough to reject it as irrelevant.

Sometimes, Olga would take Sofka out shopping: an ornamental egg from Fabergé to give at Easter time or a drive down Nevsky Prospekt. I walked up and down, identifying the shops they'd have known. These days, Nevsky has regained some of its former *élan*; once more there are stylish shoppers in this central avenue, clutching carrier bags or sipping drinks in colourful canalside palaces. Gogol's ironic comments make sense again: 'There is nothing finer than the Nevsky Prospekt, not in Petersburg anyway: it is the making of the city . . . There are numbers of people, who, when they meet you, invariably stare at your boots, and when they have passed, turn round to have a look at the skirts of your coat.' I kept finding myself staring at the strangely pointed shoes with Aladdin-style upturned toes, which were worn by male and female fashion victims alike.

In Sofka's day, Nevsky was a shopper's delight: clothes, furs, chocolates, books, cigarettes, scents, jewellers', banks, and the Russian 'Fortnum and Mason'– Yeliseyev, who thought little of bringing lobsters from Holland and oysters from France. Sofka would be fitted for her blue serge coats and sailor suits at the popular English shop on Nevsky, which supplied a vast array of Anglo-Saxon essentials and delicacies to the city's many Anglophiles. Money was never discussed or even exchanged on these trips; Olga never handled it, and considered it unnecessary and horribly vulgar to discuss prices. The *homme d'affaires* would receive the accounts later and deal with these details.

Olga's existence may have seemed dull to her granddaughter, but it was solid, weighted by generations of demarcation and prescription. You knew who people were, how they counted, and what was correct. Now, we read about this life's bizarre excesses and what seem exotic delights in books with regretful titles like *Lost Splendour*, *Once a Grand Duke*, or *A Princess Remembers*. Then, it seemed a way of life that would surely go on for ever.

CHAPTER 3

THE LITTLE BOLSHEVIK

May you live in interesting times!
– Chinese curse

It is only with hindsight that 1914 appears to be the year when everything began to change; the start of what made the Revolution possible; of what altered the course of Sofka's life. That summer must have seemed fairly typical of Sofka's childhood; characteristically, she was far from her parents, who no doubt had more interesting claims on their time than holidays with the Child. Sofka's summer holiday in 1914 was spent with dreary Miss King in Zyametchina, the Dolgorouky estate with the unfriendly village children.

That August, Olga was in Vienna, visiting her married daughter, now Princess Dietrichstein, from where she proceeded to Marienbad for a 'cure'. She didn't take much notice when news filtered through of an Austrian archduke murdered at Sarajevo. When war was suddenly declared, Olga found herself unable to get home. By the time a diplomat friend in Berlin helped her leave, and she and Louise had made a long, uncomfortable train journey (no dressing rooms this time) back through neutral Denmark, then Sweden and Finland, Petersburg had become Petrograd. Anything German, including a name, was despised and optimism was in the air; Berlin would be taken in no time.

Women and men rallied to the war effort. Both Sofka's parents left for the front: Petya with the Horse Guards, and Sophy as a doctor with her mother, Nadezhda, who set up a Red Cross first-aid unit. The Empress Alexandra established a military hospital in the palace at Tsarskoe Selo, some twenty miles outside the city, where she and her daughters worked every day. Olga did what she had done in the 1904 war with Japan, and turned the Dolgorouky ballroom into an assembly point for parcels destined for prisoners of war. Once again, she and her daughters rolled bandages, knitted scarves and made themselves useful.

People didn't know yet that most of the gigantic Russian Army was made up of poorly trained peasants with insufficient clothes and inferior weapons. Some had no boots. Village boys were sharing old-fashioned rifles. Within a year, several million Russian soldiers were dead and the country's enthusiasm had dulled to a dreadful sense of doom.

For seven-year-old Sofka, the routines with Miss King and her grandmother continued much as before, distant from the horrors of war. As the city became grimmer (street lights dimmed to save fuel, thieves lurking in dark corners, general misery), they spent more time in Olga's wooden dacha, just outside the palace gates at Tsarskoe Selo. This turning away from wretchedness and disorder was just what the Romanovs were doing too: Empress Alexandra became quite allergic to public life, while the people became suspicious of her eccentric ways. Cloistered like the Tsar's children, Sofka went for pony rides (with Simyon close by) and walked in the beautiful, well-guarded royal grounds. When her father came on leave, he brought her a white woolly puppy, named Pupsik (who was doted on by Miss King for the next ten years), and she even had a well-trained pet goat. Marie would pull Sofka along on roller-skates and come up to her bedroom, hooves clicking daintily on the wooden stairs.

The war's second year was even worse; the lack of men in the villages led to poor harvests and consequent food shortages. Still, it was not the city's bread queues that were the greatest shock for Olga. When Petya arrived home on leave, Sofka enjoyed the time with her affectionate, boyish father, going in to wake him at lunchtime, jumping on his bed and conspiring over secrets. It was probably obvious to her that something was afoot when she overheard her aunts whispering about 'the tragedy', though she might not have guessed that it involved her handsome, scented, teasing father. Petya had announced that he wished to marry Anna Michaelovna, the woman who had already borne his child, and whom he loved.

'People looked at the marriage with great disapproval,' explained a Russian émigré who had heard the stories. 'They said that he went off with a gypsy singer and had lots of bastards. It's easy to scoff now, but you have to realize the tremendous strength of social snobbishness at that time. A man with a great Russian name was marrying a possibly quite nice woman, but one who was spoken of in the same way in which one spoke of a prostitute. Actually it was very noble of him to marry her, so that she wouldn't be left penniless if he was killed in the war – the Horse Guards were suffering appalling losses. Many men would have taken advantage of the situation.' Although Petya ended up having six children with Anna, his mother never received this daughter-in-law, who was certainly not 'born'. Indeed, Olga declined to acknowledge her existence. Sofka never met her stepmother either, but her father's wayward and scandalous insistence on following his heart was a significant

Granny always dressed in full mourning clothes after her husband died. She expected 'the Child' to behave with perfect manners and was keen to install some 'backbone' in Sofka after her young parents separated. The lamb is untraceable, but was perhaps a companion of Sofka's pet goat, Marie.

example in going contrary to convention, tradition, advice and family. It was as though Petya helped immunize his daughter against keeping up appearances or ignoring the powerful pull of love; she would never be dogged by these dilemmas. Sofka's mother might have been the obvious revolutionary, but her father was the great romantic and, in his way, just as much of a rebel.

'Of course, everyone blamed Rasputin for the disastrous situation,' said Uncle Kyril. He remembered listening to the grown-ups' obsessive, anxious discussions during the First World War, waiting on tenterhooks for news of loved ones and mourning their deaths. His father (a liberal) would return from sessions at the Duma, where relations with the Emperor were growing steadily worse. Many believed that Rasputin was influencing the Tsar's decisions and feared that the entire country was being pulled into the demonic grip of a village madman. Even Sophy, normally so serious, had been curious to meet this wild-eyed, straggly-haired, black-bearded 'holy man' from Siberia. Just before the war, she'd begun studying the infant subject of psychology, reading Freud and working in 'lunatic asylums' – a new branch of medicine which she compared to 'entering a vast maze blindfolded'. She was intrigued by the stories about how Rasputin mysteriously stopped the bleeding when the young haemophiliac Tsarevich was unwell. She knew how close Rasputin was to Nicholas and Alexandra (calling them 'Papa' and 'Mama'), but she'd also heard about the drunken feasting with gypsies and the orgies with society ladies; 'you must sin first to find redemption' was his conveniently persuasive philosophy. Wanting to see this phenomenon for herself, Sophy managed to visit Rasputin at 64 Gorokhovaya Street, on one of the days he 'received', queuing up with a crowd of overexcited, bejewelled ladies. She found him repellent, she told Sofka later, but couldn't help sensing the strength of his dominant personality and the power of his piercing blue eyes. 'Some sort of hypnotism' was how she explained his success with the sick boy and his desperate parents.

In the spring of 1916, Sophy returned to Petrograd with malaria and two St George Crosses – the highest award for bravery in Russia. 'I did nothing brave,' she said, setting herself up as a daunting model of courage. Sofka visited her mother on the English Embankment, where she lay sweating and shivering in her darkened bedroom. Ice-packs and hot-water bottles were alternated by Natasha, Sophy's dark-eyed, dignified young maid.

Sofka later admitted a sense of inadequacy beside her remarkable mother. She sprawled on Sophy's rose-coloured bed and listened to the stories. During the winter of 1914–15, Sophy's first-aid post was just behind the Polish front. It was desperately cold, there were inadequate supplies and the pitiful Russian Army was being constantly pushed back by the superior German forces. At one point, Sophy was retreating through a snowy forest with some soldiers – ready with a shot of morphine for the wounded. Just as they were emerging from the woodland, they heard blood-curdling shrieks from a man in agony, behind them. Nobody turned back. The screams continued. Sophy called an orderly and headed back into the trees, towards the enemy. Finding a man covered in blood and with a shattered leg, Sophy gave relief with her 'merciful hypodermic' and the orderly carried the man back to camp. She never knew whether he lived or not. 'It was not bravery,' she insisted, though of course it was. 'I knew I could never live with myself hearing those screams for the rest of my life.'

If the cutting Russian winter had been dreadful, with its frostbite and frozen bodies, Sophy's next posting was worse. She was sent south to the Turkish front, to blistering heat, sandstorms, a lack of water, days on horseback, stinking gangrene and gruesome amputations in stiflingly hot tents. Flies, mosquitoes, snakes and scorpions added their own weapons to those of the Turks. One day, as Sophy was dressing, she felt something bulging in her sleeve. Realizing it must be one of the tarantula-like spiders with a deadly bite, she grabbed the lump, squeezing hard, until the poisonous creature was dead. I'm not quite sure what she got her second medal for, but she surely deserved it just for that. I picture her telling the story deadpan in her quiet, low voice to eight-year-old Sofka.

Sophy's convalescence was predictably brief. She took Sofka and Miss King down to Crimea for a holiday, but quickly became restless. She had formulated another bold scheme and signed up with the military flying school at Gatchina (just outside Petrograd), where she already had her own plane. Nearly a century later, it seems extraordinary that a woman should have been allowed to train as a bomber pilot, but she was not the only female fighter. Petersburg had already seen Maria Botchkareva and her Battalion of Death – an uneducated peasant girl who led 1,500 women (with shorn heads and special epaulettes) to the front. Like Sophy, she was also awarded the Cross of St George for bravery.

Sophy had been among the first women who learned to fly at the Ecole Militaire d'Aviation at Chartres in 1913. 'There was no dual control in those days, so you learned the theory,' she explained to Sofka. 'You practised moving the controls on a stationary plane and then took off. The most disconcerting thing was glimpsing the earth through the gaps in the floor under your feet.' When she returned to Russia, Sophy brought a plane back with her, keeping it at Gatchina: 'the greatest and most enjoyable extravagance of my life'. Sophy's friends were incredulous when she told them of her latest acquisition. She must have enjoyed imagining their exclamations when she arranged to fly past them as they assembled for picnics on the shores of Lake Ladoga.

'Every flyer knows the splendour of those morning flights,' Sophy wrote in her memoirs. 'The nervous tension of the beginner, the feeling of joy and peace alone above the clouds, then the first rays of the rising sun and the long gliding descent down onto the earth.'

It was just after Sophy was awarded the wings of a military pilot in late 1916 that her friend Prince Felix Yusupov killed Rasputin. Well known for being vastly rich and handsome and having a (lasting) penchant for cross-dressing, Felix was married to Irina, the Tsar's strikingly lovely niece. He also smoked opium, something in which Sophy joined him. This seductive pleasure offered her a new intellectual fascination, opening up uncharted areas of the mind, and fleetingly giving the answer to everything, even if it was forgotten afterwards. It was another example of Sophy's open-mindedness and her desire to cross boundaries; she didn't imagine that the drug's lure could ever prove stronger than her own forceful will.

Rasputin's gruesome end is well known but too compelling to entirely ignore. Like the busloads of tourists I saw from my Petersburg window, arriving each day at the sumptuous Yusupov Palace, I was fascinated by the grotesque details, the powerful archetypes; it's no chance that the museum's most popular tour (requiring an extra ticket) is the basement, where kitsch wax-works depict the murder scene. We all want to know about the specially furnished cellar, 'Yankee Doodle' on the gramophone, the bearskins, the ivory crucifix, whether or not the almond cakes and wine were poisoned; and lecherous, drunken Rasputin in an embroidered silk blouse and black velvet breeches, smelling of 'cheap soap'. Felix may have been a delicate, camp, sybaritic opium smoker, but he was forceful enough to persuade a grand-duke, a doctor and a member of the Duma to help him with the murder. It was nearly a botched job, more likely due to the amateur status of the anxious murderers than Rasputin's alleged supernatural powers, though Yusupov described the 'evil genius' returning to life after being shot, frothing at the mouth and attacking him. Finally, in the middle of the night, the men managed to kill the person they believed was destroying their country, wrap up his body, drive it to a bridge and throw it into the icy river.

The killers were never tried or imprisoned. With or without Rasputin, the country was already spiralling into disaster. Sophy was ready to leave for the front as a fighter pilot in the Squadron of Flying Ships, but there was now barely a front to go to. Few believed the Tsar could save them. Everything was unravelling: there were food shortages, soldiers deserting, workers on strike, street demonstrations. Temperatures in Petrograd plummeted to forty degrees below zero – even the trains couldn't run. The soviets (councils of workers, soldiers and peasants) grew steadily more powerful, and revolutionaries began to believe they might actually have a political future beyond plotting in smoky rooms. Revolutionary propaganda needed little to persuade people who were hungry, war-weary, cold and frightened.

Olga and Sofka stopped going for their daily drives. It was hard to enjoy them with lorries careering down Nevsky Prospekt full of armed men waving red flags. Banners proclaimed: DOWN WITH THE TSAR, DOWN WITH THE GERMAN WOMAN (the Empress), ALL POWER TO THE DUMA. In March, the Emperor abdicated in favour of an ineffectual provisional government, but the chaos and violence continued. Simyon told Sofka that people were starving and she responded by smuggling biscuits from the tea table so he could pass them on to the needy. Sofka's paternal aunt, Varvara, lived close by and often visited. In her memoirs (*Gone Forever*), Aunt Varvara described the problems of being out in the streets: 'Often, in the daytime, the red soldiers, driving about in town, would shoot without any reason or aim.' Once Miss King had to push Sofka behind a stone parapet on the English Embankment, when shots suddenly rang out and hit a wall nearby. At night, fires burned and buildings were looted. Aunt Varvara was terrified when 'a crowd gathered in front of a prison, not far away from my house, to set the prisoners free. The yelling of the crowd was sinister and indescribable, as the mob was breaking through the door of the prison.'

One day, soldiers came to Varvara's house.

'My butler managed to keep them in the kitchen, calling me down to them. They wanted my car and being in the kitchen asked for some food. The chauffeur being out, they simply broke the lock and to my disgust drove out with a big red flag fixed to my car. Every evening they brought it back and asked for food until one day they came to say that it was broken and I could fetch it in such and such a street and have it mended.'

Varvara was still indignant about this many years later, writing, 'I certainly did not have it fetched and mended for them to take it again.' Meanwhile, at the Bobrinsky home, orders to destroy stocks of alcohol were carried out. Sofka's uncle recalled Igor, the old doorman, 'livid with fear and indignation' as a group of soldiers barged in, smashing bottles of twenty-five-year-old Château d'Yquem and green chartreuse, and wading 'knee deep in a fragrant pool of most exquisite French wine'.

The Emperor and his family were under house arrest at Tsarskoe Selo, and various Romanovs were being sought out. One day, a lorry of armed men came to search the Dolgorouky house in the hope of finding someone important, and although nobody was hurt, Olga was understandably upset. It was increasingly hard to look the other way and pretend that it would all pass quickly. No doubt Sofka, Olga and Miss King were completely unaware that on 16 April a short, snub-nosed man known as Lenin arrived to a grand, popular welcome at the Finland Station. Perhaps they heard when Lenin set up headquarters in Kshesinskaya's opulent palace – after all, the exquisite ballet dancer was celebrated and had had more than one Romanov lover (she apparently suggested the title *Fifty Years under the Romanovs* for her memoirs, but it was declined by the publishers).

When Olga learned that her old friend the Dowager Empress had made her way down south to the Crimea, she decided to take Sofka and follow suit.

* * *

The journey to Simferopol took several days by train, and there were many delays along the way. But Olga managed to reserve eight compartments so it was hardly uncomfortable. Sofka was happy to be returning to the place she adored: 'To a child the Crimea was a place of infinite enchantment. Roses. Huge blossoms of every shade from which I would pluck the green-gold beetles nestling at the heart . . . The joy of lying sun-baked in a vineyard, head and book in the shade of a loaded vine; or stretched on the broad flat silvery branch of a fig tree where one had only to put a hand out for a juicy sun-warmed fig . . .' This peninsula, sticking out into the Black Sea, was like heaven on earth for the citizens of cold, damp, foggy Petersburg.

My own journey to the Crimea came seventy-seven years later, flying bumpily from Petersburg with Aeroflot. The popularity of holidays on the Black Sea didn't end with the Revolution; in fact two weeks in a state sanatorium became routine for vast numbers of Russians from around the Soviet

Union. The grand palaces and villas dotted along the coastline were turned into health spas where tired workers could rest (with the nicest ones reserved for the *nomenklatura*). These days, people organized their own holidays, and my fellow passengers looked like the last batch of pale northerners heading south for a taste of sunshine before the long, hard winter. They all carried too many bulging plastic bags and made a good deal of noise.

Sofka and Olga took a horse-drawn carriage from Simferopol, across the interior of the Crimean peninsula, down to Yalta on the coast. I went in a taxi with a police speed-radar detector. I could smell the different atmosphere immediately: pine trees, warm earth, mountain air with a salty hint of the sea. As an adult, Sofka never wanted to return to her 'picture of near paradise' with its 'intoxicating scent of sun-baked wildness'; she feared seeing it tamed and ruined by 'the ubiquitous tourist'. Once, though, unexpectedly, she was suddenly transported back while travelling in Bulgaria. 'Don't you find that of all things smell is the most evocative?' she wrote to my father when he was a student. 'You get the scent of some plant in the sun, or rain on earth, or tar in a street . . . That was one of the things that got me about Bulgaria – the smells of the Black Sea are those of the Crimea and through all vicissitudes of existence, that has remained "home".'

The Crimea became Russian when Catherine the Great annexed it from Turkey, gaining valuable access to the Black Sea, and the Romanovs helped turn Yalta into a fashionable resort after they built estates there in the nineteenth century. The area was always a rich melting pot of peoples: a microcosm of the Black Sea, with its unique combinations of Europe and Asia, wildness and civilization. Its history had seen Tartar invaders, Genoese settlers, Roman armies and ancient Greek colonies.

Russian visitors encountered Tartars, Armenians, Georgians, Greeks, Jews and merchants from all over the place. 'It's the Tartars who are the problem,' said my Ukrainian taxi driver. 'They're lazy and they smell.' He didn't mention the dreadful persecution they'd suffered, from Stalin's time onwards, when many were exiled to Kazakhstan, their homes and land confiscated.

The imperial family's arrival marked Crimea's 'velvet' season, when the 'cotton' one was ending and ordinary holiday-makers in hotels and rented rooms returned north for work. Perhaps the Silver Age artists and writers were something in between: 'silk'? Chekhov went there to write, the famous bass Chaliapin rented a dacha on the Dolgorouky estate (Sofka sometimes heard him through the trees, booming Russian songs), and Akhmatova described her love for this 'pagan, unbaptised land' with 'an ancient, half-Greek, half-barbarian, deeply un-Russian culture'. As the mellow, fading summer blurred into autumn, high society went mushroom-picking in the woods or picnicking up on Ai Petri, the craggy peak that dominates Yalta's coastline. They swam in the sea, collected pebbles and dipped them in candlewax until they shone, and rode through the countryside on ponies accompanied by Tartar grooms. There was sailing, fishing, hunting and informal parties; a far cry from the tightly corseted etiquette of Petersburg.

As in the French Riviera, there were two coast roads: one near the sea, linking the fanciful villas and elegant palaces, and another, higher one snaking through the picturesque Tartar villages. The estates ran in generous swathes from the wooded foothills down through the vineyards, greenhouses and estate workers' cottages and then the flower-filled gardens and wooded paths leading to the rocky beaches. Everybody wanted their private paradise. When the Emir of Bukhara decided to build his splendid oriental palace, at around the time of Sofka's birth, he found the best position with ingenuity. He killed seven sheep and placed each in a different potential site for his building. After one week, the carcasses were examined, and the one that was least decayed revealed the best, driest air. And that's where the Emir ordered the foundations to be dug.

I didn't know what had happened to the Dolgorouky estate at Miskhor, but I'd managed to book a hotel somewhere close to a village of the same name. The taxi driver dropped me off at a vast, unappealing holiday complex, filled with vividly sunburned Russians in very few clothes; this was evidently the 'nylon' season. The place was a hideous hangover from the old Communist style of tourism, but Dmitri, the nice young hotel 'administrator', told me that now the Ukrainians were independent, they were trying to improve things. He added that his mother was an experienced guide to the region and could surely help me with my quest.

My room was an anonymous box, up on the ninth floor of an ugly block – one of many that stuck up awkwardly and incongruously from the astounding patchwork of green trees. The Communists had tried very hard to destroy this Garden of Eden, but you could still see what it had once been. I stood on my balcony, looking at the wooded slopes that ran down to the deep cobalt sea, where white horses were breaking – 'the bluest black sea in the world', as a Khrushchev-era song went. The skies were huge and filled with strange, multi-coloured clouds at sunset. I wondered where the house at Miskhor had been and whether anything remained. Maybe it was under this very hotel.

I'd had some luck, however, in my search. When I'd visited Andrei Gagarin of the Petersburg Nobility Association, he'd dug out a photocopy of memoirs by Varvara Dolgorouky, Sofka's aunt, which I'd never seen before. Among the many photographs was a small black and white one of Miskhor; a two-storey white house, elegant but not grandiose, with a pillared porch and gothic arched windows. I now had a copy of the picture and hoped that this would help me find at least the site where Sofka spent her last two years in Russia.

By the summer of 1917 Olga's oldest son, Sergei, was already at Miskhor. He was equerry to the Dowager Empress who was under guard some miles along the coast at Ai Todor, with her daughter Grand-Duchess Xenia and her family. Sergei had made a late and unexpected marriage three years earlier, and his wife, Irina, had been married to a Vorontsoff (the owner of the vast, splendid Alupka estate). She already had four children when she fell in love with the handsome (if increasingly chubby) Sergei, but she got divorced, and the couple now had a two-year-old daughter named Olga. It must have been a horrible shock, then, for Sofka and her grandmother when they arrived in Yalta, repaired to their favourite café for chocolate and were informed that Irina was dead. She had been ill, possibly with pneumonia, and had taken too much medicine. Gossips said it was suicide; life had become unbearable for her after discovering that her marriage was a convenient screen for Sergei's long-standing affair with the Grand-Duchess Xenia.

If Xenia knew the full story, she didn't give the game away: 'Poor Seriozha [diminutive of Sergei],' she wrote in a letter to her brother-in-law. 'I feel terribly sad, he doesn't allow anyone to come near him, how he suffers and how lonely he is now. Never will I believe that it was intentional that she took poison – she loved the children too much . . .' Whatever the case, Sofka, Olga and Miss King (who favoured the suicide version in whispered conversations with her charge) arrived at Miskhor to find a house in mourning. It was Sofka's first (and 'reassuring') sight of death as she was taken in to kiss Aunt Irina's cold hand; 'one of the most beautiful women imaginable', surrounded by white roses.

Some hours after I fell asleep, to the dull thump of disco music blaring from loudspeakers by the hotel pool, I woke up to find myself out on my dark, vertigo-inducing balcony. I was clutching my sheets and blankets, trying to escape. In the morning, it seemed like an echo of all Sofka's fleeing; a sign that I was sleepwalking in her life. I took her book with me to the complex's canteen, where the breakfast was spectacularly unappetizing: fatty sausages floating in water; fly-blown bananas chopped into segments with the blackened skin still on; and glue-coloured, salty, gulag-style *kasha* (porridge). All of a sudden, I felt terribly lonely.

Clutching my photocopied picture of Miskhor, I walked out of the holiday camp to the main road. Opposite the grannies selling home-knitted sweaters and aromatic, juniper-filled cushions was a group of bored-looking taxi drivers. 'If it's Miskhor, it'll be down the road,' said a pot-bellied Azerbaijani with grey hair and beetling black eyebrows, when I told of my search for the white house. 'Here we're in Marat – you know? It's named after the French revolutionary.' We drove five minutes or so along the coast, with a running commentary about how awful the Tartars are ('Stalin was quite right in what he did to them, and if we hadn't had Stalin, we'd all be Nazis now. *Heil Hitler!*'). The driver pulled up by another gaggle of taxi drivers, playing backgammon and smoking under a tree by the side of the road. My photograph was handed around to general amusement, until one of them jumped up, shouting, 'It's just down here! Come, with me!'

The man strode off down a shady driveway, and I followed him, pursued by several taxi drivers who were evidently up for some entertainment. Through the trees, I could see a white building. 'It's yours! You should take it back!' shouted the Azerbaijani, getting overexcited. 'If you have the money, it's yours.' I stopped, comparing the three-storey house in front of us with the two-storey one in the photograph, counting the slim, gothic-arched windows. Some changes had been made, but this was definitely Sofka's beloved Miskhor. The drivers were smiling almost as much as me, sensing my happiness. I gazed around, taking in the towering cypresses and the view up to the white ridges of Ai Petri and down to the sea.

'It's a rest place and sanatorium for workers,' said one taxi driver, pointing to a sign saying LOWER MISKHOR LODGE: MEDICAL-THERAPEUTIC CENTRE. Over by a large stone fountain, some

I had no idea whether Sofka's beloved Miskhor still existed. Eventually, some Azerbaijani taxi drivers helped me find it, and there was no mistaking the house. The gardens still had an 'intoxicating scent of sun-baked wildness'.

residents sat on green park benches, eating fried things out of grubby plastic boxes. They eyed our unusual party suspiciously. The drivers were already pulling me up the steps to the front door (now missing its old porch) and calling to the 'administrator', an unfriendly peroxide-blonde. She knew nothing about the Dolgorouky family, she said. The house had belonged to a 'Prince Naryshkin'. She showed us a nasty reproduction portrait of a nineteenth-century soldier, hanging accusingly in the sitting room, as if hinting that my claims were fraudulent. The whole building was now divided up into small bedrooms for the guests – there was nothing to see. She briefly showed us a miserable little cell to prove it. Whatever the administrator's opinion, I was certain that this had been Sofka's house; I could sense it was the right place, and I had the photograph to prove it. Asking whether I could wander around and maybe come back later, I said my thanks and goodbyes to the taxi drivers, who left, whispering conspiratorial encouragement.

I walked slowly around the gardens, scented with rosemary, pine, juniper and cedar. There were no roses now, but mauve wisteria wrapped itself around the terrace at the back of the house. Above it was where Sofka had her 'schoolroom' for lessons with Miss King. I followed the shady, winding paths away from the house down towards the sea. Through the tall oaks and cypresses came the noise of waves breaking on the shingle, just as Chekhov described in 'The Lady with the Little Dog', his wonderful story of adultery set in Yalta. 'The monotonous, hollow roar of the sea that reached them from below spoke of peace, of that eternal slumber that awaits us'. It was easy to picture Sofka, aged ten, climbing trees or hiding in the bushes as Miss King called in vain from the terrace and Simyon was sent out to search. In photographs she has a wry tomboy expression, notwithstanding the pair of long, thick, glossy plaits tied with bows; she had already discovered the joys of going against the grain. I followed some steps down to a scruffy little pier and a haphazard arrangement of beach huts, where I lay down on a decrepit wooden sun-bed near a family of chubby Russians who were eating fruit. Sofka used to come down here in the mornings. She would go out early, taking Rim, her Great Dane, who was so large he could be saddled with bags, donkey-style, and used to collect firewood when fuel became scarce. Several times that winter, she saw dead bodies washed up on the rocks. They were pale, naked and crawling with crabs. People said they'd been executed in Yalta and flung into the sea.

I'm not sure where Sofka got Rim, but maybe he was another present from her adoring father, to add to Pupsik, who also made the journey south. Petya soon arrived in the Crimea too, bringing his new wife and children to his own estate on the other side of Yalta, and although his second family was treated by Olga as invisible, he visited Miskhor alone from time to time. Preferring the intrigues of friendship to parental duties, he kept Sofka supplied with contraband cigarettes – almost certainly Papirosy, the ubiquitous Russian brand with an integrated cardboard mouthpiece. She smoked them furtively with her friends up in the flat-topped fir tree, chewing wild garlic afterwards to hide the smell from Miss King.

At Miskhor, Sofka's natural rebelliousness was given plenty of space in which to flourish; this period was the most intense of her childhood, and also the happiest. The grown-ups were too worried about the 'troubles' to fuss much about 'the Child' or her lessons, and Sofka's preference was to run wild. Her new friends were Vanya and Shura, the lodgekeeper's grandsons, whom she felt would not be considered suitable playmates on account of their uncompromisingly revolutionary beliefs. She crept out to meet them first thing in the morning, before Miss King awoke. In between fighting with pine cones, picking walnuts and hazelnuts and raiding fruit gardens, their conversations opened Sofka's eyes to another side of 'the troubles'. It was this friendship more than anything else which was to remain with Sofka from her days in Crimea, and which transported her from the narrow, circumscribed world as depicted and lived by Olga and Miss King. Shura, the older, more charming and voluble of the brothers, explained the logic of the Revolution: why should Sofka have all the advantages of comfort, money and lessons with governesses, when he was much more intelligent than her, yet was barefoot and uneducated? Later, when their father became a member of the local soviet, they told Sofka about projected raids on local houses: 'Why should the Ivanovs have cakes when so many people were rationed even for bread'? She learned to keep quiet when she heard the adults' foolish speculations at home.

Backing up Shura's theories was Simyon, the footman, who had discussed such things with Sofka before. He'd take her fishing down on the rocks and talk about the injustice of wealth and poverty, and about his own miserable village childhood. The Revolution would cure all this, he believed. Needless to say, when Sofka tried airing a watered-down version of these theories to her other playmates or her grandmother, she was berated for being a 'Red' or a 'little Bolshevik'.

For the first few months, life at Miskhor seemed quite normal. Olga played Solitaire in the long drawing room or took Sofka out in the landau to visit friends. Cousins and young people gathered at Miskhor to play tennis, which had the only, much-coveted tennis court in the area. One day, Olga invited her old friend Marie, the Tsar's mother, to tea, and 'the Child' was scrubbed and groomed for the occasion. Miss King repeated instructions for teatime etiquette: 'speak when spoken to, say "Your Majesty," eat with your left hand, and teacup to the right of your plate'.

'No wonder I was deeply and profoundly horrified,' wrote Sofka, 'to see the Dowager Empress of All the Russias, beside whom I was sitting, hold a biscuit in her right hand and place her cup somewhere to the left of her plate. Had nobody told her? At last I could bear it no longer. I leaned towards her and in what must have been a strident whisper informed her that the proper way to behave was . . .'

Olga's shocked dismay at Sofka's *faux pas* dominated the next twenty-four hours, until the following afternoon, when Empress Marie drove up and asked for Sofka to go with her, unaccompanied, for a drive. Sofka remembered this and other subsequent drives with pleasure; the old woman (sister to Britain's Queen Alexandra) had huge charm and 'a slightly monkey-like vitality and humour and a gleam in her eyes that appeared to see what you were thinking'.

That autumn, things began to change. News (adulterated with hearsay) filtered through: 'Citizen Romanov' and his family had been sent to the Urals; the Winter Palace had been stormed; and somehow, within the chaos, Lenin, Trotsky, Zinoviev (no relation – he changed his named from Apfelbaum) and the Bolsheviks had grasped power. The Red Army finally arrived in the Crimea and soviets were established; every village, including Miskhor, was now ruled by a commissar. It was whispered that they wanted to execute the Dowager Empress; at this stage, everything was rumours. In December, Sofka's father was among the tsarist officers who tried to defend Yalta but were routed by the Reds. Many were killed, but Petya managed to escape; they knew this because a notice specifying a reward for the capture of Prince Peter Dolgorouky was posted on his mother's house (to

Olga's horror). One wet winter evening, some time later, the household was disturbed by a knocking at the front door. Nobody wanted to open it, as raids were increasingly common and the worst things seemed to happen at night. Eventually it was Miss King who identified the voice outside, claiming to be 'a friend'. Sofka didn't recognize the soaking, trembling man who staggered in, dressed in a torn coat and Tartar cap, until her governess instructed her to kiss her father.

There was a tense moment when Petya asked the servants present whether they would help hide him, but ultimately even Simyon, with his revolutionary opinions, agreed. His Grace had always been good to them. People were not yet too afraid or too brutalized to abandon loyalty. Petya was hidden in the attic and nursed through pneumonia by Louise, Olga's devoted maid. When he was well enough to leave, it was Simyon who helped organize his escape to Moscow, driving the scruffy figure in the Tartar clothes to a secret meeting point with the truck which would take him to Sebastopol.

Miskhor's commissar commandeered Olga's carriage and pair of ancient black horses for his own use, but he was evidently a thoughtful man, as he sometimes sent it down for her. On one occasion he passed her walking and to her consternation insisted on giving her a lift. A more improbable couple than the old Petersburg princess and the Bolshevik commissar is hard to imagine, but life in 1918 was full of contradictions. Simyon and other members of the Dolgorouky staff joined the local soviet, but they still served dinner at Miskhor, dressed in livery. Despite the severe lack of food, Olga, Miss King and Sofka continued to change for dinner, and the butler produced a menu, which might proudly announce *'pommes de terre au bacon'*, meaning a few boiled potatoes with some fried onion and a small quantity of lard.

Once, Bolsheviks arrived to search the house for weapons. Two drunken sailors brandished their revolvers in Olga's face, as she led them, frightened but dignified, through the rooms. 'Don't be afraid, madam. Don't be afraid,' they repeated as Sofka stuck close to her grandmother, watching curiously. On leaving, the order was given that all women and children should cultivate the land to grow food, and the subsequent sight of Olga, Miss King, Louise and Sofka slowly digging up the lawn must have been a tragi-comic shock for the servants. Sofka enjoyed the novelty, but for Olga, who couldn't even button up her own boots, planting potatoes must have been a humiliating trial. I imagine Louise commiserating in the evening, smoothing cream on to her mistress's pale, soft, manicured hands, which had never done a day's work.

* * *

The next day I met Olga, the hotel administrator's mother. She was brisk, intelligent and friendly – a redhead in her late forties, wearing a shiny trouser suit. Hopping on to hotel minibuses (waving her 'guide' badge authoritatively), she took me to Yalta, explaining along the way the differences between Crimea before the Revolution, under Communism and now as part of independent Ukraine. She talked about how even teachers can't afford to live on their salaries these days, and have to take a second job, or sell off their possessions in the market. Then there are the rich 'new' Russians and Ukrainians who arrive to set up shady businesses and build their enormous dachas. Later, she pointed out the long line of people waiting for 'evening bread', who couldn't afford it fresh in the mornings. Sometimes, I told her, I thought the former USSR was setting itself up for another revolution, with such a painfully obvious chasm opening up between rich and poor; it's like it was a hundred years ago. 'No!' Olga insisted, showing her passion for everything noble and pre-Revolutionary. 'In those days, rich people set up hospitals and orphanages and helped all the people who were dependent on them. It wasn't the same!'

In Yalta we strode along the busy promenade, where someone enterprising had erected a series of stage sets with matching costumes for holiday photographs. There was bondage and black leather, but the favourites were the eighteenth-century palace with silks and wigs, and the *haut bourgeois* drawing room, with bustles and bonnets. It wasn't just me, it seemed, who was seeking fantasies of the past.

After a series of meetings and phone calls, we set off to see a woman who Olga claimed would be able to tell me everything. She would meet us at the archives room of the Vorontsoff Palace at Alupka. We arrived at a gigantic palace, built like a castle, with grey stone, jagged and crenellated in places to echo Ai Petri's peaks. Skirting the ticket queues, postcard sellers and holiday-makers posing for photographs, we climbed down into the bowels of the palace, to a long, dark corridor and a room full of books and files. Inside were two elderly ladies.

'This is Anna Abramovna,' said Olga, introducing me to a woman with a very pale, quiet, determined face, iron-coloured hair pulled into a bun and a wooden cross lying on her chest. She looked like someone from another era, though I wasn't quite sure which. Within minutes, she had produced a number of photographs: Sofka as a baby and a ten-year-old; her grandparents taking tea in an estate cottage (Olga in outrageously large hat, Sandik with those unmistakable white whiskers); Sophy looking like a man; Petya and his adulterous older brother Sergei. And it wasn't just pictures. Anna Abramovna reeled off all the details of their lives and ancestors, speaking of them as though she knew them, with first name and patronymic. After she had clarified exactly which son's daughter I was, she continued explaining the lives and fates of everyone connected to the Dolgorouky family. It was as though they were all still there.

There was no mistaking Anna Abramovna's favourite: beautiful Irina. During her first marriage, she had lived in this palace with its endless ballrooms, marble columns, vast conservatory and terraces with statues leading down to the sea. I heard about how she divorced and married Sergei Dolgorouky, Sofka's uncle, the tragic illness, the untimely death, and was shown a portrait of Irina, dark-haired, mysterious, feminine and elegant. 'She was buried in the Miskhor Cemetery,' said Anna Abramovna. 'We could go and see her grave.' While the older woman went off in search of flowers, Olga gave me a whistle-stop tour of a closed part of the museum, filled with belongings and pictures of the Vorontsoff family. They were old friends of the Dolgoroukys, and their estates were established at around the same time, in the 1820s, when Yalta was becoming fashionable.

We took a taxi back along the coast to Miskhor, and followed a small, rough road up the hill, stopping by a fig grove. The driver agreed to wait, and we walked up a track to a tree-covered hillock. Anna Abramovna was clutching a bunch of colourful dahlias in a plastic bottle of water and told me about Irina's funeral as though she'd been there. It had been terribly hot weather that week – forty degrees – and there'd been a great thunderstorm. The Romanovs were given permission to leave their houses to attend the ceremony. Sofka described how Irina's coffin was carried open to the graveside, and the road from the house to the cemetery was 'inches deep in roses and great ropes of them hung, like garlands, from tree to tree'. She said that she would never forget 'the singing of the choir, the chanting of the priest, the scent of the roses mingled with the incense, the intense blue of the sky and the darker reflection of the sea which seemed just at our feet as we stood beside the grave'.

The Miskhor Cemetery looked quite abandoned. Despite the evidence of picnics and drinking sessions, there was a wonderful, secret atmosphere here, perched above the sea, among the cypresses and almond trees. It had been built for estate employees, but gradually people who lived in the dachas used it too. Many of the graves were simply marked by small stone circles, and some goats had made themselves at home, lying on the comfortable, bed-sized patches of smooth earth. Further down, a young turbaned goatherd was sprawled on the cemetery wall, looking out to sea.

'Over there is what remains of the Dolgorouky olive grove,' said Anna Abramovna, pointing across at a swathe of silver-leafed trees interspersed with some shabby blocks of flats. 'It was the largest in the whole region, and produced the best oil. People from those flats come and take care of Irina's grave,' she continued, walking up to the tomb, which was placed apart from the rest of the graveyard. 'The gravestone was completely destroyed and several of us paid for a new one in 1984. We didn't announce it because it might have brought trouble in Soviet times – Dolgorouky wasn't a name to honour then.' We stood by the simple tomb, surrounded by a little wall and cast-iron railings and overshadowed by an olive tree. The stone was marked with a Russian cross and Irina's name and dates (1870–1917). Olga arranged the dahlias and Anna Abramovna picked up an old plastic bag, breaking off some pieces of biscuit which were inside.

'Are you Orthodox?' she asked me, and when I confirmed I was, she gave me and Olga a piece of soggy, stale biscuit, as though it were a communion wafer, and asked us to say a prayer for the sins of Irina and her children. 'They're all dead now,' she said sadly. Trying to banish my faint disgust at the old biscuit, but feeling terribly moved by the scene, I made the sign of the cross for my great-great-aunt.

Returning slowly down the hill, my two companions agreed to accompany me on a second visit to the house at Miskhor, and the taxi driver dropped us off at the top of the drive. 'You know, Miskhor is one of the oldest settlements on the Black Sea,' said Anna Abramovna, explaining how Naryshkin, who built the house (the 'prince' the administrator knew about), was an ancestor of Sofka's Granny Olga.

'But the original owner was La Belle Greque,' she said. 'One of the prettiest women in Russia.' I was delighted at this twist: 'the Beautiful Greek' was my favourite ancestor. Named Sophie like so many people in the story, she was a Constantinople Greek from the Phanar district. Her mother was a poor vegetable seller, who sold both her daughters as courtesans in the slave market, and Sophie quickly became known throughout Europe for her intelligence and exceptional looks. She married an Austrian prince called Witte and according to some was lost in cards to the fabulously wealthy Polish Count Potocki, who was madly in love with her. Some said La Belle Potocka (as she ended up) was a spy; others marvelled at her witty conversation, violet eyes and perfect features. Among other dalliances, she was a favourite of Potemkin, Catherine the Great's consort. The Empress (ever tolerant of Potemkin's paramours) gave the 'Beautiful Greek' a pair of diamond earrings, but what I didn't know until now was that Potemkin topped that and gave her the estate at Miskhor. Countess Potocka had ten children with Potocki before she died in 1822, and it was her daughter who married a Naryshkin and built the house.

'Sophie Potocka dreamed of founding a Greek city on the

coast here and calling it Sofiopolis,' said Anna Abramovna. The courtesan from Constantinople, across the Black Sea, was nothing if not ambitious. 'That never happened, but her daughter built a little estate within the estate – a small house and garden for children – and called it Sofievka. There's nothing left now, but everyone remarked on how it was perfectly made, with miniature furniture. The Naryshkins brought Torricelli, an architect from Odessa, to build the house, and they often shared builders, stonemasons and gardeners with the Vorontsoffs at Alupka.' Later I discovered that when the Vorontsoffs' head gardener ordered a thousand trees from Odessa, five hundred were sent to Miskhor. They created a 'pleasure garden', planted an oak grove and a laurel forest, and made a lake with Babylon weeping willows on the island. There was a water-mill, orchards, olives and vineyards with eighty thousand vines where they produced the best Riesling and Muscat wine.

'Anna Abramovna knows about all the estates along the coast here,' said Olga, as I marvelled at the older woman's encyclopaedic knowledge. 'It's been her life's work.' Later, she would even give me a list of all the estate workers during Sofka's era, and Olga and I tried to trace any descendants of Isidor Yeltsev, the coachman, who had nine children; Kapitsova, the estate baker; Chernagorov, who made the wine . . . We scoured village records and phone directories, and Olga even went off to the military offices, which had better lists. We made numerous calls to people with similar names, but all to no avail. People sounded scared: unexpected calls have a bad history in this country; it was impossible to find anyone who had any link with the estate before 1917.

'People move and change their names,' said Olga. 'They're afraid of the past. You're lucky that you can find out about your family's history. Most of us know nothing.'

'Suddenly one day the Germans were there,' wrote Sofka in her memoirs. It seemed incomprehensible to a child to see German officers marching about, 'making themselves at home'. In March 1918, the Bolsheviks signed a peace treaty giving the Germans huge tracts of land and swathes of population. One enemy was replaced with another.

Ironically, life under the Germans took on more of a semblance of normality again – restrictions vanished, food reappeared. Nobody believed the wild rumour in July that Nicholas, Alexandra and their family had been killed; a party planned by Felix Yusupov was not even cancelled. The horrible secrets of Ipatiev House in Ekaterinburg were not to emerge for some time. Later, they would learn the haunting details: the funny, pretty daughters, whose quick death from bullets was prevented by the pearls and diamonds sewn into their underclothes; the terrified haemophiliac boy who was never allowed rough games. Jimmy the spaniel killed too. Bayonets, blood, screaming. Even the imperial corpses were considered dangerous (potential martyrs, perhaps) and were burned, broken, buried. Among the servants and companions was Dr Botkin, who had also been the Dolgoroukys' doctor in Petersburg. Olga's nephew Vassily Dolgorouky, who had gone to Ekaterinburg as Nicholas's aide de camp, was killed separately.

'Poor Nicky,' said the Tsar's mother to Sofka's grandmother at tea, refusing to listen to the wicked stories. Perhaps things would still work out. Even the Bolsheviks denied that anything had happened.

At around that time, Sofka's mother arrived unexpectedly at Miskhor. Despite the dangerous and chaotic situation (anyone connected with the tsarist regime was an enemy and liable to arrest and even execution), she managed to get a train from Petrograd. After the last ten months' lack of news, Sophy hoped to check that her daughter had survived, and was astonished to find life carrying on almost as before; games of tennis, servants waiting at table, tea parties. It was a sharp contrast to Petrograd's tension, fear, cold and hunger. Sophy had been working back at her old hospital – they needed doctors for the ever-growing numbers of casualties from hypothermia and malnutrition, as well as shootings. She was sharing her flat with an old friend, the Marquis de Saint Sauveur from the French Embassy, as he supposedly guaranteed diplomatic immunity – there was an official paper pinned to the door – but there'd already been several raids. Sofka didn't say whether she was glad to see her mother, or whether she minded when Sophy left again after a few weeks, apparently preferring the looting, violence, ration cards and breadlines to life with her daughter.

Some months later, an explanation for Sophy's journey back north became apparent, when Sofka received a surprising letter from her mother. By the autumn, it was hard for any news to get through: there were no newspapers, letters or telephones. A civil war was raging, with the White Armies in the south, led by Generals Denikin and Wrangle, trying vainly to defeat the Red Army. Sophy's messenger took two months to reach Miskhor. Having caught typhoid along the way, he delivered the missive and died. The letter was read through and then burned to avoid infection. It announced that Sophy was getting married.

Given Sophy's rebellious, open-minded character, and her liberal manner of taking lovers after her divorce, I'd have imagined her choosing a revolutionary intellectual, someone like the writer Maxim Gorky perhaps, who crossed and merged the dangerous boundaries between White and Red. Sofka remembered a string of men whom Miss King drily called 'the suitors', including the Austrian Prince Hohenlohe and Prince Paolo Borghese, who removed the little-finger bone from

Sophy's anatomical skeleton and then wore it on his watch chain. Prince Pierre Volkonsky had been among the visitors, but hadn't appeared a likely choice as husband. Thirteen years older than Sophy, he had been a diplomat in Rome, London and Berlin and spoke six languages. Deeply religious, strongly conservative, fanatically erudite and precise, he was obsessed with family genealogies. The fact that he was known as a homosexual only increases his improbability as Sophy's fiancé. But as she herself declared (not one to mince her words), 'He was the only man I ever met who was more intelligent than I am.' He was also gentle and kind. Pierre and his old mother were still living in Petrograd, somehow managing to remain in the Volkonsky Mansion, which they called 'the Little White House' – somewhat inappropriately, given its frontage of fifteen windows. Following the wedding, Sophy joined him there.

* * *

By 1919, Yalta and its coast were filling up with refugees from the north, some of whom still believed that General Denikin's White Army would beat the Bolsheviks and take their new capital, Moscow. There was help from the mostly British and French Allied troops. One morning Sofka wrote, 'Miss King appeared to go mad, shouting, crying, waving her arms at a long grey ship flying the Union Jack.' A number of English people were evacuated, and there were increasingly urgent conversations amongst the Russians about whether it would be better to flee, at least until 'the troubles' settled down. A little later, HMS *Marlborough* anchored off Miskhor and the captain arrived at the jetty, with orders to take Queen Alexandra's sister, the Dowager Empress. Olga's carriage with the elderly black horses was sent off to Ai Todor with the message, but Empress Marie refused to abandon her relations and friends; she wouldn't leave unless everyone in danger was evacuated, she announced regally.

There was a period of waiting. It was a delicate situation: not only were there many who now wanted to leave, but King George V was extremely worried about giving British asylum to the autocratic Romanovs; there were fears of a backlash encouraging Labour Party support and increasing republican sentiment. Maybe the Dowager Empress should go to her native Denmark? Meanwhile, Miss King took tea with various British officers and 'strange delicacies such as Quaker Oats and corned beef' appeared on the Dolgorouky table. At last, a day was appointed for the evacuation and some other Allied ships arrived in Yalta. Crowds of people rushed to the port, abandoning their cars and carriages in the panic, pushing forward to find a way of leaving.

Sofka was told to prepare a bag of personal possessions, so as to leave with the Dowager Empress the next day. 'All I wanted was a favourite ikon, silver mug and bright coloured scarf and Rim,' Sofka wrote half a century later. The Great Dane was too big, they said. And it was not the idea of abandoning her home or the separation from her parents that caused Sofka most unhappiness; it was leaving the dog – 'the first real sorrow of my life'. Waking early on her last morning, the eleven-year-old raced down to the sea with Rim, 'howling in impotent agony at the thought of leaving it all'. She said goodbye to Vanya and Shura 'with the passionate misery of children', discussing the possibility of her hiding and remaining with them. But they 'seriously decided against it. The Red Army might not know that I was "all right" and I might as well live.'

At first, Sofka, Olga and Miss King were taken aboard a destroyer, the *Grafton*, but during the wait they were transferred to the *Marlborough*, where they joined the more select company, including the Dowager Empress and her daughter, Grand-Duchess Xenia, with her five children. Altogether there were 1,170 evacuees, including nineteen members of the imperial family, with servants, governesses and officials, and whatever anyone could salvage in the way of jewels and precious objects. One of the young officers organizing the operation was Francis Pridham, who later wrote a book about his experiences, and was greatly impressed by the 'dignity of the Russians on board'. The elderly Empress Marie was given the captain's cabin and people were made as comfortable as possible; extra bedding was sent for from the imperial houses so that at least the older people had mattresses and sheets, and dormitories were set up wherever possible on the cramped ships. Olga had a cabin, while Sofka and Miss King found a corner in which to sleep. Under the governess's high-necked blouse, a valuable rope of pearls pressed secretly against her pale breast – Sophy's wedding present from her parents in 1907, which she had given to Miss King for safekeeping on her recent visit.

After bad weather and repeated delays, the boats departed on 11 April. It was a grey, sombre morning. Elizabeth Zinovieff (a relation on the other side of the family, who was on the *Princess Ena*) recalled grey sky, grey sea and a great grey battleship veiled in a film of dense fog: 'The mist lifted slowly and a lonely, black-robed figure stood on deck, dignified and sorrowful. It was Empress Marie.' Nearby, was the magnificently tall Grand-Duke Nicholas (the Tsar's cousin and former commander-in-chief of the Russian armed forces), dressed in a long, military coat and grey astrakhan Cossack's hat. They were an improbable group of refugees, with their fine manners and elegant clothes. There in the haze they sang the Russian national anthem, 'God Save the Tsar'. Pridham noted later that this was the last time this 'beautiful old tune' was sung to a living member of the imperial family within Russian territory. Russians and British sailors alike shed a tear at the sad scene.

> *. . . Reign strong and great*
> *For our glory, our glory.*
> *Reign to the fear of our enemies,*
> *Tsar of the Orthodox Faith . . .*

Sofka remembered her 'last glimpse of the battlemented peak of Ai Petri' and saw this departure as marking 'the end of childhood'. Nevertheless, for the children on board, the journey seemed rather an adventure. Sofka quickly made friends with Vassily, Grand-Duchess Xenia's youngest son, who was two years her senior. A handsome, animated boy, who was soon very popular with the crew, Vassily had brought his canary with him,

It was a grey, foggy day when HMS Marlborough *finally left Yalta. The murdered Tsar's mother, Empress Marie, cut a lonely figure on deck and many wept when the Russian National Anthem was sung.*

93

and the family's smooth-haired, black dog Toby, the offspring of Sofka's Pupsik, who was also on board. Certain gossips said that Vassily might be Uncle Sergei's son, which would have made him Sofka's first cousin, but nobody took the rumours very seriously. The children played quoits, danced on the quarterdeck, exercised the dogs, talked with the kind British officers and listened to Felix Yusupov singing to his guitar. The camaraderie was unusual enough to be fun. Vassily didn't really understand when he heard an adult cousin murmuring, 'What fools we all are.'

Pridham admired the Russians for their stoical, long-suffering attitude, and was enchanted by Xenia and her mother, describing how the Empress gave him a parting gift of some extravagant ruby and diamond cufflinks, which he later made into various jewels for his wife. He described how the only complaint on

On board ship, Sofka became close friends with Vassily, the attractive, lively nephew of the Tsar. Vassily's dog, Toby, was the offspring of her dog, Pupsik, and both animals accompanied their young owners into exile.

board came from 'one of my own countrywomen', a governess to some of the children, 'an extremely plain and unpleasant-looking woman', who objected strongly to Russian men being allowed to have their makeshift sleeping berths in the passage outside her cabin. I hoped it hadn't been Miss King.

There was some delay at Constantinople (which Miss King declared 'filthy'), partly because it was still not agreed in England that all these undesirable Romanovs could just move in. While they were waiting, Sofka's other grandmother, 'Granny Bob', arrived. She was still leading a Red Cross unit after all these years, this time trying to reach the White Army fighting near the Persian frontier. About a year later they heard that she had died from typhoid, collapsing while still tending the sick and wounded.

The Russians' next stop was Malta, where they stayed for about a week. Miss King had a favourite story about the hotel manager screening off part of the dining room so as not to embarrass the 'poor refugees, only to find his indigent guests coming down in full albeit old-fashioned evening dress and glittering with jewels'.

All in all, it took a month before the evacuees arrived in Portsmouth on HMS *Lord Nelson*. One warm May day, 'there was a terrific smartening up of everything and everybody' and a parade on deck as Alexandra, the elderly Queen Mother, stepped aboard to welcome her sister. A special train was laid on, taking the Royals and the 'in-waitings' through the unfamiliar English countryside to Victoria Station, where King George V and Queen Mary awaited. Some of Xenia's Russian servants fell to their knees before the bearded, blue-eyed King (and first cousin of Nicholas II), believing him to be the Tsar, somehow miraculously restored. After all the presentations, Olga, Sofka, Miss King and Louise were taken away by Olga's sister, Sophy, whose husband, Count Benkendorff, had been the last Ambassador of Imperial Russia in London. It didn't seem too bad. The idea was to sell some jewels, live relatively frugally and wait until the old life could be resumed.

CHAPTER 4

THE REFUGEE

If to do were as easy as to
know what were good to do.
  – Shakespeare, *The Merchant of Venice*

Olga sold her pearls and then did what she had always done when she was tired or harassed: she went for a rest cure. With Sofka, Miss King and Louise in tow, she took a suite at the elegant Spa Hotel in Bath – a large mansion boasting a staircase decorated with copies of the Elgin Marbles, set in grounds that included croquet and tennis lawns, a lily pool and even a classical temple. Olga easily established the sort of familiar routines she had perfected in Marienbad or Vichy, walking into town to sip the waters and taking afternoon tea on clipped grass under the copper beeches and cedars of Lebanon. News arrived that all her four daughters were safe, and perhaps there were times when the old woman forgot the calamity behind this particular recuperation. It was still too soon to give up hope of return or to feel what Nabokov called the 'animal aching yearn for the still fresh reek of Russia'.

Bath was the first taste of a country Sofka had heard about endlessly from Miss King. During their six years together, the governess repeatedly assured her that everything – from food and clothes to manners and morals – was better in England. Team games, in particular, encapsulated the very essence of the noble English spirit. Sofka was naturally sceptical towards Miss King's insular outlook, and she had never played team games, but she was impressed by England's small, neat houses, the tidy green fields with hedges, the helmeted policemen.

A photograph from the summer of 1919 shows Sofka in an old white cotton dress which is slightly short. She probably hadn't had any new clothes for a while. A river of dark hair falls loose over a shoulder and she looks out of place, standing against a dark brick wall. She *was* out of place. Not yet twelve, her expression is one of knowing mixed with innocence. She might have been among the earliest of the waves of twentieth-century refugee children, but she probably didn't feel like a refugee. She was already accustomed to travel and separations; it was really only later and with hindsight that these early days of exile took on significance.

Sofka may have seen more than many girls her age, but she was also sheltered enough to have thought she was dying when she found blood on her nightdress one morning. Her shock and bewilderment were allayed by Miss King, who explained the occurrence, but added that from now on Sofka would spend a day in bed each month due to this unfortunate development. On the other hand, the Child was adventurous enough to enjoy the rebellious intrigues of her first kisses. Geoffrey was a seventeen-year-old midshipman from the *Lord Nelson* who visited Sofka in Bath, and afterwards in London, whenever he was on leave. Later, Sofka was puzzled as to what this youth saw in her. Certainly from her side, Geoffrey had 'too many teeth' to pass muster as a fitting picture of true love. But she was happy to let him kiss her behind the bushes in a way which was 'not entirely platonic'.

Sofka had not seen her mother for almost two years when Sophy arrived unexpectedly, rather as she had the previous time in the Crimea. Again, she only stayed briefly. She had left Russia through Finland and wanted to check up on Sofka, of whom she had heard almost nothing. Having established that her daughter was safe and much grown, Sophy rapidly became restless with the peaceful tedium and quaintness of Bath. For several weeks she endured drinking tea with the old princess, taking her daughter for drives into the country and playing Patience in the evenings. But she was deeply worried about Pierre, her new husband. He was supposed to have followed her out of the country with his mother, but she had received no news. Reports in the press described widespread arrests in Russia and even mass executions. Sophy's desperation (and dry humour) reveals itself in a letter she wrote to Pierre, which never reached him: 'Contrary to all physical laws, the force of your attraction not only does not decrease in inverse ratio to the square of distance, but the farther I go, the stronger I seem to feel it. The moment approaches when neither reason nor motherly affection will prove capable of retaining me here any longer.'

Everyone said Sophy must be mad to return to Bolshevik Russia, however worried she was about Pierre. It was unheard-of to take that direction – like turning back into the eye of a dreadful storm. It was known that Lenin wanted to exterminate the bourgeoisie; why hand yourself over to people who wanted you dead? Perhaps this spurred her on; still only thirty-one, Sophy couldn't resist a challenge. Early one morning she took leave of her former mother-in-law. Olga was still in bed, but blessed Sophy with the sign of the cross, presumably wondering whether she would ever see this wilful young creature again. At Bath railway station, Miss King was unable to control her sobs as they saw Sophy off. Sofka was unperturbed. Whereas her mother believed this was due to youthful ignorance, Sofka later claimed that already, for her, partings were too commonplace to be upsetting. Whichever is the case, neither felt a strong bond; it was enough that each was safe.

In London, Sophy spent some days preparing for her trip. She obtained visas, discussed plans with disapproving diplomat friends and ordered a big box of supplies from Fortnum and Mason, imagining the joy it would give her starving friends in Russia. Tormented by fear and rumours, the Russians in London veered between trying to dissuade Sophy from her mission to rescue Pierre and making all kinds of requests: to visit an old mother or to check on a house. On her arrival in London Sophy had been put up at the Ritz by her uncle ('Oh, the joy of luxury!' she wrote in her diary), but now she went to stay with her friend Felix Yusupov and his wife, Irina, at their Knightsbridge flat. She recalled it as having been filled with extraordinary people, none more so than her host. Sophy enjoyed unpredictability, in others as much as in herself, and though she was intolerant of frivolity she enjoyed Yusupov's witty butterfly hedonism. 'He knows the secret of rendering his faults as attractive as his good qualities. If not more so . . .' she wrote in her memoirs. 'As if we love people for their virtues!'

As Sophy set off by boat from Newcastle to Sweden and then on to Finland, Sofka was taken by Miss King to Margate. They stayed in a boarding house and Sofka was deeply offended when she was given a bucket and spade and expected to play on the sand. This seaside was very different to the rocky, wild Crimean one she had so recently left behind; even the dreary, placid donkeys which plodded along giving rides compared badly to the mad dash clinging to a donkey's bare back at Miskhor. Every night, for a long time to come, Sofka went to sleep thinking about beloved Miskhor, her image of home: Rim, Vanya, Shura, the pine-scented path down to the sea . . .

By September Olga had set up home in London at 46 Gloucester Place: a five-storeyed furnished house, close to her sister. She was joined by 'Little Olga', her motherless young granddaughter (Sergei's child), who came with a nurse and a governess, Miss New. By the time Sofka arrived there was a cook, a parlour-maid and a housemaid in residence, as well as Louise. Olga was clear that these were conditions of 'strictest economy'. Every day of her life, she once said, she had repeated the words of the Lord's Prayer, 'Give us this day our daily bread.' But she never imagined the time would come when she would have to give them a literal meaning. Thinking about this period, some fifty years later, Sofka observed that, austerity measures notwithstanding, it still 'took seven people to care for three female Dolgoroukys, aged respectively sixty-nine, twelve and four'.

London in the autumn of 1919 must have seemed deeply unfamiliar. I imagine that, as a voracious reader, Sofka would have already read some Dickens, about this 'black shrill city' with its sky's 'leaden canopy'. And perhaps she came across descriptions in Sherlock Holmes stories of the dreaded 'peasoupers', which still regularly enveloped the capital in thick, greasy, yellow fog. The disasters of the First World War had only recently ended: a generation of young British men had been eradicated; and the Spanish flu epidemic had just killed hundreds of thousands throughout the country. Russian refugees were not the only families around to have faced loss and tragedy. But the Russians' past troubles were magnified by unfamiliarity with the present and insecurity about the future. Surprisingly, perhaps, many Russians felt the cold in England. At home there had always been plenty of wood to keep the tall stoves burning, and even in the frozen winter months houses were warm. Here, they had to buy woollen underclothes and huddle around fireplaces or miserable gas stoves. The dowdy English food was only remarkable for what it was not: familiar tastes of home. Anna Akhmatova wrote, 'Like wormwood smells the bread of strangers.' Exile leaves a bitter taste in your mouth; other people's food is a constant reminder.

While in London, Sophy had chosen a school for her daughter – Queen's College in Harley Street, as it offered 'more education and less games'. This was Sofka's first taste of institutionalized education and she loved it. School provided a refuge from the past and from worry and sorrow at home. It was an opportunity to reinvent herself. Dressed in a navy-blue tunic, she entered a safe, cloistered, orderly world which reminded her of the popular Angela Brazil books – *A Patriotic Schoolgirl*, *The Jolliest Term on Record*, *A Terrible Tomboy* and *Bosom Friends*, to name a few. Sofka's bosom friend was Violet Cyriax, the daughter of two doctors, who, like Sofka, wanted to become a doctor. Both girls belonged to the more serious set, who hoped to attend university and pursue a career; they scorned what they called the 'giddy set' – girls whiling away the time with a little French, elocution and drawing until a good marriage settled their futures.

Miss King's eulogies about team games had evidently fallen on deaf ears, as Sofka's reports indicate a lack of attention on the netball court. But after the previous two years of haphazard, monotonous and solitary lessons with Miss King, Queen's College was refreshing and exciting. Furnished like a smart London house, there were colourful rugs, framed portraits on the walls, lacy curtains, flowers in vases and an art room filled with classical busts. As Sofka's gregarious nature was stimulated by spending her days amongst a seething mass of teenage girls,

Miss King became increasingly tetchy. With too much time on her hands at home, the governess grew abnormally obsessed with Pupsik, the fluffy, white dog which Sofka had been given by her father at the beginning of the First World War – only five years previously, but already a bygone age.

The young émigrée's school reports record that she did well (sometimes passably) in a wide range of subjects, including Latin, Greek, botany and natural philosophy as well as the more usual lessons. Even the unaccustomed end-of-year exams were enjoyable for their novelty: the quiet tension in the hall; the wooden desks with their piles of foolscap; the severe gaze of the invigilator. The teachers included various 'characters' such as Monsieur Cammaerts, a bearded Belgian poet who thundered out Molière and Racine, and young, pretty Miss Sutcliffe (the object of many 'crushes'), who brought Shakespeare alive. In her first year Sofka wrote a short piece for the school magazine on 'The Russian Revolution', which I imagine must have impressed her cloistered young classmates, whose contributions were more along the lines of 'On Holidays Spent in Devonshire'.

. . . The Bolsheviks grew stronger and stronger, because if the peasant men did not give up their corn, the Bolsheviks killed their wife and children, and lastly, tortured them . . .

If they took a Russian officer a prisoner, they would cut off his nose, ears and tongue, poke out his eyes, and do even worse. In Odessa they slowly put the prisoners into boiling oil, drove splinters under their nails or tied a number together and threw them in the sea . . .

The revolution has been going on for three years now, and does not seem to be diminishing, but I hope that, for the sake of Russia and Europe, it will soon end.

Russia in London

ANOTHER CHARMING
AND DISTINGUISHED
VISITOR

THE
PRINCESS SOPHIE
DOLGOROUKY

These photographs of the Princess—and her dog—were taken specially for Eve. *Princess Sophie, who is studying painting, literature, and French at Queen's School, Harley Street, is one of the many members of the Russian nobility who found sanctuary in England after the tragedy of the Revolution. Her family have lost all their possessions in Russia*

Photos. by Malcolm Arbuthnot

The Princess Sophie Dolgorouky

Princess Sophie Dolgorouky is living with her grandmother, Princess Olga Dolgorouky, in Gloucester Place. She and her family left Russia five years ago, and spent two years in the Crimea before coming to England in 1919. Princess Olga is the daughter of the late Count Pierre Schouvaloff and the sister of the well known Countess Benckendorff, whose husband was for many years the Russian Ambassador at the Court of St. James's. The Count died only a few weeks before the Russian Revolution. His only daughter, Countess Nathalie, married the Hon. Jasper Ridley, the uncle of the present Viscount Ridley, who comes of age next year, and has three boys and a girl

Sofka's provenance was still of enough interest for an English women's magazine, Eve, *to interview her. Not yet fifteen, the young émigrée looks uncharacteristically demure, holding Pupsik.*

A year or so after Sofka started at Queen's she was photographed for *Eve*, a popular women's magazine of the day. The title is 'Russia in London: Another Charming and Distinguished Visitor. The Princess Sophie Dolgorouky'. Smiling gamely for the camera, she is wearing a dark tailored dress and clutching Pupsik. The article describes Princess Sophie's school studies and how she is 'one of the many members of the Russian nobility to have found sanctuary in England after the tragedy of the Revolution. Her family have lost all their possessions in Russia.' There was still enough glamour attached to their titles and romance associated with their drama to give a few lucky refugees such as Sofka and her grandmother the sense that their former lives were valued by others. Most didn't have pearls to sell and were victim to the racism so many refugees and migrants always have to face; in Paris it was common to hear people mutter, '*Les sales Russes*' after the deluge of 'White Russians' poured into the city. On the other hand, Olga was considered important enough to be invited to hand out the cups at Sofka's school prize-giving ceremony and English visitors were intrigued by her grandeur. Among Sofka's papers I found a letter she received some sixty years later, following a television interview:

> I realized that you must be the little girl who used to come
> to my parties when I lived at 'Leigham Mead' in
> Streatham . . . My governess, Miss Whitford, was a friend
> of your governess Miss King. I can remember you and your
> lovely long hair and beautiful eyes and you were Princess
> Dolgrouke (have I spelt that correctly?). My governess used
> to take me to London to tea with you and I can remember
> your grandmother . . . and being told to do a little curtsey
> when I met her.

But defunct titles are flimsy qualifications; they wouldn't go on impressing people for long.

If school was lively and pleasurable, holidays were a dull endurance test: long, grey London days, closed in Olga's matriarchal domain, with only the prospect of games of Whist with Louise and the two governesses, or slow, damp walks with her tired, ageing grandmother. Her cousin, Little Olga, was too young to be interesting and I don't imagine there was much laughter or physical affection. Russian visitors were pitifully obsessed with the past and their misery. One notable exception was Olga's lively, humorous and cultured sister, Sophy, who lived close by and who was a favourite of Sofka's. She was energetic and practical and, unlike Olga, surely knew how to put on her own shoes and stockings. Her husband, Count Alexander Benkendorff, had died just weeks before the Revolution, while posted as London's Russian Ambassador, but the family had rooted itself in English society. Countess Benkendorff's gatherings and parties were attended by an appealing mix of diplomats, English high society, writers, celebrities and Russians and her friends included H. G. Wells and Maurice Baring (Aunt Sophy had enough talent to paint whimsical illustrations for a book of his fairy tales).

Hearsay and news filtered through sporadically from Russia: Olga's favourite aunt, Sasha Naryshkin (descendant of the original owner of Miskhor), had died. Sofka remembered visiting her in Russia, when she believed this bent, bony woman to be the oldest person in the world. She never forgot the small gold bell with a carved black handle which she rang to call the maid. The story of the ninety-year-old aunt's death sounds melodramatic – the sort of thing the refugees might have embellished – but Sofka described the incident as though it was historical fact, so maybe it was.

Apparently the old lady was summoned before a revolutionary

tribunal, and challenged the court from her wheelchair. She said that she didn't fear death and wanted the tribunal to know exactly who she was. She probably didn't mention that the Naryshkins prided themselves on bearing a name that was above all titles except grand-duke and tsar, but she listed her own formidable court positions and the additions she had made to public life: the town's library, orphanage, teaching college, dowries for moneyless brides and so on were all funded by her. Then she paused. 'And now let me tell you who you are,' she enunciated clearly to the Bolsheviks before her. 'You are murderers and assassins, cut-throats and rebels, tyrants, robbers, scoundrels . . .' Her cause of death was officially listed as a heart attack, but the story goes that a guard shot her then and there.

* * *

Meanwhile, Sofka's mother was experiencing the most taxing and dramatic phase of her life. Although Sofka knew nothing about Sophy's adventures at the time, she later realized that this highly significant period had been her mother's turning point, after which everything would be different. Sophy's bravery and heartfelt determinedness (recounted in her memoirs, *The Way of Bitterness*) always remained a dauntingly impressive example for her daughter. Heroes are not usually the easiest parents; emulation looks hopeless and competition doomed to failure.

When Sophy learned that Pierre had been imprisoned, she became desperate with worry. Hoping to pass back into Russia the way she'd left, she spent weeks in Helsingfors (Helsinki) trying to sort out her papers. The wait seemed endless, the setbacks insuperable, especially when it emerged that she had been blacklisted by British Intelligence as a Bolshevik agent. Sophy passed those late summer days and nights pacing up and down the streets and smoking and sobbing in her tiny hotel room. Uncharacteristically (was she inspired by Pierre's traditionalism and piety?), she even resorted to praying in church. I imagine her in the dark comfort of an Orthodox chapel, murmuring her beloved's name: not 'Pierre', the French translation of the Russian Pyotr, which she gives him in her book, but Petukh, or Cockerel, the inappropriate nickname by which her mild, scholarly husband was widely known.

When the impossibility of entering Russia through Finland became apparent, Sophy crossed the Gulf of Finland to Tallinn, a sleepy town which had suddenly woken up as capital of the newly independent Estonia. A centre of Russian exile, Tallinn was seething with intelligence officers, refugees, agents, officials and black-marketeers. Sophy's habitual cool, logical efficiency was replaced by nerves and tormented insomnia. She described her 'feverish impatience' and long lonely walks. 'And through it all, making my pulse race and my hands tremble, the thought that soon, very soon, I should see Pierre.' Among the Russian refugees in Tallinn was the Zinovieff family (my future grandfather, Leo, was fourteen, while Uncle Kyril was nine), and Sophy visited them frequently during her stay, grateful for tea and conversation to break the miserable anticipation.

At last, Sophy obtained a way back into Russia. Having paid under the counter for a stolen Estonian Communist Party card, she packed a small bag with personal belongings: some linen, a few toilet things, her new fountain pen, a small electric torch and a bottle of Guerlain scent. 'Every object was chosen with the greatest care and deliberation, as though for an expedition to the South Pole,' she wrote. She had also hidden a lethal dose of morphine, given by her old professor of surgery, after she persuaded him that a quick, clean death would be preferable if she fell into the wrong (Red) hands. With difficulty, Sophy had clung on to the precious, still unopened Fortnum and Mason box, and lovingly pictured Pierre savouring the biscuits, chocolate, sardines and old brandy in his Soviet prison.

The journey, by train and then military lorry, was risky and uncomfortable. Worse, Sophy's bag was stolen and she was left without even a change of underclothes. The final part of the journey, from Gatchina to Petrograd, was the hardest of all. Trains were not running, there were no cars for hire and Sophy reluctantly decided that her only option of covering the forty-two *versts* (twenty-eight miles) was on foot. She hated walking at the best of times, but strung a bag across her shoulders and tied a shawl over her head – she was amazed at her transformation: 'I could have easily been taken for some local schoolmistress,' she remarked. It took her two exhausting, frightening days, trudging on bleeding, blistered feet and sleeping the frosty November night in a ditch. The last miles were covered by horse-drawn carriage, after she swapped some Turkish cigarettes for a lift from some unsuspecting Soviet workers.

It was bizarre to be home again – unwashed, worn out and in pain, but home. After spending the night at her old hospital, Sophy hobbled (everyone now walked everywhere) to the place that had been her home since her marriage to Pierre, the Volkonsky Mansion or 'Little White House'. Standing at the gates in the Fourstadtskaya was the old butler, Ivan Adamovitch. He didn't recognize Sophy at first. The house had been requisitioned by the Red Army and was now a barracks. Everything inside was broken or stolen; furniture was burned in the stoves and the family portraits were stabbed with bayonets through their eyes. Sophy paused before asking the old man what had become of Pierre; waiting for the answer seemed like a roulette of life and death: 'Now in a moment, I would know . . . Everything: the present and the future, the happiness, the very meaning of life. What would it be? Heads or tails, red or black?' Sophy nearly fainted from relief when she heard that her husband was alive in Moscow's Ivanovsky prison camp.

Pierre's elderly, increasingly deaf mother had moved with her maid into a small building at the back and was apparently too self-absorbed even to realize she should help her daughter-in-law. It was bad enough for Sophy that Princess Volkonsky (a former society beauty who was something of a domineering old diva) had practically caused Pierre's arrest by insisting on staying at home, knowing her loyal son wouldn't leave her. Now, when Sophy needed somewhere to stay, the princess said she would invite her, but the dining-room lamp was broken – how could she stay in the dark? Sophy left, incredulous, wondering where to go; most of her friends had fled or were in worse trouble than her.

> *A different time is drawing near,*
> *The wind of death already chills the heart*

wrote Anna Akhmatova in 1919 about 'this savage capital', which was no longer a capital. Petrograd was a dangerous place to be wandering around without papers. Eventually, however, Sophy found Marianna, a friend who had never been particularly close, but who gladly took her in. Countess Marianna Zarnekau had recently become an actress; even hunger, prison and terror did not preclude theatre. Not only did Marianna let Sophy sleep on her sofa, she introduced her to Maxim Gorky, who may have been a natural revolutionary – a man of the people – but was sensitive to others' woes. Sophy didn't describe where she met him, but she probably went to his capacious flat at 23 Kronverksky Avenue, which was famously filled with visitors, friends and artists, some of whom came for tea and stayed for years. Residents all had nicknames (Gorky was 'Duke' at home) and, in spite of the horrors outside, they created a light-hearted atmosphere of amusing stories and games. Baroness Moura Budberg (later mistress of H. G. Wells) was among the more exotic permanent residents at this time, with her feline smile, beguiling ways and risky Mata Hari tendencies. (There is a book and 1934 English film, *British Agent*, about her affair with Bruce Lockhart, the British Consul during the Revolution.)

Gorky was renowned for his moderation and for pleading the cause of intellectuals, artists and detainees. Dogged by tragedy and drama since being orphaned as a child, he was easily moved to tears and passionate about the arts, which he feared were facing annihilation by the Bolsheviks. Prior to his celebrated career as a writer, he had been a ship's cook and a painter, had walked around Russia, been in prison, and had once attempted suicide. 'Toothache in the heart' was how he described his youthful misery. It was no chance that his pen-name meant 'bitter'.

Long before I read Sophy's book, I had the sense that Gorky was a good person. It had filtered down the generations without my knowing why. For my twelfth birthday, my father organized a marathon film projection of *Gorky's Childhood*, *My Apprenticeship* and *My Universities*. I have no idea what the twenty pubescent London girls, dressed in 1970s bell-bottom jeans, thought of these scratchy black and white Soviet films from the late thirties: street urchins, big beards, peasants in padded coats and vistas of the Volga River. My father didn't spell out anything about why we were watching the extraordinary trilogy or what I should think about the Soviet Union (was it that year or another when he offended the neighbours by flying the hammer and sickle from the house?). I remember, though, that between slices of cake and fizzy drinks, I sensed Gorky's humanity. It was only later that I learned how my great-grandmother had warmed to this walrus-moustached man of the people, with his booming voice and irresistible laugh.

'Without his help,' Sophy wrote, 'I should probably have perished.'

Armed with the necessary documents, Sophy travelled to Moscow by train on 'an official mission' as a music instructress – an irony as she knew no music. She had heard that a first cousin of Pierre's, Sergei Volkonsky, had moved to Moscow and although she didn't know him well, she knocked on his door. Formerly the director of the Imperial Theatre in Petersburg, Sergei had supported Diaghilev's early career and was now living in a communal flat in Sheremetevsky Pereoulok with four women including his young niece and the apartment's old housekeeper. There was no hesitation in welcoming Sophy as the sixth member of the crowded household.

Prison visits were on Sundays and Sophy took her place in the queue long before the appointed time. It sometimes seems that all of Russian literature is littered with pale, terrified women standing outside prison walls in the snow. Akhmatova described the months waiting in line when her son was imprisoned and how one day a woman with 'bluish lips' whispered: '"Can you describe this?" It was some comfort to reply: "I can." Then something that looked like a smile passed over what had once been her face.'

Sophy barely recognized what had once been Pierre's face across the small prison courtyard. Gone were the tidy, downward-sloping moustache and the oiled hair with its precise, off-centre parting and his controlled, quizzical expression. His scrawny cheeks, long, unkempt locks and straggly beard had turned him into a stranger. What can you say in these circumstances? Her 'Hello!' was greeted with perplexed confusion by Pierre, who could barely take in what an extraordinary thing his wife had done in coming to find him. The brief fifteen minutes were scarcely enough to explain before 'Time is up, citizens,' and visitors were roughly pushed towards the door. Pierre was not the only person to be impressed by Sophy's bravery; all the prisoners commented on the unique occurrence of a woman returning from abroad to rescue her husband. The gossip quickly spread around Moscow and people automatically compared this courageous Princess Volkonsky to another, almost a hundred years before: Maria, the beautiful, cultured young wife of Prince Sergei Volkonsky (cousin Sergei's grandfather), who was exiled to Siberia for his part in the Decembrists' uprising. Maria travelled four thousand miles across snowy wastes to live in exile for twenty-six years.

Sophy took the risk of breaking her cover and spent the next weeks approaching authorities to plead Pierre's case and struggling to find contents for a food parcel, which could be delivered to the guards each week. After all the effort, Sophy's box of Fortnum supplies hadn't made it; the man who agreed to fetch it for her from Gatchina disappeared along with the delicacies. Now, in the bitter Moscow winter, with frozen potatoes and millet practically the only foodstuffs available, Sophy could only weep with thoughts of the chocolate and brandy. Each day was taken up with trying to procure enough fuel and provisions with which to survive, and something in addition that might prevent Pierre starving. He was already unwell enough to have been excused manual labour and was working in the prison library, but death had become an indiscriminate, everyday occurrence, even outside the prison walls. The Civil War was ripping the country apart, but it wasn't only Reds and Whites who were killing each other; Muscovites were dying by the thousand from hunger and cold. Lorries piled high with coffins passed through the streets, and people were reduced to hauling their dead along the pavements on toboggans.

Sophy used a small sledge to pull Pierre's parcel to the prison every Wednesday, about an hour's walk from home. Prison rules permitted a short list to accompany the contents and the Volkonskys learned to sneak in some words of correspondence:

Food Parcel for P.P. Volkonsky
kasha,
bread,
a bottle of milk,
cigarettes,
have had good tidings,
although uncorroborated,
do not lose courage.

From P.P. Volkonsky, January 21, 1920
Corridor VII, Cell 80.
1 net bag,
1 round pot,
1 bottle
The toast was excellent . . .
Would you like the idea of trying to send message to your daughter
by applying to the English parson, Reverend North . . .?

When the weeks turned into months, Sophy found a job as a medical assistant in a hospital, while continuing the dispiriting rounds of pleading with officials to grant Pierre's release. Gorky's plea on his behalf had fallen on deaf ears; 'innocence' was no longer relevant (prisoners were regularly executed without explanation); and Sophy tried to push Pierre's claim as an Estonian national – the family had an estate near Tallinn. Evenings were spent at home in Sergei Volkonsky's communal apartment, where it was so cold that everyone wore their fur coats constantly, even sleeping in them at night. Reading was done with gloves on and in bed, and English novels were avoided for their accounts of large and frequent meals, although food was the overwhelming topic of conversation. Sophy found it humiliating to dream of sweets and pastry, and criticized the irresistible composing of imaginary menus as 'mental flagellation'. Sometimes someone would arrive with a sack of flour or potatoes, leading to a flurry of distribution and cooking; everyone in the household contributed to its survival.

Sophy had experienced hardship and war, but she had never before carried out basic domestic chores. The water pipes had burst and she had to queue at the icy pump before bumping unwieldy iron buckets up several flights of stairs. More laborious still was hauling up heavy logs and sawing them for the stove: 'When, during the fourth year of my medical training,' wrote Sophy, 'we learnt to perform amputations on corpses, the Professor used to say: "The technique is quite simple; saw the bone in the same way you saw a log of wood." Possibly, the other girls knew how to saw wood. For myself, the experience was reversed; when my saw got stuck in one of those big frozen logs, I tried to think of the operating table: the same movement as when sawing through the tibia.'

Sergei was a close friend of the poet Marina Tsvetaeva, who often visited. She gave him the nickname 'Cedar', apparently after the trees he planted on his estate, and she idolized this tall, distinguished man, calling him 'the best friend of my life'. Although Sergei was homosexual and decades older than

Tsvetaeva, she thought him 'the most intelligent, fascinating, charming, old-fashioned, curious and most brilliant person in the world'. Sergei's memoirs were dedicated to the poet, and in them he described the appalling circumstances in her bare Moscow apartment where 'the dark and cold came in from the street as though they owned the place'. This was the year that Tsvetaeva's younger daughter died from starvation.

Within a year or two, both Tsvetaeva and Sergei would have left Russia. While he achieved some late success lecturing and writing in émigré publications, she was always torn by the empty homesickness of exile, which plagued so many writers. She felt:

> *Stunned, like a log left*
> *Behind from an avenue of trees.*

Finally, unable to bear émigré life, Tsvetaeva returned to a Soviet Union which then destroyed her. Perhaps her eventual suicide didn't surprise many, but it was emblematic of the dreadful, often unbearable choice facing Russian writers and poets. Uprooted, they lost their milieu, their readers and often their voice; they longed to be surrounded by what Tsvetaeva called 'the milky call' of their native tongue. But home was unrecognizable, drenched with bloody 'Red terror'.

Sergei and his female household were regularly woken in the middle of the night for searches by the Cheka, the secret police. Even the sound of a car in the darkness was enough to stop all conversation (nobody but the Cheka had cars), but it was usually a rude banging at the door at 2 a.m. that announced their arrival. Armed men would spend hours rifling through every drawer and throwing papers and underclothes on the floor, while the inhabitants awaited their fate. The dread and humiliation was horrible; it was clear that the smallest detail could suffice as a reason for being taken away, imprisoned or executed. Like many survivors of Communist persecution, Sophy was left with a terror of unexpected visitors.

Part of the 'war against the palaces' was forced labour for the bourgeoisie. When Sophy received an order one day, to present herself at the police station, it probably reminded her of her marriage to Pierre, which had taken place only a year before. On the documents they were given at the Liteiny Commissariat in Petrograd, Pierre described himself as 'philologist', Sophy as 'housewife'. As they left, they noticed a huge red banner reading SHE IS AWAITING HIM. 'How sentimental,' said Pierre, who shared Sophy's dry attitude to overdone emotions. 'The bride waiting for the bridegroom.' Then they saw the full sentence: THE BOURGEOIS WANTS THE GUILLOTINE. SHE IS AWAITING HIM. There is no record of whether they shivered or laughed, but it was under this proclamation that Prince and Princess Volkonsky had begun their new life together. Now, in Moscow, Sophy regularly joined a pitiful group of supposed 'public enemies', with worn clothes and frightened faces. They were marched through the icy streets and given pointless or humiliating tasks such as shovelling snow or cleaning lavatories (though Sophy managed to avoid this). The armed guards smoked and laughed, jeering at their exhausted, degraded enemy until at dusk they were dismissed with a pound of damp, black bread, which often contained straw and even bark.

One sunny, icy day in February 1920, just when hope seemed impossibly distant, Pierre's release was ordered. Sophy was delivering her Wednesday parcel when she heard her husband's voice behind the prison gates:

'I am free!'

Sophy asked why he didn't just come out and was astounded when he replied, 'There is no hurry.' He wanted to pack and take leave of his companions, and requested that she return some hours later with a sledge for his box. Pierre's methodical lack of spontaneity at the end of his nine-month prison term was as remarkable as it was characteristic.

After all they had been through, Sophy and Pierre saw no alternative to leaving Russia. Staying would be too perilous and painful. They might have managed to sneak out secretly, as Sophy had entered, had it not been for Pierre's mother, who was sending increasingly desperate letters from Petrograd: her jewels were gone, she couldn't leave her bed, and the former servants were hitting her. The only option was to try to acquire Estonian papers and leave legally with Maman. They returned to Petrograd with more false papers; this time, Pierre was a fictitious university lecturer at Balt-Flot, a fictitious university. Again, the problem was where to stay: the Little White House was still a barracks; Sophy's apartment on the English Embankment was occupied by Red sailors; and the Bobrinsky house had become a museum. It was Sophy's old friend Anna Akhmatova who came to the rescue. She had been allotted a room in the newly established House of Arts and although life was as hard for her as everyone else (she wrote no poems in 1920), she was living elsewhere and didn't need it.

The House of Arts was in a large mansion on the Moika canal by Nevsky Prospekt. It had belonged to Yeliseyev (formerly the prosperous owner of the fanciest food shop in Petersburg) and was now being used for cultural events and to house a number of poets, writers and artists, frequently amongst the least fortunate of Petrograd's desperate citizens. The Volkonskys found themselves inhabiting Yeliseyev's old study, which still contained his desk and framed photographs of the plump merchant and his family. Sophy's book makes no mention of what they slept on (camp beds? Certainly others slept in dormitories), and she gives away nothing of her relationship with Pierre. After all her trembling anticipation and evident passion before they are together, afterwards she unequivocally closes all doors, including the bedroom's. Pierre leaves no trace of his qualities as a lover except that he was known for preferring men. So it is hard to imagine them as a youngish (thirty-one and forty-four), newly married couple. I hope that despite the hunger and worry there was something of a second honeymoon (I don't think there was a first). I picture them laughing in quiet irony at their surreal camp in Yeliseyev's plush study, with its mahogany furniture, flamboyant replica Egyptian sculptures and gilded plasterwork. I suppose they sometimes also wept, looking out of the windows to the extravagant Stroganov Palace opposite and the iron Police Bridge crossing the grey, misty waters of the Moika.

You can still see Yeliseyev's study. Its gaudy, *nouveau riche* Art Nouveau decoration was revamped after his house underwent yet another metamorphosis for the twenty-first century. For years it was the Institute for Marxism and Leninism, but it is now a fabulously ostentatious club with restaurants and a hotel, which has reconstructed Yeliseyev's glory days. Rich businessmen play roulette in a casino with a ceiling depicting 'The New Being of Socialism'; they are looked down upon by determined workers shovelling fiery coals and strong, rosy-cheeked peasants amongst red flags and silver birches. Photographs of Yeliseyev's family once more adorn the walls, there is a strict dress code, and oysters are brought in from France for dinner. Prices are in dollars and beyond the wildest dreams of ordinary Russians. Like the city's name, the sense of inequality has come full circle, though the creative writers and artists have not yet returned.

In 1920, sunlight shot colourful sparkles through the showy crystal chandeliers, but below them, those who had been

Petersburg's finest writers and artists were emaciated, dirty, lice-ridden and clad in worn, inadequate clothes. Unidentifiable darned grey garments dangled depressingly on inside washing lines and people drank 'tea' that was really grated carrot soaked in water. Like Gorky's establishment the House of Scholars (and his publishing house, World Literature, which had given Pierre a translating job the year before), the House of Arts was supposedly a safety net for Petrograd's dying intelligentsia. In theory, the newly established Petrocommuna (the first city commune) provided food and certain necessities, and a system of canteens was meant to serve the whole population, with rations varying according to class and work. Writers, artists and journalists (defined as 'a non-working element') and bourgeois were placed in the lowest category along with tramps and criminals. They received 'just enough bread so as to not forget the smell of it', as Zinoviev cruelly ordered. But even this system didn't work and food just wasn't available. Although this phase later looked tame in comparison with the appalling starvation during Leningrad's nine-hundred-day siege, the suffering was serious. In desperation, people were driven to eating domestic animals. Gorky's beloved Great Dane, Diane, was assumed to have had that unhappy fate, after she failed to return from a solitary expedition.

House of Arts food was customarily dreary boiled millet and a thin soup of *vobla*, the nauseating, spiky-boned salt-fish nicknamed 'Soviet ham'. 'How can I convey the real meaning of the word *vobla* to the mind of the European reader,' wrote Sophy,

for whom 'fish' is naturally associated with the appetizing picture of *sole frite* or *turbot au vin blanc*? What comparison shall I find to give with sufficient strength the repugnance of taste, smell and even sight inspired by that meanest member of the whole ichthyological family? A mixture of bad egg with caster-oil, asafoetida with dog's bile . . . Only those who have been through it themselves will know that in the long run the horror of rotten fish can overshadow even the horror of the firing squad.

Sometimes the House of Arts organized a function and everyone would gather in the mirrored hall and the huge wood-panelled dining room in their best clothes (some newly sewn and noticeably matching the heavy brocade curtains). The young poet Nina Berberova described how the old Yeliseyev servants would hand around tea and greyish biscuits off heavy silver trays. Strauss waltzes were played as duets on the two grand pianos, while stars of the Silver Age like Nikolai Gumilyov (Akhmatova's first husband) and Andrei Biely would come and discuss their latest work. Berberova attended Gumilyov's poetry classes (he encouraged his students to play Blind Man's Buff), and was intrigued by this slightly older generation of poets, with 'their conservatism, anti-modernity, mannerisms, the exquisite parting of their hair, their sublime handkerchiefs in their breast pockets, their foot-shuffling, hand-kissing, and special enunciation of certain vowels . . .' These congregations of 'old society' did not go unnoticed by the city's puritans and bureaucrats, who disapproved, reporting 'dinner-jackets with asters in their buttonholes, fantastic trousers, glossy hair, French conversation and silk stockings'. What seems remarkable now is that they could muster any of their old silvery affectations in such a hard age of iron.

When H. G. Wells came to visit Soviet Russia in 1920, he was invited to a lavish dinner in the House of Arts; even the starving inmates were given meat. An academic, Pitirim Sorokin, tried to make a speech about the murderous situation faced by the intelligentsia, but Gorky butted in, saying that such words were inadmissible. This attitude brought Gorky lasting opprobrium among many writers, while he was also considered increasingly unreliable by numerous Communists. It was not long before Gorky realized that he couldn't continue and he too left in 1922, regretting 'the triumph of stupidity and vulgarity'. By that time, most intellectuals and writers were dead or gone. Their finale began with the funeral of Aleksandr Blok in 1921, which symbolized for many the grim end to a glittering era. It was confirmed by the subsequent mass-execution of various intellectuals on trumped-up charges, including thirty-five-year-old Gumilyov. It was the destruction of one, if not two, generations of Russia's intelligentsia. After many years of exile, Gorky returned to a hero's welcome in the USSR (streets, parks and even a city were named after him, statues erected, films made), but even his death in 1936 had an enigmatic, inconclusive nature, which some believed was Stalin's doing. 'Terror fingers all things in the dark,' wrote Akhmatova after Gumilyov's shooting. There were to be many more years of darkness.

Pierre's mother, poor Maman, was now in a pitiful state, ill and swollen from starvation, and Pierre's quiet manners were not helpful in the attempt to obtain Estonian papers for them all. Sophy, the more practical of the two, became responsible for their physical survival. Initially she sold her linen sheets – part of the trousseau from her first marriage, which she had brought to the Volkonskys' home. Then she discovered there was a way to sell books to the Soviet Library Committee and acquired a paper enabling her to return to her adored flat on the English Embankment to requisition some volumes. Sophy's arrival was overshadowed by her own memories, but the visit became haunted by the death of Natasha, her lovely, devoted maid, who had stayed on in the apartment with her husband. The previous year, Natasha had told Sophy that she was depressed . . . But then everyone was depressed. Natasha hanged herself from a nail in the wall. It was so low that she had to double up her legs. To add to Sophy's distress, she felt deeply wounded by the sight of the Red sailors living among her treasured possessions – there were still framed pictures of Sofka on the tables. She was repulsed by the idea that they slept in her bed and ate off her china. She didn't admit her identity to the men, but merely showed them the paperwork and took down her carefully collected medical tomes from the glass bookcases. The door to her study was locked, so she couldn't even search for her papers. It was her last sight of the familiar panorama across the pale, wintry Neva; a picture that remained through years of exile as a reproach to the seedy, unloved Parisian streets she later looked out on.

Sophy was accompanied by a man from the Library Committee, 'a bright little Jew'. Nowadays, her anti-Semitism cannot fail to offend, though then it was surely so common as to pass unnoticed by her peers – 'God save the Tsar and beat the Jews!' was shouted by many loyal Russians. When Pierre's beautiful, intelligent niece (who had shared the communal flat in Moscow) married a Soviet official, Sophy unhesitatingly labelled him 'a spiteful little Communist Jew'. The more I found out about Sophy, the more complicated she appeared. I admired her bravery and her accomplishments, and was intrigued by how she masked her extremely sensitive emotions, but I sensed a coldness running through her. This was something which Sofka was later to experience. Sophy's dark, dry descriptions of the appalling suffering around her reveal a hardness in their sharp intelligence which is sometimes reminiscent of the writer (and later Nobel laureate for literature) Ivan Bunin. Like him, she has an eagle's eye, but her clear-sighted cleverness leads to a cynicism which outweighs her compassion for her fellow human beings.

When the money from the books ran out, Sophy reluctantly applied for a medical job, something she had avoided doing because doctors under forty were often obliged to serve in the Red Army. Citizen Volkonsky was employed by the Petrocommuna to supervise the inoculation against cholera and typhus of Petrograd's bakery employees. The daily ration of a pound of bread (and a few sweets once a month) was probably what saved her and Pierre from death, but the city itself seemed to be dying and rotting away: houses were boarded up; shops were empty and abandoned; people's bellies were swollen from hunger; typhus was rampant. On Nevsky, street urchins sold small matchboxes containing 'typhus-lice', supposedly taken from the body of a typhus patient and liable to infect a healthy person. Nobody thought it odd that someone might want to buy these potentially deadly parasites (to escape mobilization in the Red Army perhaps, or to avoid arrest), but they ridiculed the gullibility of those who believed the enterprising children were offering genuinely infected lice. However, when Sophy first discovered she was infested with 'the grey horror', she was sick with disgust; her doctor's objectivity failed when it came to herself. She tried everything, rubbing stinking ointments all over her body and scrubbing all her clothes, to no avail. Everyone was crawling with them; there were even placards on the streets at one point saying IS THE LOUSE GOING TO CONQUER COMMUNISM?

Some comfort was found in drugs. Cocaine was wildly popular, providing an exquisite, if brief, spell of joyful intoxication. All private trade was banned by the Bolsheviks, but black markets supplied any number of things. Gangs hung around the cigarette factories, making deals with the women workers over cigarettes, jewellery and cocaine, and barbers and hairdressers became the prime suppliers of 'snow'. Soldiers and sailors were habitual users and it was particularly popular amongst actors and in the Cheka. In hospitals, the preferred (and widely available) escape was morphine. Sophy wrote disingenuously that these drugs made her unwell, but it is hard to believe that she didn't ever indulge. She described how 'after a hard day's work, the night nurse would laughingly offer you a box of [morphia] ampoules: "Take a sweet?"'

It was early in 1921 when Sophy and Pierre eventually obtained their papers to go to Estonia. They were exhausted and thin and Sophy had been horribly ill with dysentery. To worsen the pain, there were those among their friends who disapproved of people who left:

> *I am not with those who abandoned their land*
> *To the lacerations of the enemy*

wrote Akhmatova. (She refused to go, but paid the price throughout her life in persecution and suffering.) Someone had a friend who was mistress of the Commander of the Soviet fleet, and consequently the Volkonskys had a car to drive them to the station. The old princess wore a bulky black hat and a fine fur coat but was now hideously emaciated and yellow-faced. She was unable to walk, so they carried her in an armchair (there were no stretchers) on to one of the empty goods trucks that were their transport. They laid her on an air mattress with blankets, and took their places close by, along with the old family butler Ivan Adamovitch, who happened to be Estonian and was taking his family out too.

It took two uncomfortable, agonizingly tense days to reach the border. There were searches and delays and it drizzled continuously. One woman screamed hysterically as she was taken away for having a jewel in the heel of her shoe. Nobody knew until later that old Maman had hidden three gold coins in her clothes; she gave money to the priest every year for taking prayers at the family chapel near Tallinn, and why should the Bolsheviks change that? The border was nothing remarkable – a bridge over a small, muddy river – but the moment was overwhelming. Maman called out in trembling French, as she had done every few minutes for two days: '*Sommes-nous arrivés?*' Sophy collapsed sobbing and Pierre made the sign of the cross, gazing back towards Russia.

* * *

Nearly two years had passed since Sofka had seen her mother. After spending several months recuperating in Estonia at the Volkonsky estate, Sophy arrived in London with Pierre. After all the terror and suffering she had witnessed during two Russian winters, it must have been strange to see before her a contented, well-fed London schoolgirl; a young woman of fourteen, who attended dances and made plans for an English future with Violet Cyriax. Did they bridge the gulf with literature, I wonder? Certainly it had been a link between them in Sofka's childhood and she had already begun a lifelong habit of keeping notebooks, filled with poems and quotations she liked. Her entries for 1920–1 are written in black ink with a tidy, rotund hand given to the occasional girlish flourish. She favoured the romantics – pages are filled with Byron, Shelley, Tennyson, Swinburne and Robert Louis Stevenson. Kipling's bold rhymes spoke to her most of all and he remained one of her favourite poets.

Having taken rooms in a nearby boarding house, Sophy introduced Sofka to her stepfather for the first time. Sofka never described her reaction to the man she called Uncle Peter, but I have the impression that she always liked him for his mild benevolence, even if his exquisitely old-fashioned manners and quiet scholarly character made him somewhat remote. Sophy sold her pearls, which Miss King had been guarding ever since Crimea, so there was some money to buy clothes and to tide them over until they found work. Sophy imagined she would continue her medical career in England or France, but enquiries brought an unpleasant shock: Russian doctors' qualifications were not recognized in either country, and to qualify she would have to return to schoolbooks and take exams along with eighteen-year-olds. The effort and humiliation seemed too great to take on after all she had been through.

This time it was Pierre who came up with a practical solution. What remained of the old Russian establishment, now in exile, offered him a diplomatic post. Financed by the old Ambassadorial Fund, he would go as representative of a non-existent, imperial Russia to Hungary, which had not yet recognized the Soviet regime. As Chargé d'affaires, he would have no authority, but he would do the diplomatic rounds in Budapest and be paid a salary.

Before they left for Hungary, Sophy took Pierre and Sofka to stay with some old friends for the weekend. Sophy had known the Duke of Hamilton from pre-Revolutionary days when he had hunted with her family in Russia, and he now invited her to Ferne, his country estate in Wiltshire. The Douglas-Hamiltons' household must have brought back memories to Sofka of the old days in the Bobrinsky or Dolgorouky homes: footmen in livery carried the suitcases upstairs; maids laid out the clothes; grooms fetched the horses; and one of the eleven gardeners brought in flowers and fruit from the walled garden. Coulsey, the butler, took charge, always heading the line of servants for household morning prayers and announcing visitors in his nasal tones.

There were endless meals and constant visitors. The family might have been proud of being the next best thing to Scottish royalty, but their eccentricities were very English. Their large Georgian house was crawling inside and out with animals: cats, canaries, goats, tamed foxes and even monkeys were welcomed by the duchess, who liked quoting a Chinese proverb: 'To love with the heart of a dog, one must see with the eyes of a god.' Lolling on the best armchairs were numerous canines of every size and breed; guests were asked to choose one to take to bed.

The duke had long been partially paralysed after a dramatic accident during his time in the navy, where he'd been known as 'Pocket Hercules' for his diminutive size and great strength and courage in diving exercises. Attempting to swim under a large battleship in what some said was a dare, he suffered a massive stroke, and by the time he met his future wife he was already going about in a bath chair. Now, he was a small, weak, shadowy figure, who lived in separate quarters from the rest of the family and was accompanied everywhere by his piper Matheson and pushed about by Shepherd, his intimidating secretary. It was his wife Nina, the overpowering duchess, who dominated life at Ferne. Handsome, six-foot and dauntingly energetic, she was a fanatical vegetarian who allowed no meat in the house. She had founded the Society for Animal Defence and Anti-Vivisection, and was deeply preoccupied with spiritualism, reincarnation and the philosophy of universal love. Her constant companion was a bossy Swedish woman known as Miss Lind-Af-Hageby. A spiritual ancestor of today's animal activists, she was generally disliked by the family, not least because she ultimately persuaded the duchess to leave Ferne to her and the animals rather than to her offspring.

The Douglas-Hamiltons had seven children, who were then mostly teenagers. Tall, good-looking, robust outdoor types, they lived 'a full-blooded life', as one of their children later recalled.

Life with the seven Douglas-Hamilton children was full of action and noise. Sofka loved being part of a large family and quickly became close friends with Margaret (in the middle).

Douglo, the eldest, was already at Oxford (later to be known as 'the Boxing Marquis') and Jean was doing her first season as a deb. After Geordie (the only book lover) came Margaret, who was sparklingly pretty and almost exactly Sofka's age. Cecil Beaton later described her in his diaries as 'golden-haired, with love-in-the-mist eyes and russet cheeks', adding that 'she has masses of equally healthy-looking giants for brothers'. Sofka and Margaret took to each other immediately. Both had a wild, mercurial streak, which they recognized and encouraged in each other. It was later to bring them trouble, not to mention a reputation. By the end of the weekend, Sofka was popular enough to be asked to stay on for the rest of the Easter holidays by herself.

Sofka probably appeared quite exotic compared to the young county set who usually visited – a vivacious, dark-eyed Russian princess with a slight accent – but she was quickly absorbed into the Douglas-Hamiltons' entourage. She enjoyed learning their ways: eating porridge at breakfast while walking, Scottish style, around the dining room; riding out on the downs; and reading *Tatler* and *Country Life* by the fire after tea. Sometimes they would push back the furniture and dance to the latest records on the gramophone: Al Johnson singing 'Coal Black Mammy' and a jazzy foxtrot called 'Forty-seven Ginger-Headed Sailors'.

Sofka noted that nobody read books as she did; there wasn't time with all the expeditions, escapades and exercise. It was a high-octane existence, which the Douglas-Hamiltons continued in later life: all four boys became skilled pilots. They rushed from tennis to lunch, from riding to dressing for dinner, from making apple-pie beds to telling ghost stories. This was a huge contrast to the staid life with Granny and Miss King and far removed from Sophy's intellectual austerity.

The holidays ended and Sofka returned to London, but she sensed she had found a home. She was invited to return whenever she could, and began to spend her holidays at Ferne and on the duke's Scottish estate, Dungavel. Matheson would play his pipes outside the house each morning to wake the family and came in to play in the evenings, when Sofka learned to dance Scottish reels. The males of the family would don their kilts, worn barefoot to cross the moors, and for dinner with green velvet evening jackets and lace jabots. There were games all the time – Sardines was a favourite, with hot, giggling teenagers squeezing themselves into corners and cupboards around the large house as their pursuers chased and called. It was Sofka's first taste of rumbustious family life with other young people, and she loved the security and fun of being part of a pack. She adopted the duchess's ethical outlook (if to a less obsessive degree), becoming a vegetarian for several years, and even as an adult she used Scottish expressions like 'Och, well'. Queen's College had given her an inspiring school life in England, and now the Douglas-Hamiltons were becoming her family. With them, she could live each moment to the full. It was wonderfully refreshing after the melancholy backward gaze and paralysing fear of the future so prevalent in her fellow émigrés. Like so much in Sofka's life, however, this happy set of circumstances was not to last.

CHAPTER 5

THE EUROPEAN

To live is the rarest thing in all the world –
most people exist – that is all.

– Oscar Wilde

Olga was restless. By 1922 it was dawning on her that she
would not be returning home to Russia soon and she felt
isolated from her friends and relations. Whereas large,
bustling 'Little Russias' were taking root in Berlin, Paris and
New York, London was home to relatively few White Russians
of her sort. Olga used London's gloomy, damp weather as a
pretext – a not entirely convincing one, given the awful
climate of the city she longed to return to. They would go to
Rome, she announced. The Mediterranean would be better for
her old bones. Probably more to the point, she had two
daughters and a number of close friends already living there.
Sofka was horrified. Just when she had established a life for
herself, everything was being taken away from her again.
School had been going so well, but now she would not even be
able to stay to take her matriculation that December. As to her
new-found security and happiness with the Douglas-
Hamiltons, it seemed to count for nothing. Sofka pleaded with

her mother, but Sophy was implacable: Granny needed her and she must go to Rome.

Sofka remembered the deep sense of injustice and misery brought on by the prospective move and with hindsight it appears strange that her needs were so brusquely ignored. It is also ironic that Sophy wanted her daughter to be brought up by her conservative, old ex-mother-in-law. But after all the traumas everyone had suffered, these issues were evidently not considered a priority. At nearly fifteen, Sofka might have acquired a woman's body, but she still wore long, black-ribboned plaits down her back and was considered a child. Sophy collected her daughter at the end of the summer holidays from Dungavel and accompanied her to Rome. Thus began several years of messily criss-crossing Europe.

Olga had established herself in a furnished flat overlooking Piazza Flaminia, where Mussolini's Blackshirts gathered for rallies. Sofka didn't take much notice of the political developments, but they watched from the balcony that October when crowds of men assembled for Mussolini's famous 'March on Rome'. There were five bedrooms to accommodate Olga, Louise, Sofka, Little Olga (now seven) and the two English governesses, who loathed each other. To avoid extravagance, an Italian cook and a maid came in during the day. While Sofka's spirits plummeted, her grandmother's revived; she was not too infirm to insist that everyone still changed for dinner. There were frequent visits to other elderly Russians, who would shed salty tears into their weak, lemony tea. 'Tea is the centre of all our nostalgias,' said the exiled Stravinsky. Together, the émigrés shared memories of a lost world which was beginning to sound like ancient history. Nabokov wrote of 'the remote, almost legendary, almost Sumerian mirages of St Petersburg and Moscow, 1900–1916 (which, even then, in the twenties and thirties, sounded like 1916–1900 B.C.)'.

Compared with Sofka's life in England, Rome was suffocating: tiresome lessons with an increasingly crotchety Miss King were interspersed with tutorials in Italian literature, and history lessons from an eccentric German professor. The Russian archbishop came to impart 'law of God', and was subjected to Sofka's already confrontational nature as she tried out some early arguments against Christian dogma. It is easy to imagine that the Duchess of Hamilton's theories of reincarnation did not go down well with His Eminence. Far more interesting and memorable than lessons were the visits from her father, who was living with his second family outside Florence. Sofka later suspected dwindling funds as a motive for his regular appearances – Olga might have disapproved (and never even referred to his wife), but she couldn't refuse her darling youngest boy. Petya would whisk his daughter off on jaunts around Rome, shouting applause with the crowds from the cheap seats at the opera; eating fish by the sea out at Ostia or drinking wine in some unsuitable dive in Trastevere. Above all, Petya taught Sofka about *dolce far niente* – the hedonistic pleasure of just being – in the country that coined the phrase. Having left a note for an infuriated Miss King, Sofka skipped lessons and they would sit perfectly happily for hours, sipping coffee, smoking and watching the world go by.

Sofka was thrilled by her affectionate, boyish father, with his zest for life. He was not yet forty, and must have been delighted to find such an attractive, fun-loving, curious young creature with whom to pass a leisurely day away from his noisy infants and frequently pregnant wife. This reckless grasping the moment and to hell with the consequences flew in the face of everything Sofka's mother stood for, but her impetuous father made the seductive charms of the approach quite evident. And Sofka embraced his way for ever – an inherent trait encouraged by what life had already shown her: that everything might (and quite often did) end tomorrow.

Soon the cards were thrown up in the air again. During the Christmas holidays of 1922, a letter arrived from the duchess: Margaret had been expelled from school and Sofka was invited to Ferne to share a governess for the next six months. Sophy's permission was sought in Hungary, and granted, and an ecstatic Sofka was soon packed up and travelling to England. If Margaret's school had found her 'unmanageable', Sofka was not the person to change her ways, and the two fifteen-year-olds spent the first half of 1923 being unmanageable together. The duchess had a propensity for adopting strays of all species, and she had evidently taken a special liking to Sofka. A 1923 letter to Sophy describes her as 'a most dear child and I find her so thoughtful and helpful and <u>really</u> in earnest'.

These sentiments were unquestionably *not* shared by an unfortunate Miss Scott, who was put in charge of the two adolescents. The governess's ideas about reincarnation matched those of the duchess and the pupils were set to learn little else but Egyptian hieroglyphs. Miss Scott described her previous life as a pharaoh and explained that ghosts of her long-deceased dogs still came for walks with her; she was often seen calling to invisible four-footed companions as she set out from the house. The teenagers behaved more circumspectly when the duchess was at home, but as soon as she was away (which she very often was) they were ruthlessly naughty. They would sneak out after breakfast and go riding until lunchtime, not caring if Miss Scott got cross. At night, they would get up and creep around until the pitiable governess chased them, red-faced with fury, along corridors and down the back stairs. By the early summer Miss Scott could bear it no longer and was reduced to flinging whatever was to hand, including the inkpots, at the girls. But they didn't even give her the satisfaction of showing remorse, and laughed mercilessly as the governess packed her bags and left.

After a summer in Scotland, Margaret was sent off to Miss Spalding's school in London and Sofka was faced with returning to Granny. It was with a heavy heart that she left her adopted family once more and set off for Rome. Her sense of not belonging anywhere must have been exacerbated by the fact that she no longer had a nationality, a state or a normal passport. Like all White Russians, she now had a special new document, invented by Fridtjof Nansen, the Norwegian polar explorer, who was the League of Nations' Commissioner for Refugees in 1921. The Nansen passport gave no security, rights or homeland, it provoked delays at borders and its very existence was a humbling, physical proof of the émigré's painful limbo. But at least it enabled these non-citizens to travel and work.

The situation in Olga's female household had deteriorated. The bad blood between the two governesses, Misses King and New, had progressed beyond quiet loathing. Miss King had become increasingly vague and eccentric and her exaggerated affection for the ageing, moth-eaten, eczema-ridden Pupsik and her peculiar demands that he receive special treatment were driving Miss New to paroxysms. The beak-nosed, mean-spirited and cannier Miss New not only detested dogs but believed that Miss King was mad and planning to kill her. Meanwhile, Louise was becoming gradually more grumpy and bossy, and was really only interested in serving Olga, who in turn was declining as she proceeded through her seventies. To add to the hysterical crisis, the Italian cook was threatening to leave if someone didn't take charge of things and do the accounts.

Sofka was turned to. It was the first evidence of her practical, no-nonsense side, which always ran parallel to her chaotic, fun-loving nature. Though she was not yet sixteen, she was soon organizing the monthly budget, ordering meals, paying the rent, checking the shopping and going through the accounts each month. 'A salutary training', she called it. This unlikely-seeming down-to-earth streak wended its way down the generations. When I was eleven and my parents separated, I lived with my father and proved perfectly capable of shopping and cooking my way through the havoc. And my father, though he was always known as a wild, unreliable Russian (long before he ever set foot in his parents' motherland), could be relied on to set up a stylish home wherever he found himself and cook a good borscht (with proper stock). All four generations, from Sofka's parents onwards, lacked a conventional family environment, and in its way, it provided us all with a salutary training.

Notwithstanding her youthful responsibilities, Sofka's appetite for adventure and excitement was as intense as any other teenager's, and she soon discovered alternatives to the claustrophobia of home life and the lacklustre lessons with loopy Miss King. At Rome's Russian Club she found relations, family friends, and familiar names and faces: old Princess Yusupov (Felix's mother) ran the Red Cross bazaars; Prince Borghese appeared, still with the little-finger joint from Sophy's skeleton hanging from his watch chain; and there seemed to be far more boys than girls, eager to welcome her into their midst at the Saturday-night parties and charity balls. For the first time, Sofka began to enjoy the attentions of admirers. 'After all,' she wrote archly in her memoirs, 'I could dance, my nose was powdered, I was really older than my age and had seen more of the world than any of them. Success was assured.' No doubt the Douglas-Hamilton social life had added to her self-assurance and experience of young men, and she also discovered that by being sufficiently decisive (a leaf she could have picked from Sophy or

Olga's book), 'one could rule'. When she ordained a picnic in Villa Borghese or a walk in the Forum, the others followed. After all the upheavals, it was gratifying to find herself queen bee of Rome's Russian youth and to receive flowers and poems and have young men waiting for each dance.

Notwithstanding the tumultuous gaiety, Sofka retained her hunger for books, and regularly visited the English library by the Spanish Steps. She was still young and politically innocent but she was thrashing around, searching for meaning, and grappling with ideas that would only take shape after many years. Among the many and varied authors she recalled as having influenced her at the time were two Americans: Theodore Dreiser (whose supposedly amoral writing was censored in his native country) and Ernest Poole, a left-wing journalist and Pulitzer Prize winner whose positive perspective on the Russian Revolution reminded her of those early conversations with Vanya and Shura, the lodgekeeper's grandsons at Miskhor.

Home life in Rome had its roots firmly in the nineteenth century; Miss King was a Victorian at heart and Granny still favoured floor-length black skirts and large-brimmed hats with trailing veils. Sofka, on the other hand, was a virginal *femme fatale* embracing the Roaring Twenties. And she didn't find it hard to dissemble to Granny and Miss King, whose strict rules on chaperonage she circumvented whenever possible. Tricks, lies and forged notes were all part of the weaponry used to fight for an independent life of parties and romance; sneaking out had already become a lasting habit. Along with her contemporaries, she was now learning to kick up her heels for the Charleston, her hemlines were rising, and though she didn't cut her hair into a boyish crop, she favoured cloche hats. In later life, she rejected all thought of fashion as superficial and superfluous, but pictures from this era show her to have been surprisingly elegant and ladylike. Her high heels, silk stockings, fancy patterned overcoat and dark felt hat pulled low over her eyes belie the old woman's story of having better things to think about. As a young woman, she evidently put some effort into her appearance and it was having the desired effect.

Sofka's heart was eventually won by Alexander Daehn, a friend from the Crimea days. Four years earlier, they'd climbed trees together and made war, throwing pine-cone missiles at the children of General Wrangel, who lived in one of the Miskhor dachas. Alexander's parents now shared a villa up on the Gianicolo hill with one of Olga's daughters, Countess Sophy Fersen, and the two old playmates renewed their friendship, sharing books, practising dance steps and spending hours discussing life and its elusive meaning. As Alexander was part of the family's intimate social circle, the pair found plentiful opportunities to meet – Olga and Miss King were happy to take the tram with Sofka up to Villa Sforza, and then there were all the Russian Club *soirées*. It was only gradually that they realized they had fallen in love, an event which Sofka's memoirs describe with mocking acidity, fearful probably of sentimentality, for which she shared her mother's intellectual antipathy and secret propensity. After weeks of prevaricating, the two finally admitted what they felt. 'We kissed, bumping noses. And it was spring in Rome,' she wrote.

It was Olga's restlessness that brought things to an end yet again after three years. Once more the climate was blamed (Rome's humid heat was deemed stifling and insufferable), and she decided to move to the milder climate of Nice and join her friends and relations in its sizeable Russian community. There is no record of Sofka's reaction, but presumably she was as distressed at the prospective change as she had been before leaving London. The bitter blow must have been sweetened though when, in early summer, Olga's household moved out of the flat in Piazza Flaminia

*Aged fifteen, Sofka was starting to enjoy the Roaring
Twenties. She was gratifyingly popular with Rome's
Russian youth, and didn't hesitate to trick Granny
and Miss King into allowing her out unchaperoned.
It was here that she fell in love for the first time.*

and joined Aunt Sophy and the Daehns in the roomy Villa Sforza, with its large, shady garden on the cooler heights of the Gianicolo. Sofka and Alexander suddenly found themselves living together. They began to arrange secret meetings at night; Alexander would whistle softly from the garden and his Juliet would appear on her balcony. Sofka slithered down into Alexander's arms and sometimes they would boldly go down into Rome together, but mostly they would stay in the warm, scented garden, talking Russian through the night and 'shyly kissing'.

It was Miss King who raised the alarm on finding Sofka's bed empty one night, and who ran the couple to ground in the garden: 'And there we were, moongazers, lying cheek to cheek on the grass. Oh, the disgrace, the row, the sordidness,' wrote Sofka in her memoirs. This may have been innocent first love, but in an environment where chaste kisses on the hands were usually as far as it got, the scandal was deemed large enough to send for Sophy. Sofka's mother surely smiled to herself when she arrived and discovered what had really happened, but she decided for the first time in over a decade to take her daughter in hand. She was now settled with Pierre in a large apartment in Budapest and she announced that Sofka would go back with her. Miss King was found another position and, having piled insults on Sofka, finally left. The Russian Club organized a dance in Sofka's honour, with toasts, speeches and bouquets of flowers; she had evidently made her mark there. The parting from Alexander was heart-rending. As all young lovers do, they believed their feelings would last for ever. They never met again.

* * *

I don't suppose Sophy was very sympathetic to Sofka's love-sickness as they travelled by train across Europe to Hungary, or after they arrived at the flat on the Király utca. She was far more concerned about her daughter's intellect, and after all the years of maternal neglect was suddenly worried that her only child had not received sufficient education. According to Sofka, her mother also wanted to give her the opportunity to taste something of 'the old life' – the elegant diplomatic receptions and dazzling parties given by the Hungarian aristocracy, who were having a glorious swansong.

Sophy's life had vastly improved since her hungry days with Pierre in Petrograd's House of Arts. They now lived on the first floor of a mansion and had two Croatian servants. To Pierre's delight, his home in Berlin (where he was posted before the First World War) had retained its diplomatic immunity, and all his belongings were brought over to Budapest: an imposing black seventeenth-century cardinal's desk; a polished mahogany dining table with twelve chairs; a gigantic divan covered with rugs and cushions; and numerous portraits of Volkonsky ancestors, who now stared down from the walls.

Sophy's two-pronged plan for Sofka was quickly put into effect: tutors were brought in, and 'my black-ribboned pigtail was assembled into an overweight chignon and I was "out"'. Sophy was only too pleased to send Sofka off to official functions in her place. She had never enjoyed socializing and was now busy working under a Hungarian surgeon in a hospital – the source of great happiness. So the heartbroken teenager found herself having to cope with elaborate dinners and polite conversations with pompous diplomats, while accompanying her formal stepfather on his rounds. It might have been fun to pretend to be an adult occasionally, but Sofka felt herself vulnerable to making gaffes in public and was not cut out for diplomatic life. She found the existence a strain, although she attended some marvellous parties. There had been a ball in an

Esterhazy chateau: gleaming-booted officers; long white gloves, silver cotillion favours and the sort of sparkling, candle-lit glamour her grandmother had described in nineteenth-century Petersburg.

As to Sophy's educational reforms, they were not an unqualified success. While Sofka was enthralled by her first proper introduction to Russian literature, and plunged happily into Pushkin, Tolstoy, Dostoevsky, Turgenev, Gogol and Chekhov, she was intimidated by her mother and Uncle Peter. Both were pale-faced, quietly spoken and studious, but exuded a volcanic intellectual tension. They wrote poetry and spoke numerous languages; if Sophy was passionate about science and logic, Pierre knew the genealogy of every princely family in Europe. Their day-to-day conversation was astoundingly erudite, razor-sharp and labyrinthine, 'with casual references to literary characters, historical events, mythology, the sayings of the philosophers'. The atmosphere left Sofka feeling doltish and ignorant and although she always admired her mother she could not warm to her. Sophy heightened her daughter's feelings of awkwardness with her teaching methods: believing that few know how to pursue logical thought to its conclusion, she determined that Sofka should be taught how to think, and would set problems (how electricity works, say, or the main difference between Dostoevsky and Tolstoy). Her daughter would be instructed to work it out without books and return later with the answer. It was well meant, but Sophy's lack of maternal feeling made the cerebral onslaught dry and threatening – it couldn't have been a greater contrast to Sofka's indulgent, affectionate father.

Perhaps Sophy did help stretch the adolescent's mind, but the months in Budapest confirmed in Sofka a lasting sense of intellectual inferiority and ignorance, which even decades of avid reading did little to amend. 'To be honest, I'm not really very intelligent – but I manage to conceal that,' she confessed in a letter to Jack, in her fifties.

When, in the autumn of 1924, everything came to an end, Sofka was not unduly concerned. The Hungarian government had recognized the Soviet Union, so Pierre's position representing imperial Russia became immediately untenable. Sophy didn't hesitate. Her short experiment in parenting and education over, she dispatched Sofka by train back to Granny in Nice. One can only speculate as to who breathed the greater sigh of relief.

Olga had known Nice half a century earlier, when her father, Count Peter Shuvaloff, had a villa above the town and when the '*train des grands-ducs*' brought half of Petersburg to the Riviera for holidays or convalescences. Once more, Nice had large numbers of Russians, but this time they were impoverished and insecure. Nowadays it was the Americans, like Scott and Zelda Fitzgerald, who gave big tips and swaggered down the Promenade des Anglais; the Russians were their waiters, doormen and seamstresses. According to the memoirs of one émigré, the Russian dustmen of Cannes were famous for cutting a dash in their old officers' uniforms, while the Cossacks took to the hills and kept chicken farms.

Olga too was now feeling the pinch, and her cramped apartment on the Boulevard de Cimiez reflected their reduced circumstances. By the time Sofka arrived, there was only one daily help and the household was already ruled by the iron hand of Little Olga's governess, Miss New. The tight-lipped spinster made it clear she had not forgotten the scandal in Rome and that she believed 'the worst'. Although Olga was increasingly feeble and forgetful, she was still able to make the rounds of her old friends, whose society was ruled by her sister-in-law Mary

Benkendorff. More weak tea with lemon and raking over their losses filled the afternoons, while Sofka was absorbed into the Russian youth, much as she had been in Rome. There was a round of socializing; *thés dansants* at the Negresco (spotting Isadora Duncan amongst the glamorous customers), tennis parties, swimming expeditions and games of mah-jong – the latest craze.

Less entertaining was the *lycée*. Suddenly, at the age of seventeen, Sofka was draped in a navy-blue school overall, inserted into a class of younger girls and expected to go through the exhausting drilling for the *baccalauréat*. It was too late for this. She had seen too much of the world to enter such a formal, cloistered environment and her conversational French was not up to the strenuous demands of the fourteen different subjects and copious homework. She tried for a while, before giving up what appeared a hopeless task. Olga was not bothered in any case, and Sofka was able to bluff her way along, skipping lessons as she went and damn the consequences.

Sofka gave up any serious attempt at studying and was absorbed by the frivolous party-going crowd in Nice. By now, memories of Alexander had faded enough for her to enjoy male attentions again. According to her memoirs, there was no single important attachment during this phase; rather there were boisterous, if sexually innocent, groups of boys and girls gallivanting from one party to another. She continued to read by herself and was increasingly preoccupied with searching for a meaning in life. Aged fifty, she wrote a letter to Jack, recalling this period and her lack of interest in success as measured by money, position or achievement: 'The success I desired in youth was different: it was to *be*, if you like: to find a way of living, a rule, an answer. To achieve happiness possibly – that was always the thing I wished for at New Year. But not just contentment – an active happiness, which is quite different. So all my young years I was groping and searching and did discover that the more you give away of yourself the richer life becomes.'

The most important man in Sofka's life at this time was almost certainly her father, who continued to appear sporadically. Dressed in her finest, Sofka was only too pleased to play Freudian games and pretend to be Petya's inappropriately youthful wife when they visited the Casino at Monte Carlo. As in Rome, they favoured walks and picnics, driving to Cap Ferrat or up winding roads into the lavender-scented foothills of the Alpes Maritimes. They drank wine, smoked Gauloises (French cigarettes became a lifelong preference) and recited their favourite poems to one another. At the cinema, they watched the new heroes of the silent era: Rudolph Valentino as the dark-eyed, turbaned lover in *The Sheik* and Douglas Fairbanks, tautly muscular and athletic on a magic carpet in *The Thief of Baghdad*. Of Petya, Sofka wrote: 'He was gay and gallant and charming and made me feel beautiful and important to him – surely the highest achievement for any man, especially a father!'

It was just after Sofka's eighteenth birthday in October 1925 when a telegram arrived announcing that her father was dead. He had been planning to go and stay with his mother and daughter in Nice to convalesce after an operation in Paris for an abscess on the lung. Sofka and Olga had been thrilled at the prospect, discussing how they would care for him and what fun it would be to spend some time with Petya. Now they learned that he had died from 'complications' during surgery. He was forty-two. Olga was so shocked by the death of her favourite, youngest child that she had a mild heart attack and was unable even to make it to the funeral in Paris. Sofka didn't go either, feeling obliged to stay and care for Granny. The young émigrée already knew about loss, but this was her first experience of grief and it was the person she loved most; the emotions were savage and raw. It was still normal then to wear mourning clothes (even girls of her age donned long crape veils), but Sofka refused to conform. Perhaps the fight gave her some purpose in her wretchedness as she already had a taste for swimming against the current. What she remembered was that it felt inappropriate to dress so sombrely in memory of such a joyful person as her father – he'd have surely wanted her decked out in feminine colours, not swathed in tear-stained black.

After Petya's death Sofka remained closeted in her grandmother's grief-laden apartment. Her heavy black notebook became dominated by poems about death, written in a greyish, faded ink. Several were by Maurice Baring, whom she knew from her London days:

> And yet I cannot think that Death's cold wind
> Has killed the flame
> Of you forever, and has left behind
> Only a name.

Christina Rossetti, too, features prominently:

> Yes, I too could face death and never shrink.
> But it is harder to bear hated life.

Isolated in her despair, Sofka tried to make contact with her mother, writing letters and hoping for consolation or warmth. But Sophy was unable to respond with the comfort or answers that Sofka was searching for: 'She wrote about my future,' recalled Sofka, 'trying to find some career that would suit me, at a time when I was seeking a key to eternity.'

* * *

Olga went into a steep decline after Petya's death, and although Sofka stayed with her in Nice it must have become obvious that her grandmother's home was a sinking ship. There were two life-rafts which became increasingly important over the next year or so. The first was the Douglas-Hamilton family, which continued to welcome Sofka for frequent holidays. The duchess sent generous cheques for travelling expenses, which Sofka used to buy clothes and then travelled third-class. The other was Paris. When everything fell apart in Budapest, Sophy and Pierre had moved there, quickly finding themselves in a similar predicament to the hundred thousand or so other Russian émigrés already in the French capital. The Volkonskys moved several times after their arrival in 1924, ending up in a small house (three rooms and a kitchen on the first floor with a bathroom on the ground floor) near Porte de Clichy. They dubbed it the 'Little Grey House', in an ironic reference to the magnificent 'Little White House' in the city that had now been renamed after Lenin. The cramped rooms were overwhelmed by Pierre's grand furniture, overbearing, gilt-framed ancestors and heavy, burgundy velvet curtains embroidered with birds of paradise, most of which they were gradually forced to sell off over the years.

Having arrived several years after most White Russians, Sophy and Pierre were perhaps at a disadvantage, in spite of their culture and qualifications; others had found work and homes and had used up what sometimes seemed limited supplies of French good will. Pierre managed to find some translating jobs, but work was erratic and he was painstakingly scholarly and dreadfully slow. For a while he became a part-time accountant in a small Russian printing firm, but he suddenly seemed much older and more vulnerable. Sophy was bored to desperation by the drudgery of ordinary domestic chores and both of them bore psychological scars; an unexpected knock at the door was enough to provoke a fit of trembling. A dark cloud of depression hung threateningly over the Little Grey House.

Sophy found it hard to accept the humiliation that her new life entailed. And the worst was not the poverty but the reflection of herself in other people's eyes. After she arrived, she contacted her old friend Armand, Marquis de Saint Sauveur, hoping that he might help her and Pierre. Armand had shared Sophy's English Embankment home during the dangerous year after 1917, when his post at the French Embassy gave valuable diplomatic immunity to the apartment. He was now married and held a high position in the French Foreign Service. He answered Sophy's letter warmly, gave her and Pierre a splendid lunch and never contacted them again. Sophy was terribly hurt by this snub, expressing her emotions in a poem which seems to hint that Armand had been her lover:

> *How can it be you now care nothing*
> *For those who once you claimed were dear?*
> *Was the real you in times forgotten,*
> *Armand? Or is this you today?*

The poem ended:

> *Since all those fervent words you uttered*
> *Were rippling water, wind on grass.*

Sophy's unhappiness was compounded by a series of unsatisfactory jobs. As in England, her doctor's qualifications were not recognized, and although she did some nursing, she was not actually even a trained nurse. She also acted in films (as an extra, I imagine, like many Russians), knitted clothes and gave gymnastic lessons (God knows where she learned to do that). Later, she spent many years as secretary and reader to a blind Baron Ginsberg, but when Sofka came to stay in the mid-twenties Sophy was working as a taxi driver. At least this combined her passion for cars with a love of freedom, and she liked working nights – nothing happened during the day, she said. There were numerous Russian men, particularly officers, who took to the streets in taxis; was it perhaps viewed as less demeaning than other menial jobs? By the Second World War, nearly half of Paris's seventeen thousand taxi drivers were said to be Russians.

Although Sophy and Pierre were absorbed into a social life based on St Petersburg traditions (the Association of Ladies-in-waiting or the officers' regimental clubs ignored any downturn of circumstances, valuing only former titles and positions), they were increasingly humbled and saddened by Parisian life. They surely would have agreed with Akhmatova's opinion

> But to me the exile is forever pitiful,
> Like a prisoner, like someone ill.

Sofka, however, experienced something very different when she began to visit them for holidays. Paris in the mid-twenties was a thrilling place. Artists, writers, performers and those in search of something new were converging from around the world, attracted by the artistic and sexual freedoms it promised: Pablo Picasso, Joan Miró, James Joyce, Ernest Hemingway, Ezra

Pound, Gertrude Stein, Josephine Baker ('the Ebony Venus', whose cabaret included her pet cheetah) and Alistair Crowley (with his black magic recommendations for sex, drugs and dancing).

In addition to the crazy Dadaists, Cubists and 'cultural anarchists' (as Satie and Cocteau were called), there was an extraordinarily talented collection of Russian composers, dancers, writers and poets. The glamorous Tamara de Lempicka and her colourful, slickly erotic paintings of semi-naked women and shiny cars encapsulated Paris's complex allure of modernity and decadence, elegance and brashness. The cafés of Boulevard Montparnasse, previously the haunts of plotting Mensheviks and Bolsheviks (Lenin and Trotsky both favoured La Coupole), were now filled with Russian aristocrats and intellectuals. The Reds had been replaced by the Whites and around the edges of this grey city there were glints of silver as artists of Russia's great twentieth-century blossoming tried to continue. It was often desperately hard for the Russian writers to 'keep body and pen together' as Nabokov put it, but they were certainly trying. They could be spotted in the popular cafés or Russian cabarets, eking out one coffee or brandy over an entire evening or perhaps working as *garçons* and doormen before heading back to a freezing garret to write in their own language.

Sofka, on the other hand, was too young to be bitter. She belonged to the *je m'en fous* generation and Paris was just what she wanted. Not giving a damn and to hell with the future was some kind of defence for an eighteen-year-old: it protected her from humiliation (her awful Nice *lycée* failures and her mother's unrealistic expectations), from insecurity (the incessant changes and shifting homes) and from loss (her father, her country, stability in England and her first love). She had nothing to lose, except her virginity. It was in this rebellious mood in a milieu characterized by rebellion that she experienced what she later saw as the greatest emancipation of her youth.

The factors in this emancipation were many, but the strongest catalyst came in the form of her Obolensky cousins. Related to her on both her father's and mother's sides, the three Obolenskys came from an even more complicated background of divorce and remarriage than Sofka. They now lived much of the time with their disorganized, impoverished, but affectionate and easygoing mother, Elena, in a large apartment which they shared with another family. Elena scraped by with nursing and knitting, but the teenagers didn't care about money, possessions or even food. If there was nothing to eat, they would read poetry instead. The cousins consisted of Sashka (nineteen years old, handsome and already a lady's man), Andy (Sofka's age, with dark hair, grey eyes and a serious expression) and Alyonka (a beautiful blonde, blue-eyed girl of seventeen). During the holidays they led a chaotic existence, sharing books, ideas and when necessary clothes, and often ending up sleeping on mattresses pulled together in one room, so that they could go on talking and reciting poems until they dropped off in the middle of the night. They walked the streets in worn-out shoes (they couldn't afford to reheel them) and sometimes Sofka would take them to her mother's house, where they would fit up to ten friends on Uncle Peter's gigantic divan, lolling in an ecstasy of literature and annoying their elders with their noise and carefree exuberance. Whereas Sofka had known carefree high-jinks with the Douglas-Hamiltons, this was different: it was Russian, it involved literary and intellectual excitement, and the Obolenskys were outsiders like her.

Sofka spoke only Russian with her Obolensky cousins and they all became obsessed with twentieth-century Russian poets.

They learned Akhmatova, Blok, Gumilyov and Gippius, becoming drunk on their words (it was now that Sofka was thrilled to learn that the strange woman who recited poems by her mother's Petersburg fireplace had been Anna Akhmatova). The teenagers were not alone in enveloping themselves in whatever they could salvage from their homeland. In Russian districts such as Boulogne-Billancourt (where the Volkonskys ended up), it was barely necessary to speak French. The poet Nina Berberova described this Little Russia in wonderful stories called *Billancourt Fiestas*, published in a newspaper column. She immortalized the former White Army officers with military bearing, thousands of whom now worked as labourers for Monsieur Renault at his car plant by the river, and who kept their regimental distinctions, medals and epaulettes at the bottom of old trunks. In Billancourt there were Russian shop signs (Pyshman's grocery sold Moskva toffees, icons, *pirozhki* and painted wooden spoons); Russian cafés, cabarets and night clubs, where gypsy singers made everyone cry with their nostalgic songs; Russian lawyers and doctors (who got struck off when discovered by the authorities); Russian presses printing books, pamphlets and newspapers (the *Latest News* – in Russian – sold thirty-five thousand copies daily). Even those who hadn't previously cared particularly for religion lit a candle in the Russian Orthodox churches and shed a tear at the beautiful singing.

Sofka sometimes crept into Ballets Russes rehearsals at the Théâtre des Champs-Elysées and sat captivated. She wasn't alone. Parisians were not always welcoming to the stateless émigrés, but they were certainly influenced by these first refugees of the century. The French had been introduced to Diaghilev's spectacular ballets many years earlier, but they were still entranced by Stravinsky's startlingly modern music and Leon Bakst's dramatic, colourful costumes and sets. And if Nijinsky was now too insane to dance, there were still exquisite performances by other stars like Anna Pavlova. And everyone knew that Picasso had married one of Diaghilev's dancers, Olga Khoklova. Sofka must have become aware that Russian style was all the rage. Magazines showed Coco Chanel abandoning her streamlined classic designs to make Russia *à la mode*, with daring, oriental colours inspired by the Ballets Russes: tango orange, jade green, crimson, silver, Persian blue, and gold thread all over the place. Chanel employed pale, sad-eyed Russian girls as models and saleswomen, and it was Russian hands that embroidered haute couture fabrics for her in a workshop run by Grand-Duchess Marie; every other Russian gentlewoman in Paris had taken up needles to sew and knit her way out of poverty. Suntanned, crop-haired and gamine, Chanel flirted with Stravinsky (giving him an astrakhan coat and Hermès scarves) and took up with the much younger, handsome Grand-Duke Dimitri Pavlovich. Though penniless, he was the perfect model for the new fur-lined cloaks and embroidered blouses she was promoting and he also helped her create a new blended flower-based perfume. It was sold in an unusually plain, square-cut bottle, and came to define the era, if not the century: Chanel No. 5.

It was during this whirlwind infatuation between Paris and a glamorized image of Russia that Sofka and her cousin Andy Obolensky fell in love. It was the Easter holidays of 1926 and they were both eighteen. 'This was far more delirious than anything I had ever experienced,' she wrote in her memoirs. 'We were in an ecstatic state when we could stand side by side on the back platform of a bus or strap-hanging in the metro, tense and silent and still, lost in one another's eyes and oblivious to all.' I picture them, dark-haired, scruffy, pale-skinned and rebellious, murmuring in Russian among the well-dressed, slightly disapproving French passengers.

Sofka returned to Nice transformed. She still hadn't even kissed Andy, but that did nothing to diminish her emotions. The sunny Midi had become a dull prison, keeping her from her love, and it was all she could do to mark off the days until she could go to Paris for life to begin again. The pair wrote letters almost every day and Sofka began to save money for her return, giving English and maths lessons and avoiding every unnecessary expense. It probably wasn't until the summer that she made the eighteen-hour railway journey north to Paris again. She remembered the exhausting experience of the overcrowded third-class night train: hard, slatted wooden seats (if you were lucky enough to find one); French sailors swigging from bottles; smoke; singing; and smells of garlic and cheese.

This might have been Sofka's *je m'en fous* period, but she was also deeply romantic; an obvious and lasting contradiction in her character. She felt as though she and Andy existed in a dream world, where nothing else mattered and where everything was coloured and changed by her experience of love. It was the only time in her life she remembered this metamorphosis, where even her perception of poetry and painting was altered by her overwhelming feelings. Sophy's continued attempts to imbue some logic and rationality in her daughter were, needless to say, useless. She still made Sofka open the *Larousse* or *Oxford English Dictionary* and then try to define a word in her own way – presumably a kind of torture for someone who is dreaming of kisses. The disorganized Obolenskys were not Sophy's preferred choice of company for Sofka in any case, and she was almost certainly not happy about the romance, but there was little she could do. Sofka often just avoided the Little Grey House, preferring Aunt Elena's happier, chaotic evenings or wandering about Paris with Andy.

By the Christmas holidays, the nineteen-year-olds were in a

frenzy of mutual obsession, though they had not slept together. Sofka may have embraced sexual emancipation later, but she claimed that in spite of Andy's increasingly 'urgent' embraces she was still a virgin. I have no reason to think she should have lied; she was always quite open about sex. The teenagers spoke of marriage, but although it might have solved certain issues, it was practically impossible given their age and lack of finances. Even within the madness, some tiny grain of common sense helped Sofka return to Nice at the beginning of term. It can't have felt like that though when, some time later, Andy's daily letters dried up and it became apparent that he was involved with someone else. Alyonka, his younger sister, finally broke the bad news. Sofka was plunged into a despair as all-consuming as her love had been. Like her father's death, this was another devastating loss; it was useless even to pretend not to care. Later, she rationalized Andy's departure: her absences and the limitations of her physical response were highly unsatisfactory for a passionate young man. She also described it as her one agonizing experience of being left in love. It was added to the list of things she never wanted to let hurt her again; in future, she made sure she did the leaving.

Olga's stale, poky apartment in Nice didn't help the heartbreak; an elderly widow, two ageing spinsters and a young girl were hardly the ideal distraction. When the time arrived for the *baccalauréat* exams, Sofka realized she was not prepared; she had barely worked for months. But she didn't care. After seeing how hopeless her case was on the first day's exams, she left the flat each morning and then went sunbathing on the Californie beach instead.

The summer of 1927 closed an era. Olga had been unwell ever since Petya's death and had started her old game of blaming the climate. Summers in Nice were too hot; she would move to

Versailles and join her oldest daughter Mary Troubetskoy. Following her return from a Douglas-Hamilton summer in Scotland, Sofka learned that her grandmother was not expected to live long. She went to stay with friends in Versailles and visited her every day, until one morning Louise opened the door weeping. Sofka didn't record her feelings about this death; certainly it was not the shocking, sharp wound of her father's, nor comparable to the gnawing pains of lost love. But Olga had provided a home for Sofka since she was five: she had clothed her, fed her and told her stories. And though she was a strict *grande dame* of the old school, she had doted on her favourite grandchild and had been her one stable point of reference in the dangerously shifting sands of her young life. Olga's natural *hauteur* and confidence almost certainly rubbed off on her granddaughter, and although Sofka was never pompous, she could sometimes alienate people with what appeared to be a lofty superciliousness. But that was decades later. There was a big funeral for Olga and she was buried at Neuilly with her beloved son Petya. Already scornful of 'the cult of the tomb', Sofka refused to be doing with flowers and tearful visits to tend the grave.

It must have been hard for Sofka, staying with her mother and Uncle Peter in the Little Grey House. Their gloomy pessimism now reflected her own feelings and she would have agreed with Sophy's adage that fate was a bully; it liked to kick you when you were down. Still, things were not exclusively bad and some of their friends and relations were doing quite well in Paris. Sophy's maternal uncle Alexander Polovtsoff evidently had a knack for surviving: despite being a camp aesthete and a vastly rich nobleman, he had been valued enough by the Bolsheviks to be allowed to spend several years after the Revolution saving countless art works and treasures from private houses which were in danger of being lost, burned and pillaged, and preserving the buildings as museums. Now, in Paris, he was doing well in the antiques world and his elegant wife had opened her own haute couture business. Meanwhile, Pierre's nephew had married the daughter of Serge Rachmaninov, and Sofka accompanied 'the parents' to the composer's house and listened to him playing the piano. Taking advantage of the current penchant for Russian style, Felix Yusupov and his wife Irina had founded the Irfe fashion house (named with a play on their first names) and, though it didn't prosper, sad-eyed Irina still wore the Yusupov pearls and Felix was as elegant as ever, dining out on his past as a murderer. The glamorous couple often visited the Volkonskys, and Sofka remembered lounging on Uncle Peter's divan, listening to Felix gleefully recounting gory details of Rasputin's demise to an entranced American visitor.

Perhaps Felix and Sophy smoked the odd opium pipe together, though Sophy's taste for oblivion might have already become a more private vice. She discovered that she could obtain prescriptions for laudanum (opium in alcohol), claiming it was to apply externally for neuralgia. She would then inject the liquid and escape into blissful peace for some hours, blaming her isolation on headaches. If the drug had once opened up her mind to existential answers, it had become the best method of fleeing life's hopeless dreariness. Sophy was now forty, middle-aged and without security or a future. But despite her unhappiness, she still had a creative urge. Even after driving her taxi through the dark city, she found energy to read and write. Her friend Jock Balfour, whom she had met at the British Embassy in Budapest, gave her a subscription to the *Times* Library, enabling her to have any book sent from England. To help make ends meet, she reviewed them in the Russian émigré press, and it was at this point that she wrote her book about rescuing Pierre in 1920.

While her mother took drugs, Sofka tried to soothe her

broken heart with visits to the popular Russian church in Rue Daru. It sounds improbable now, in view of her later Communism, but she always admitted a respect for religion and an appreciation of its aesthetics. In later life, she sometimes described herself as 'a non-believing Christian'. She also took a course to learn French and English shorthand and typing, remembering an offer the duchess had made, that she would be able to work as her secretary when she was grown-up. And sure enough, in the spring of 1928, a letter arrived from Ferne inviting Sofka to begin in the autumn. To cover the months until then, Sofka worked in a variety of jobs: salesgirl in a hat shop; assisting with book-keeping for a knitting business; and selling evening cloaks. Her first experience of being tipped made her blush with shame, though she soon learned to accept the coins.

A more effective medicine for the heart than prayer or work was a renewed social life. There were plenty of other young people who liked cheap wine and poetry, and Sofka even helped found a literary circle, where members stayed up half the night trying to answer life's great questions and discussing books. Later, she wrote that this was also the first time that she 'applied that unfailing panacea for love's woes: if anything goes wrong with one, console yourself with another. There were plenty of people to flirt with who had been hovering on the edge of my obsession. I flirted.' Having been proposed to by three men in one evening, she felt much happier: 'Vanity was quite healed and, after all, it plays a very major part in the disillusion of youth.' This sounds as though hindsight tidied up what was actually a frightening mess of emotions, but there's no doubt that Sofka proceeded to use amorous distraction as prevention and cure against being hurt.

* * *

Sofka was just twenty-one when she arrived to take up her post as secretary to the duchess in November 1928. She must have felt quite at ease at Ferne – a part of the family really – although with her £2 a week salary, plus free food and board, she was now technically an employee. It was such an upturn in her finances that she was able to send half her money to Sophy in Paris.

Life had moved on for the Douglas-Hamiltons and none of the younger ones was now at home: all four sons were away studying or pursuing political or military careers; Margaret was living in London, a bright young thing surrounded by beaux; Jean, the oldest daughter, was married; and Mairi, the beautiful, blonde baby of the family, had died of an illness the previous year, aged twelve. The duchess marked her grief by dressing only in white, summery clothes and appeared even in winter in white socks and gym shoes (no leather) under pale skirts. She had now thrown herself with even more of a vengeance into saving animals: a growing menagerie – wild and domestic, injured, sick and cured – was housed at Ferne. Her obsession with the fashionable fad of spiritualism was also strengthening, as she invoked psychic powers to contact the dear departed, using mediums, séances, ectoplasm and auras.

The duchess had numerous 'animal women' (as one daughter-in-law put it) and curious hangers-on, but she and her Animal Defence Society were still dominated by Miss Lind-af-Hageby. Although younger Douglas-Hamiltons tended to see the wrinkled, scowling face of a dubious con-artist, the duchess stood firm by her Swedish friend; whatever else anyone said about the duchess's bizarre beliefs and peculiar ways, they all describe her great loyalty, benevolence and warmth. In a maudlin little book she wrote about young Mairi's life, the duchess claimed that her daughter had always remembered the Swedish woman in her prayers: 'Please, God bless dear Miss Lind and let no more cruelty, vivisection and Jewish custom be.' The 'Jewish custom' referred to the two women's abhorrence of Jewish slaughtering methods; they both wrote regular letters which were published in *The Times*, demanding that the meat not be sold in Christian shops. Whether this was direct anti-Semitism or just an overwhelming concern for animals is now hard to ascertain, though I suspect it might have succeeded in killing two birds with one stone . . . Sofka later described what she believed was 'the inherent anti-Semitism of the British "upper"', saying that it 'has always made me snarl'.

Sofka was hardly overworked. She knew the daily routines: prayers in the hall, with the servants grouped on one side; hearty breakfasts under silver lids in the dining room; and walking some of the numerous dogs – a photo shows her with Deirdre, the gigantic Irish wolfhound. She would stroll through the gardens, past the ponies clad in special leather shoes, pulling mowers over the smooth expanses of lawn, and maybe down to the hothouses to pick some scented Muscat grapes on the quiet. She also typed letters and invitations and often took the duchess's place opening fêtes or giving anti-vivisection talks. As Princess Dolgorouky, she was a perfectly good stand-in to cut a ribbon or hand out a prize, and she was doubtless entertained by the Defence Society tours around rural England. The villagers must have been astonished as the two women emerged from their van: the statuesque duchess with piercing blue eyes and a large stone crucifix permanently hanging on her chest, and her pretty young Russian companion. The pair would then display the horrific instruments used in animal experimentation; Sofka was quick to pick up on her employer's techniques, and was soon able to shout passionately about humane killing techniques in Switzerland and the duchess's model abattoir in Letchworth.

There were still the trips to Scotland and periods spent in London, but Ferne was the base. At weekends Sofka would be joined by Douglas-Hamiltons of her age and went riding on the Downs and dressed for dinner as if she were a regular house guest. Presumably, in a milieu where etiquette was highly valued and titles in constant use, it would have cut some ice when Coulsey addressed her as 'Your Highness'. Sofka's favourite was still 'Lady Margaret', who would arrive breathless from London, turning her fur coat inside-out so as not to catch a scolding from her mother and telling stories of flappers' parties and daredevil escapades. She would invite Cecil Beaton over, and the photographer, who lived close by at Ashcombe House, snapped her splendid profile, privately drooling over her brothers – 'athletic, God-like creatures'.

Douglo, the future duke, had his own open-cockpit biplane – a Moth, made from wood and fabric – in which he took Sofka and others for spins and loop-the-loops over the Wiltshire countryside. Perhaps the risky freedom of these flights made Sofka think about her mother. A few years later Douglo would be celebrated as the first person to fly over Everest; 'down currents were just as bad flying over the Grampians', he said afterwards, and during the war he and his three brothers were all RAF pilots and squadron leaders. (It remains a mystery as to quite why it was to the new Duke of Hamilton's Scottish home that Rudolph Hess parachuted in 1941, hoping to arrange a peace settlement.)

Most attractive among the brothers to Sofka was Geordie, the family's second son. A godchild of George V, Geordie would later become Earl of Selkirk and have a distinguished military and political career. Even at twenty-two (a year older than Sofka), he was remarkable in the family for his sharp mind and love of reading. This was in contrast to his siblings; Margaret's daughter remembered how her mother would get annoyed if she even saw someone with a book, shouting, 'What are you doing? There's so much to do!'

It appears that an element of romance existed between Sofka and Geordie, though no proof remains. Sofka spoke of them as having been 'very close' and my father (who was later made Geordie's ward after his own father died) always understood that they had been involved at some point. After Geordie was ill in the late twenties, it was Sofka who was seconded as 'companion' for his convalescence at Ferne. She remembered them both smoking pipes, reading Plato, Hegel and Descartes and going to bed early after high tea. Maybe they also held hands, or even 'necked' – something which she discovered that men in England (unlike France) seemed to expect after an evening out. Among Sofka's papers I came across a studio photograph of Geordie – sternly masculine and dressed to the nines in full tartan regalia, with sword and silver-buckled shoes.

It was at Ferne that Sofka finally lost her virginity, but not with Geordie. Her lover remains anonymous in her memoirs, perhaps because this turned into a complicated story of adultery. She writes somewhat coyly that on her early-morning rides at Ferne she met 'an attractive young man' – a farmer's son from across the hill. I suppose she enjoyed the fact that it was secret and she certainly imagined that he would not be received as a suitable admirer in Douglas-Hamilton circles. More worryingly, he was engaged, though between kisses he claimed that he would break off with the other girl, who was away. But all went awry when the nameless fiancée lied that she was pregnant and the wedding went ahead. Sofka described it as heartbreak of a manageable sort – unlike the deep unhappiness she'd felt over Andy – and it was actually after the marriage that they became lovers.

Sofka and the anonymous farmer's son had split up when he married, but Sofka rode up to the 'old trysting place' some time later and found him waiting. 'Without a word I was off my horse and in his arms . . . I crept out that night to meet him and returned a virgin no longer.' There followed 'a bitter-sweet month or two'. She wrote that it was the only time she ever had an affair with a married man: 'I suppose I might have learned about love-making a happier way, but certainly the intensity was unequalled and one learns that it is the strength of the feeling that really counts, far more than the happiness of the outcome. After a time he left that part of the world and we deliberately ended all contact.'

I wonder whether Sofka confided in Margaret, especially given the girls' preoccupation with love and the atmosphere reminiscent of a Nancy Mitford novel: the large, aristocratic household; the eccentric parents; the bright young beaux in their motor cars, the girls with pearls and hair in wavy bobs all sound straight out of *The Pursuit of Love*. Margaret certainly told Sofka when things got serious with one of her many admirers, and after the engagement was announced in 1929, the duchess dragooned her young secretary to organize the wedding. It was to be a magnificent affair for a couple whose easy glamour turned heads wherever they went; James Drummond-Hay was as tall as Margaret's brothers, and photographs show him dressed in Scottish tribal gear – kilt and a sporran sporting a badger's head, which seems to be leaping fiercely from his groin. Some said Jimmy was kind-hearted if not too bright, and others that Margaret cuckolded him right from the early days of their honeymoon, but there is no doubt that all the stops were pulled out for their wedding. And it was Sofka who was pulling many of them. She sent out invitations to a thousand guests, who would gather at Salisbury Cathedral, and organized about 150 of them for the evening dance, with eightsome reels. There were piles of presents to list and Sofka had not only to corral the dozen grown-up bridesmaids into being fitted for spectacular dresses, velvet jackets and matching headdresses, but to be one herself.

The Times's account of Lady Margaret's 'medieval gown of cream lamé, woven with gold and silver threads' noted the multicoloured 'rainbow retinue' of bridesmaids in colours such as 'rose-pink, lavender-mauve and cherry-red'. Pamela Bowes-Lyon (soon to marry Margaret's brother Malcolm) was in almond green and 'Princess Sofka Dolgorouky, dressed in jade-green'. Photographs in the Douglas-Hamilton albums show men in gleaming spats and silken cravats and pretty girls with lots of jewellery. Sofka looks a bit anxious, or bored. Was she thinking

Sofka was the main organizer of Margaret Douglas-Hamilton's wedding to Jimmy Drummond-Hay at Salisbury Cathedral. As well as dealing with invitations for 1000 guests and overseeing the piles of presents, she was one of the 'rainbow retinue' of a dozen bridesmaids, seen here following the newly-weds.

of the farmer's son? Or perhaps the arched eyebrows and down-sloping mouth indicate she was worried she'd forgotten something in the preparations. Maybe she was just uncomfortable standing around in the February chill in those precariously high-heeled, tight-looking satin shoes and flimsy skirt, clutching a bouquet of orchids, lily-of-the-valley and tulips, tied with Drummond-Hay and Douglas-Hamilton tartan ribbons. At the edge of the high-society line-up is Matheson, the duke's stocky old piper, his chest smothered with military medals. He delighted the crowds of well-wishers gathered outside the cathedral, and then gave his best again later that evening for the Scottish reels.

* * *

Buttressed by Douglas-Hamilton wealth and comfort and absorbed by romance, Sofka had little cause to notice Britain's growing economic crisis and unemployment. However, it was Douglo's entry into politics that opened her eyes and persuaded her, for the first time, to lean leftward. As Marquis of Clydesdale, Douglo was running in Glasgow for the conservative Unionists, and Sofka was part of a group of picturesque socialites accompanying him on his campaign. As he canvassed and gave speeches, she was steadily more appalled by the extreme nature of the poverty she witnessed. The terrible contrast of their swish cars rolling into the stinking slums was hard to bear; there was something almost obscene about the Marquis and the Princess (as the papers dubbed them) crowding into a filthy, crumbling room that was living space for ten members of a hungry family on the dole. She felt shamed in front of the pale, thin mothers carrying wailing babies and the quiet humiliation of the jobless men. Sofka didn't tell Douglo when she went to one of the Labour candidate's speeches, wondering whether perhaps it offered a better solution, though it got out into the papers anyway. It had suddenly seemed absurd that someone as privileged as Douglo should represent people as poor and needy as those she had met. How could he possibly understand? She left Scotland profoundly shocked, thinking, perhaps inevitably, about Russia's experience and how drastic change was needed here too. It was still some time, though, before she actually did anything about it.

Sofka also seems to have felt a gulf within herself. She had taken up with a new admirer, the extremely rich George Sale, who whisked her about in his big car, took her out to London's most fashionable night spots and even spoke of marriage. But she was dissatisfied. Life with the duchess was beginning to pall – the spiritualism was annoying and it was hard to keep up the excitement over plaster models of pigs at the abattoir. She also found herself getting exasperated with the girls of Margaret's circle, who only spoke about clothes and horses, recognizing in herself an intellectual snobbery not unlike her mother's. In spite of her lack of formal education or satisfying career, there was probably a disapproving internal voice shouting "Frivolity!" at all this gadding about. A letter to her mother, written around the middle of 1930, gives a good impression of her verve and energy and shows a surprising degree of daughterly affection and openness. The reference to her next date gives a clue to the great changes that were soon to come:

Moppy dear,
I am going to get your book typed out as I see that it doesn't really look very clear [the English translation, by Sofka, of her mother's *The Way of Bitterness*]. How is the third part getting on?
    . . . I have at last got a permanent visa to live in England, so you can imagine my joyful feelings . . . I wrote to the

In 1930, Sofka was still enjoying high-society escapades with the Douglas-Hamilton set, but she was also starting to search for something more.

Home Office to prolong my visa for as long as possible, as I said I wanted to stay here, finding life in England very pleasant. [She doesn't mention that she 'lost' her Nansen passport on purpose] . . . So in that respect I am happy and settled. It is highly pleasant . . .

Now for G. We went out all Saturday and he is taking me out on Wednesday evening again. But the worst is that the more I see the dear man the less enticing becomes the idea of having him for good and all. And the 'thrill' of his holding my hand gets weaker and weaker. He's very nice and all that but . . . Oh, it's difficult to explain. Anyway he gets rather boring after a time, and what could be more fatal? But we'll wait and see. He is going away again at the end of August till about February. Perhaps I'll be able to work up a certain enthousiasm [*sic*] in his absence. But can you imagine his letters personified? And he keeps on repeating the same anecdotes – and I really don't think any 'glittering Rolls Royce' that 'arouses envy in the hearts of the destitute' can really make up for that, can they? So that is what I am feeling at present. As I say, it may pass off so let us wait and see.

I had a frightfully interesting evening last Thursday. I went with a girl I'm very fond of, Helen Greg (friend of Margaret's) to the house of Sir Henry Norman [politician and journalist], and there we found three other girls and as men, who do you think???? Bernard Shaw, Harold Nichols [*sic*, probably Harold Nicolson], A.A. Milne, Sir John Symons, Sir Edward Lutyens [*sic* – Edwin Lutyens, the architect], Joynston-Hicks [an MP]. And we all had about 20 minutes tête a tête with Bernard Shaw. He talked to me about the Russian character and told some anecdotes of his life . . .

Must stop now, as I am lunching at the Gregs. I had dinner with Arkadi and Freddy Chehacheff the other night. He's alright, but I'm not very fond of their type. Wouldn't trust them, somehow.

Tonight I am going out with the Zinovieff boy. He's quite different, really nice and does something, is making his way and making a career for himself (builds bridges etc.) while those two live on credit, as far as I can see and try and be men of the world. I must go. On Thursday, I think we leave for Scotland [with the Douglas-Hamiltons].

Kisses and kisses.

Sofka

CHAPTER 6

THE WIFE

*If you would know what the Lord God thinks of money
you have only to look at those to whom he gives it.*
                                                    – Maurice Baring

'The Zinovieff boy' looked older than his twenty-five years.
His thinning hair was combed down tightly on a high,
lightly frowning forehead and wire-rimmed spectacles were
wedged on a nose that hinted at a childhood break. He had clear
blue eyes, rather sensuous lips, a small moustache and enormous
charm. By all accounts he was voluble, witty, kind and unusually
attractive to women. 'He was brilliant at many things,' said his
younger sister, Elena. 'And he was so tall and graceful. He was
a wonderful dancer. When he danced, the upper part of his body
remained still, and only his long legs moved. Everyone would
stop to watch when he was on the dance floor.'

I had rung up Aunt Elena in France to talk about her older
brother. I'd only met her once as a child and I heard a pause
when I introduced myself as Sofka. When I added 'Sofka
Zinovieff', her shocked voice echoed mine down the line with
a question: 'Sofka Zinovieff?' It sounded as though she had
leaped back seventy-five years and been confronted by a ghost.

After I established that I was not her dead former sister-in-law, she became very friendly. Why didn't I come and visit her, she asked. After all, it was only two hours by train from Paris. And so, not long after, I found myself arriving at Moulin Station, one snowy February afternoon. There was no mistaking Aunt Elena waving from the end of the platform. She was almost ninety-six, but remained tall, willowy and stylishly dressed. You could tell she'd been a model in her youth: upright posture, red lips, pearl earrings and softly coiffed, white hair. She embraced me warmly.

The French housekeeper drove us home, through whitened provincial streets lined with bald, pollarded trees to a four-square, slate-roofed house, set back behind gates in a large garden. Inside there was the comfortable, polished and slightly worn feel of a home which has done its duty – Aunt Elena brought up her six children here with her French husband and there are still many visitors. The sitting room was filled with pictures of grandchildren and long-gone Russians, and as we sat down to drink weak tea I wondered how I should start talking about the woman I knew Aunt Elena detested.

'There are extraordinary people you meet in your life,' said Aunt Elena, getting straight to the point. 'And Sofka was one of them.' She paused, struggling with her conscience. 'I don't want to say bad things . . . But she was terrifying! Those dark, dark eyes. She certainly attracted men. She had a very beautiful face, with dark black hair and dark eyes – you know that's rare with Russians. She had lovely teeth – very white – and when she laughed, you'd see the teeth and white of her eyes shining. My mother was in the same set as Sofka's parents in St Petersburg, but they were very different from us. Both Sofka's parents had free love lives, whereas for us it was absolutely impossible. Sofka was completely natural in that way; it was natural for her to sleep with men and to be provocative and flirtatious.'

In the early days, Aunt Elena admitted she'd been impressed when she and Sofka 'went to the same cocktails' and Sofka (who was two years older) would predict which man would drive her home. 'She'd sit very, very close to a man and laugh, leaning against him – things that were done in old films. People probably thought that Sofka's wildness was very Russian. But in fact I didn't know any other Russian girls like her.' Before long, Elena made regular requests in her prayers that God should not let her become like Sofka.

At dinner, Aunt Elena opened some white wine and rang the hand-bell after the smoked salmon so the housekeeper could bring in the beef fillet and then the home-made apple tart. We spoke about the Zinovieff family.

'At that time we were still quite recent refugees,' she said, remembering how their money ran out completely by about 1925. 'We were very poor and it was really a struggle even to pay the electricity bills. My mother used to unscrew the light bulb and take it around the house; if we were doing lessons in the dining room she'd bring it there.' They were living at 19 Mornington Avenue, a large, red-brick, late-Victorian house in West Kensington. It was filled with people. Although Olga, the older daughter, was already married, Leo, the oldest son, had just returned from his first engineering job in Ireland, and Elena and Kyril ('les petits', as Leo called them disparagingly) were still living at home. Elena was working as a model for Worth's fashion house and Kyril was a student. Their mother kept the family going by giving Russian lessons and taking in students who wanted to live in a Russian environment as paying guests. Every available room (including eventually the dining room) was given over to a shifting population of about six young men from the Foreign Office or the military, who adored their vivacious, smiling teacher.

'We all thought the PGs were rather a nuisance,' said Aunt Elena, remembering the chaotic lack of privacy, 'but my mother was always very gay with the pupil-lodgers and never complained. She joked that she was preparing "future spies".' She was probably right: a policeman was often posted at the end of the road, presumably monitoring this unusual domestic melting pot of nationless exiles, ambitious diplomats and high-flying young officers. Zinovieff *père* couldn't find a job, and though his heart was in his history books, he did the household shopping in North End Road market and helped with housework. Kyril remembers him even emptying the lodgers' chamber pots and warning his refugee children: 'Never, never think work can be too lowly for you!'

In the basement, looking on to the rambling, one-acre garden, was Manya's chaotic kitchen, full of boiling pots and talkative visitors drinking tea – mostly other Russian servants like her. Manya had been 'given' to Leo's mother on her marriage, when both were twenty years old. A washerwoman's twelfth, illegitimate child, she was brought up in a Petersburg charitable institution (founded by Leo's maternal grandmother), where she trained as a seamstress. Tiny, pious, garrulous and devoted to the Zinovieffs, she had left Russia with them and though she wasn't always paid – often there wasn't enough money – she never contemplated leaving. 'I'm a true proletarian!' she liked to say after the revolution that turned all their lives upside-down. In exile, Manya gave up sewing fine muslin blouses and turned into a wonderful cook and family confidante. From her kitchen emerged cabbage and egg pies, cutlets, mushroom sauces and soups which smelled of home. She fed several generations of children, and even when I was growing up her legacy lurked in our kitchen, as my father urged me to add excessive quantities of butter and make the *pirog*'s pastry 'like Manya's'.

Sofka's first visit to Mornington Avenue passed into Zinovieff folklore, after she allegedly refused to remove her coat in the hall: 'I want to take it off in Leo's room!' she is said to have announced, flouncing off upstairs. I wonder whether this boldness really took place on her first meeting with the family; what was sure was the sense of invasion.

'My parents said that she just attacked him,' said Aunt Elena grimly. Was it there, in Leo's first-floor room that Sofka decided she wanted him? And how did she 'attack' him? I imagine them looking out past his small balcony to the London plane trees and red-brick mansion block. Did Leo confide how he'd wanted to be a civil engineer ever since he was a child in Petersburg? Did he tell her about when he came to England aged fifteen speaking no English, but learned it at Mr Reeve's crammer and then came out first from the City and Guilds Engineering College? There was a solidity and seriousness behind his laughing, flirtatious manner: he was clear about his ambitions, about what was right or wrong, and he had adopted his father's sense of personal honour. Perhaps this is where they first kissed – Leo tall, blue-eyed and angular, stooping slightly to embrace this soft yet fiery, dark, full-bosomed, laughing creature.

They fell in love. And Sofka was happy at Mornington Avenue: Russian chatter (all the Zinovieffs exaggerating wildly for comic or tragic effect), food tasting of her childhood, and classical music played on the gramophone. Manya, whose last job of the day was to bring up evening tea and home-made cake at eleven, would remain entranced whenever they put on Mozart or Bach. There were constant visitors: Leo's beloved old nurse, who fussed over her former charges; Aunt Vyeta, who moved everyone with her singing; and friends of the PGs dropping in. And always music: Leo played the violin and could strum a balalaika and his mother was a talented pianist. Sofka discussed

По уполномочію Временнаго

Россійскаго Правительства.

Заграничный паспортъ.

PASSEPORT POUR L'ÉTRANGER.

Подпись Владѣльца

Leo's stern expression belies his witty charm and affectionate nature. Sofka felt at home in the bustling, musical Zinovieff household, and she and Leo soon fell in love.

literature with Kyril and her future father-in-law talked about Petersburg: he'd been in the Horse Guards with Petya, and both he and his father had been marshals of the nobility. It was simultaneously refreshing and familiar. After George Sale's dullness and his ostentatious 'glistening Rolls Royce' and the privilege and snobbery of the Douglas-Hamilton milieu, it felt real.

There wasn't much money for dining out, but for a treat Sofka and Leo (and their friends) favoured the Hungaria in Regent Street – one of the most popular restaurants of the day. It was run by an Italian chef, Joseph Vecchi, who had worked at the Astoria in pre-Revolutionary Petersburg. Vecchi knew all about selections of *zakusky* to eat with vodka and how to keep things lively with Slavic panache. He introduced chicken *à la Kiev* and salmon *koulibiac* to Londoners and plucked penniless Russian singers off the street: Gregory Makaroff's Hungaria career was made when he was admired by the Prince of Wales, and the Duchess of York liked his white fox terrier, who always accompanied him on stage. Vecchi had known Sofka's father in the Astoria days and welcomed his former client's daughter eagerly: she was given a discount and, like all his Russian visitors, greeted in her mother tongue, with patronymic and title. In his memoirs, Vecchi claimed he could 'always tell a woman who has Russian blood in her'. In addition to a cultivated mind, 'there is a charm about the Russian lady which never palls. She is "different" and unexpected.' Vecchi believed this was partly on account of their interest in dress, 'unless they are interested in Revolution', in which case they cared nothing for their appearance. I imagine that Sofka would later have agreed and placed herself in the 'revolutionary' bracket, but photographic evidence indicates an attention to feminine details at this stage: beads, heels, furs and shiny hair twisted into 'earphones'. Aunt Elena, too, was mad about the Hungaria, and it was there that she was spotted on the dance floor by Mr Worth and summoned to his table for inspection as a prospective model. Afterwards when she worked for him, she was given his designs to show off on outings to the Hungaria, acting as a living advertisement for his evening wear.

Even from the early days, there were observers who noted the couple's contrasting characters: Leo shared none of Sofka's love for poetry; he saw it as a waste of time, while for her it was central to life. But these were petty details in the face of newborn passion. They had already become lovers and before long decided to get married. Later, there were murmurings that Leo was 'on the rebound' from a former girlfriend, and that perhaps it was his sense of honour which kept him with Sofka. I doubt it though; I think they were both in love and youthfully optimistic. Socially, it was viewed as a splendid joining of two old, noble Russian lines, and Leo, to whom these things counted, was delighted by his future bride's provenance. I suspect that Sofka was not interested; she certainly knew that the marriage would bring her neither wealth nor comfort. Several people were against the marriage: Leo's grandfather wrote from Rome to say that the Dolgorouky girl was not to be trusted and would bring disgrace on the family (kissing Alexander in the garden had apparently left her with a badly blemished reputation); and (according to the Zinovieffs) even Sofka's mother warned her old friends in writing that they would soon see what kind of person her daughter really was. Could Sophy really have done that? If so, what would her motives have been? The answer will never be known but, *post factum*, it definitely added fuel to the flames of Zinovieff outrage.

Speaking with Aunt Elena, I realized that Sofka had come to represent everything she (and by extension, her family) was not. Over the years, the archetypes had become stretched apart and fixed. Elena had put her energies into being good: a faithful wife, a caring mother and a practising Christian. Sofka, at the other end of the spectrum, was not only 'lazy, sloppy and immoral', she was 'bad': an adulterous wife, an uncaring mother, an atheistic Communist. Although I imagine that the Zinovieffs got on with Leo's fiancée at first, she was later condemned as a rotten apple.

It became almost a Zinovieff creed, to demarcate these divergences, which covered anything from interests to morals to body shape. Thus, while Sofka wrote about going dancing and playing tennis as a young woman, Aunt Elena claimed that her sister-in-law would never have done either ('she couldn't have danced. It was impossible – her feet couldn't have moved quickly as you had to in the foxtrot and Charleston . . .'). Similarly, Aunt Elena and Uncle Kyril said that the Duchess of Hamilton didn't like Sofka and was against the marriage to Leo, whereas this appeared to conflict with all the evidence that I had about Sofka's long-standing intimacy with the Douglas-Hamiltons (though opinions very probably changed later, especially after Sofka embraced Communism). I had the impression that it didn't suit the Zinovieffs to believe that Sofka was liked or did things that they excelled at. I kept hearing how Sofka was 'very badly built' and certainly not 'well built' – a favourite Zinovieff expression, which applied to all the tall, lean members of their family. There is no doubt that Sofka was sturdy in middle-age and huge in old age, but photographs I've seen from her youth show her ranging from curvaceous to very slim, and always attractive.

By the time I left Aunt Elena, I was convinced that she was one of the warmest, most charming people one could meet, but her perspective on Sofka was entrenched in dislike and even disgust. The resulting sense of contradiction made me feel awkward; how could I reconcile this with my picture of Sofka as complex and flawed – (who isn't?) – but fascinating and lovable? How did I fit in, as a Zinovieff, to the family which condemned my grandmother? Sometimes I enjoyed hearing the stories about Sofka's wickedness, her heartless selfishness or her crazed adulterous escapades; I was able to keep my own sense of proportion about what seemed likely or possible, and I could imagine her motives. But there were moments when I suddenly felt offended by the skewed images. After all this time with Sofka in my head, I had a sense of her judgement and was developing my own relationship and loyalties to her as a young woman. It had become almost like living with her.

* * *

After the engagement, the duchess continued in the role of adopted mother, doubling Sofka's salary and organizing a society wedding for her. BRIDAL CROWNS AND IKON was the headline in the *Sunday Times*: *Marriage of Russian Princess: Picturesque London Ceremony.* London's Russian bishop took the service on 27 June 1931 at St Philip's, the Russian church in Buckingham Palace Road (later destroyed after the war). 'The princess was a striking figure in her gown of white satin' – an elegant, clinging concoction, specially made by her aunt with the Paris couture house. She looks thin in the photographs, with a surprising porcelain fragility. I suppose she must have smelled delicious from the orange blossom in her hair, the generous sheaf of white lilies, a dab of Guerlain or Chanel and just a hint of the brandy that she'd drunk for Dutch courage. Ducky (as Sofka called Leo) positively gleamed in top hat, tails and bright white spats. The *Sunday Express* printed a picture of the bride and groom during the ceremony, clutching candles, with heavily ornate golden marriage crowns held over their heads from behind. The twelve 'groomsmen' who had this job included

Uncle Kyril ('it's terribly tiring, with your arms stretched out'), three Douglas-Hamilton sons, several favourite pupil-lodgers from Mornington Avenue and Jock Balfour, Sophy's friend from the Foreign Office. There was only one bridesmaid – Little Olga – and the bride was given away by Uncle Peter, who had come over from Paris with Sofka's mother.

Sofka and Leo's wedding was in the Russian church. Some people were against the marriage from the start, while others commented on the obvious differences in their characters.

It was a sunny day and the female guests were festooned in ruffled chiffons, flowery frocks, fox-furs and floppy hats. The duchess looked awkwardly hunched and large-nosed, like an amiable vulture in a white, pleated dress, as she welcomed the guests to the reception, held at her London house in

St Edmund's Terrace, by Primrose Hill. The marquees were stiff with titles from British and Russian society, including a sprinkling of Romanovs. Margaret (who had probably been mixing cocktails in her mother's drawing room since morning) fell into Grand-Duchess Xenia's lap while attempting to bob a curtsey. The photographer took pictures by the lily pond, a towering, white cake was cut with a sword; and the newlyweds left for their honeymoon in Guernsey. 'The bride travelled in a blue and white silk dress under a dark blue coat and a blue close-fitting hat to tone,' commented the *Times* correspondent.

The initial calm of married life looked promising. After the honeymoon Sofka and Leo moved into a rented house near Mornington Avenue, at 28 Castletown Road, along with Chip, Sofka's black Cairn terrier. To help supplement Leo's £6 salary, they rented another house in the same street and sublet it as small flats and rooms. Sofka left her job with the duchess and for a short time lived a life of relative leisure, reading avidly, doing the odd translation, lunching with female friends and learning to produce meals for her husband. She admitted that until her marriage she could barely boil an egg, and in last-minute desperation before the wedding had visited the vast, well-staffed kitchens at Ferne to pick up some tips. Soon however she was enjoying herself at the stove, experimenting with food colouring and giving surreally tinted dinners to friends: red mashed potato to contrast with blue cocktails, and so on.

Before the 1931 elections in October, Sofka went canvassing for the Labour Party, supporting the candidate for Elephant and Castle. She realized that London, too, had the gaping chasm between rich and poor that she had witnessed in Glasgow. Once more she felt wounded by the injustice and her sense of helplessness, though not enough to get more deeply involved. Her 'mildly pink activities' (as she called them later) shocked Leo and offended her in-laws. Like most Russian émigrés, they judged political parties primarily according to the harshness of their position on the Soviet Union; Labour wasn't their style at all.

The first major blow came when Leo lost his job. Suddenly the economic crisis and burgeoning unemployment stopped being the theoretical issue they'd read about in the papers. Early in 1932 the couple found themselves thrown with startling rapidity into grinding poverty. It quickly became obvious that due to the recession Leo would not be able to find another job easily, and they moved into two rooms on the second floor of their house, letting out the rest. They gave up smoking, getting awful pangs and then feeling worse when they grubbed around for their old cigarette butts. Meals declined into a depressingly dull regime based on bread and potatoes. It had been a quick jump from high-society dinners with the Douglas-Hamiltons to bargaining for something leftover and cheap on the North End Road stalls. Suddenly, they were on the 'other side'. Sofka found she comprehended exactly what her old boyfriend, George Sale, had meant when talking about his Rolls-Royce 'arousing envy in the hearts of the destitute'. Now she looked at rich people passing in their cars and felt anger at how much they had when she and Leo went hungry. It was to change her whole way of thinking about social inequality, and while Leo just saw their predicament as hopefully temporary bad luck, Sofka was convinced that there was something wrong with the system.

To add to the crisis, Sofka became pregnant. Her morning sickness turned into continual nausea, and for many months she was weak and bed-ridden, hardly able to keep any food down. The doctor inconveniently recommended that the expectant mother drink a glass of champagne every morning to combat her symptoms, and Leo somehow came up with a case of quarter-bottles. It sounds a bad mix: tipsy and nauseous, emaciated and pregnant. And poor. Very gradually, as her belly grew, Sofka began to get better. Leo got a little freelance work and Sofka started doing whatever she could to pay off the bills, from knitting (she discovered she could do it while reading) to envelope-addressing. They bought a 1914 Corona portable, and Sofka was soon busily typing out manuscripts for friends and acquaintances. That summer the Douglas-Hamiltons sent partridge and grouse from Scotland – a kind thought, but the meat was sickeningly over-rich and 'after a while, anything was better than game day after day'. They ended up exchanging it with a butcher for stewing-beef.

Although Sofka and Leo were happy together through these shared hardships, there was already a divergence in their values and outlook which went beyond the party-political. While I was with Aunt Elena, she told me a story illustrating this gulf, which she found almost too 'awful' to relate. I pleaded (half expecting tales of orgies or black magic) and eventually she agreed:

'One day, during a heat-wave in the summer of 1932, I walked over to visit Sofka after work. She was pregnant and feeling very unwell and it was extremely hot. I found her lying completely naked on the bed, reading a book, and told her, "Sofka, you mustn't, it's awful – I'll get you a sheet." But she refused to cover up, saying she was too hot and it was the only way. I was very upset, but stayed for a while. Then Leo came back from work and was so cross: "What's going on? Are you mad?" And he brought her some clothes.'

What shocked Elena as much as her first sight of a sprawling naked woman was Sofka's lack of shame. 'It was a wildness – a bit like an animal,' she said. For me, having grown up in London's hippy era, it hardly sounded like a crime – more as though Sofka was just ahead of her inhibited times. But I understood that to Elena and Leo it looked like wilful, almost unhinged behaviour. 'You mustn't put that in your book,' warned Aunt Elena. 'It would shock Peter.'

Peter, my father, was born on 26 January 1933 and named after Petya, his maternal grandfather. Sofka had been afraid that her ill-health and poor diet might have affected the baby, but he emerged 'an active six-pounder' in a nursing home near to Castletown Road. Later, she described fierce maternal emotions – the 'mother wolf instinct' – and claimed to have enjoyed the experience of having babies and 'the excitement of giving birth'. 'Given a different existence,' she wrote, 'I am sure I should have had a dozen with delight.' This was somewhat disingenuous, given her limited maternal attention span, and she admitted that, having walked home with her infant, she was terrified of being left in charge of such a small, helpless creature. It was evidently with relief that she found Maureen, a young Irish nurse, who was given a roof, meals and five shillings a week to look after the newborn while the new mother went out to earn some money. Leo too was back in regular work, converting houses in Pont Street into flats for a newly established firm, and after twelve years as a nationless exile had applied for (and later gained) British citizenship. 'Applicant appears to be a respectable man,' wrote one of the laboured, heavy-handed police reports. It looked as though they had weathered the worst of the storm. It only later became apparent how close to one another the storm had brought them.

Peter's christening was held at the Russian church where his parents had married and his half-dozen godparents included the Duchess of Hamilton and several friends from that circle (one christening present was a Harrods account). Like his mother, the baby was uncompromisingly strong-willed, and as he grew, Sofka frequently found herself locked in a battle of wills: Peter would choose to stay in his cot all day without food rather than get dressed; or when he wanted to be carried over the road at Hyde Park Corner, he remained alone on the pavement instead of walking across with his mother. (In the end, a policeman broke the impasse by carrying the toddler across himself.) Peter had his father's broad, slightly frowning forehead and his mother's dark hair, and was quickly the darling of his Zinovieff grandparents. Photographs show him toddling, naked and lordly, in their enormous garden, which became his playground and fiefdom.

According to the Zinovieffs, Sofka had already begun to have affairs: with the PGs at Mornington Avenue; with the milkman; with 'anyone passing'. Aunt Elena repeated to me what had evidently become a family maxim, that Sofka might have inherited certain physical 'needs' from Catherine the Great along the Bobrinsky line. The Empress 'couldn't even write a letter if she didn't have relations with a man', my great-aunt said. 'Her head wouldn't work properly. She wrote that in her own memoirs.' Sofka herself didn't ever admit to having such 'needs', and while she certainly recommended the joys of casual sex when she was older, she admitted its limitations in comparison to one exclusive love, which 'is something to appreciate and cherish'. In her book, she does however describe one affair she had during 1933, adding that 'cheating one's husband or lover has always seemed to me to be a lowering of one's dignity'. Whether this was a smokescreen to conceal her rampant adultery is now impossible to check; my instinct is that her marital indiscretions were less numerous than her in-laws imagined.

The backdrop to the *affaire* (as she called it) is described in some detail in Sofka's autobiography. In 1933 she took a trip to Paris for the first time since her marriage, and 'in a fit of mischief' rang up Yuri, a young man she had encountered two

*Peter often played in his grandparents' garden at Mornington
Avenue. Here, Sofka appears to be regarding her first child with
detached curiosity, while his strong will is already evident
in his features.*

years previously. At their first meeting she had been on a solitary pre-nuptial trip to collect her wedding dress, and had gone out with a group of Russian friends and cousins. After dancing at a fashionable 'negro nightclub', they ended up at La Coupole in Montparnasse, where she started talking to Yuri, the black sheep of the gathering. He had worked as a labourer since the age of fourteen to support himself and his mother. Tall, thin, with dark hair, piercing eyes and bad French, he was deeply serious, especially about Russian literature. When the party broke up in the small hours, they all arranged to meet there again the next morning, but Sofka and Yuri continued talking. 'Time flashed by,' she wrote, and at 10 a.m., when the rest of the friends turned up for breakfast, they were both still there. Nothing more happened between them, but the second time around there was an immediate intimacy and they became lovers. Sofka regretted this episode as 'one of the worst things that I have ever done'. Not so much because she was married, but because Yuri was 'too intense and single-minded a person to take anything lightly'. She didn't describe how her lover was affected, but presumably he was devastated to provoke such remorse. Nor did she reveal that they would get together again after the war, in very different circumstances.

Sofka told Leo what had happened in Paris, but he too had reason to feel awkward. He had recently met up again with Oggi, his former love, who was now married with children and living in Switzerland, and they had both been plunged into a torment of rekindled emotions. Oggi (a tall, well-dressed Russian who danced marvellously) begged that they both divorce and marry each other, but Leo felt honour-bound to his vows. When Sofka returned from Paris, she found Oggi's picture pinned above Leo's bed. At least this made for a sense of quits, even if she had been the only adulterer. But these conflicting desires inevitably created a new rift between Sofka and Leo. He began working very hard, often spending evenings back at Mornington Avenue with his parents, while she made friends with a group of local artists and started going to unconventional parties that Leo didn't like.

During the day, while little Peter stayed with Maureen and visited his grandparents, Sofka gave Russian lessons at Davies' – the crammer which specialized in Foreign Office exams. She also put herself on the books of Universal Aunts: 'Anything for Anyone at Any Time' was their motto. People could call up Knightsbridge 3101 and get 'efficiency and reliability' from a chaperone, a carpenter, a dog walker or someone to meet children off a train. Sofka offered herself for secretarial work, and had already become a dab hand at rewriting old ladies' wills and organizing society parties by the time she turned up at Cheyne Walk at eleven one morning. An Irish maid ushered her through some impressive bronze front doors into a vast, high-ceilinged room which had once been Whistler's studio. It was newly decorated, somewhat ambitiously, with heavy, pickled-oak furniture, cocktail bar, minstrel's gallery, grand piano, tapestries and impressive fireplace. Sofka was shown into a study, where a debonair young man in a silk dressing gown handed her a bundle of letters and a pile of signed photographs – her first taste of fan-mail. Several hours later, having successfully completed all the replies, she was paid her five shillings and left.

Sofka had not previously heard of Laurence Olivier, but she immediately took to him and his actress wife, Jill Esmond. The Oliviers had evidently liked her too, and soon rang to request that she come twice a week; Sofka was hardly a usual secretary, with her cosmopolitan worldliness, acidic humour and literary bent. Olivier probably appreciated her Russian traits too, as he had regularly tasted White Russian excesses at Hollywood's

Russian Club, where he and Douglas Fairbanks Jr had downed vodkas to the strains of balalaikas and complained about their wives. Although Sofka eventually became particularly close to Jill, I wonder if she and Larry (as he was henceforth known) didn't sense the dark, highly sexed ruthlessness they both had in common. They had been born within a few months of each other and their marriages were to run a surprisingly parallel course of devastation and divorce.

After a few weeks, Sofka was asked to come every morning and then full-time to help with letter-writing, book-keeping, press cuttings and minding the ring-tailed lemur, Tony, who roamed freely around the house and was given sips of cocktails. The couple were generous employers: 'Give her thirty bob!' was Jill's reply when Sofka timidly suggested 17s. 6d. for five mornings a week. And the stylish, creative atmosphere was exhilarating; Olivier was on the brink of colossal fame, moving from matinée idol to the legendary Shakespearian actor who gave a new, vigorous realism to his roles.

Sofka was soon utterly absorbed by theatrical life, spending long hours watching rehearsals at the Old Vic and never missing a first night. Olivier's astonishing versatility was made clear to her one day when she brought some letters in for him to sign, arriving during a dress rehearsal for *Twelfth Night*, in which he was playing Sir Toby Belch. As she watched from the stalls, 'a short stout man with flabby cheeks came and sat in the row in front of me', she wrote in her memoirs. 'I took no notice of him at all until he turned to me and said: "I can sign them now." It was Larry.' Sofka frequently attended Cheyne Walk parties, meeting many rising and established stars such as Noel Coward, Peggy Ashcroft, John Gielgud, Ralph Richardson and Edith Evans. She described this company as slightly larger than life, 'where "darling" was the ordinary form of address and four-letter words flicked unnoticed through conversations'. Given the hardships she had recently been through, 'it was like living in a fairy-tale sunlit world after enduring a long, grey winter'.

Sofka and Leo were not so close any more, but they were not exactly unhappy. And at least they were solvent. Although Castletown Road was becoming increasingly run-down and even slummy, they both embraced an intense London nightlife again: clubs, dances, mischievous adult treasure hunts – who can return first with a policeman's helmet and a Savoy ashtray, and so on. And endless parties. Evelyn Waugh's *Vile Bodies* gives the tone: 'masked parties, Savage parties, Victorian parties, Greek parties, Wild West parties, Russian parties, Circus parties, parties where one had to dress as somebody else, almost naked parties in St John's Wood, parties in flats and studios and houses and ships and hotels and night clubs, in windmills and swimming-baths . . .' Sofka casually mentions parties where 'promiscuous necking' was *de rigueur* and I imagine she was game enough to follow Gertrude Stein's recommendation that 'One must always yield to temptation.' Naturally, alcohol flowed extremely freely and Sofka had acquired not only a Russian aptitude for drinking but was blessed with a strong head and a powerful constitution. She rarely suffered from hangovers and could get up breezily the morning after a night's carousing.

There were also regular weekends at Ferne with the Douglas-Hamiltons. More parties. Peter was put to play with Margaret and Jean's young children, cared for by nannies, while the adults went riding, played tennis, mixed dry martinis and visited Cecil Beaton (Sofka was impressed by bedrooms with four-posters and leopardskins, and a bathroom covered with hand outlines and autographs of Beaton's rich and famous friends). Leo had become a favourite of the duchess, and Sofka also noted a growing affection between him and Jean, whose own marriage was proving

increasingly miserable. Looking back, Sofka wrote (in an autobi-
ographical report for the Communist Party) that one of the main
reasons for her 'complete incompatibility of outlook' with Leo
was that 'he yearned towards the Hamiltons in the same ratio
as I swung away'. This may have been no more than a convenient rationale, but for her it symbolized the parting of their ways.

* * *

No record exists of exactly when Sofka met Grey, but it was
probably in late 1934, when she was sent by Davies' crammer to
his flat behind Harrods. At twenty-three, he seemed very young
to his twenty-seven-year-old Russian teacher, though he was
well-dressed, favouring a bowler hat and double-breasted
jackets. One person recalled a highly attractive, 'Leslie Howard-
ish' appearance, but photographs also reveal a vulnerable,
physically slight, lost-boy quality, with melancholy brown eyes.
Perhaps this reflected his unhappy childhood: his father was
gruff and bullying, his mother bitter and complaining, and things
only went downhill after Honington Hall, the family pile in
Warwickshire, was sold following financial difficulties and the
couple divorced. Presumably it wasn't chance that Sonny (as they
called him) got involved with a woman who was so evidently
incompatible with his own insular, huntin'-and-shootin', class-
bound background, which had brought him such misery.

It appears likely that Grey was hoping to enter the Foreign
Office, although records show no mention of his having applied.
The Skipwith family story goes that he was thwarted from a
brilliant diplomatic career by his unfortunate involvement with
a much older, married, man-eating, Russian *femme fatale*. However, the Foreign Office made no stipulation that applicants could
not be married to a divorcee, and Grey might have been just as

hampered by the fact that he abandoned his history studies at Cambridge after only one year in 1931, thus leaving without a degree (it is not known why). Though he looked like the sort of regular public-school chap who might soon be posted to some colonial embassy, in fact he had a sceptical, questioning mind. He soon proved himself quick-witted, emotional and a keen linguist – by the time he started Russian lessons, he had already spent periods abroad acquiring German, French and Spanish.

It wasn't love at first sight, and though the lessons were pleasant enough, Sofka was busy with the Oliviers, family life and party-going. Grey gradually increased the lessons until he and Sofka were meeting every day, and there was a point where Sofka realized that she missed him when they were apart. They began to go to parties together and dine out at the Hungaria, but Sofka wrote in her memoirs that their relationship remained purely platonic. Her friends assumed otherwise, playfully calling Grey 'Young Woodley' after the public-schoolboy character in a popular 1920s play who falls in love with his housemaster's wife (Grey's family used the same expression later, with distaste). The way Sofka puts it, 'It was not until one day we bumped in a doorway and found ourselves kissing that I understood how serious it was. That evening I spoke to Leo. "Don't see him for six months," he said, "and you'll get over it."'

I have to admit that, though I prefer believing Sofka, her writing about this period doesn't quite ring true. The leap from bumping into Grey's embrace and the realization that she had found the love of a lifetime was surely much greater and riskier than it sounds in her jaunty prose. Her subsequent claim that she and Leo decided to have a baby together, despite realizing that their marriage was possibly on its last legs, is equally unconvincing. Admittedly however there is no overwhelming evidence that her second child was Grey's, so perhaps it was a

Sofka's relationship with Grey began as a playful flirtation but developed into something which overwhelmed them both. Sofka did not hesitate in breaking up her marriage for him and Grey's family believed that he had sacrificed a potentially brilliant diplomatic career for a disreputable older foreigner.

'mistake' with Leo. Sofka once confessed to my father that she had tried to abort one of her pregnancies with quantities of gin and hot baths, and I suspect it was this one. By the time Sofka was hospitalized, in the autumn of 1935, pregnant and seriously ill with pyelitis, the situation was evidently painfully chaotic. I'm not sure whether Sofka actually waited the agreed six months (she said she did), but she had definitely decided that she was going to leave Leo for Grey once the baby was born. Thus, although Leo was at her bedside in the nursing home, it was Grey who wrote to Sophy in Paris to inform her of her daughter's condition. His hurried, late-night epistle on Basil Street notepaper conjures up an odd set of circumstances:

> My dear Princess,
> Thank you very much for your letter and for the extremely generous attitude which you have taken towards me.
> Please do not take anything I may say as the absolute truth, but I am trying to tell you the position as far as I can gather it. That is to say that I waited outside the nursing home until Leo left after seeing the doctor, and I dined with him tonight.
> . . . The doctor's report is a little more difficult to get accurately. Apparently he explained to Leo that if the child was taken out Sofka would be perfectly well within half an hour. As you know that is not easy to arrange in this country (although Leo was very anxious for it).
> . . . Apparently the doctor wants to do everything possible to avoid taking the child away for another fortnight in order to make sure that it will live. In any case there seems to be every possibility after tonight's report that they will get Sofka completely well, and that the child will be born quite normally in December.

All did turn out well, and Ian was born shortly before Christmas. On the baby's first visit to Mornington Avenue Manya exclaimed, 'Just like Grey!' And though Leo was categorical that *he* was the father, there were many who assumed otherwise. An incriminating letter was found by the 'char' who cleaned both Mornington Avenue and Castletown Road: it was from Grey to Sofka (or was it Sofka to Grey? – nobody could quite remember), indicating that he believed himself the father. Having fished it out of the bin, the cleaner passed it on to the Zinovieffs, provoking even more pain and anger. Nevertheless, although it sounds logical (and I initially suspected) that Ian might have been Grey's son, I came across nothing in my searches through Sofka's writings and my talks with people close to her to indicate that Leo was not the father. Surely the secret would have come out at some point? And given Sofka's taste for shocking people and her undying love for Grey, this appears to be another point in favour of something closer to her official version.

I hesitated before raising the matter of his paternity with my Uncle Ian. I knew that as a young adult he changed his name to Fitzlyon (as did Uncle Kyril) – a sign perhaps of wanting to leave his past behind. I was struck too by Ian's adoption of a safe, conventional, Middle England style, as if he had tried to move himself as far as possible from the Bohemian, Russian, unpredictable muddle which characterized both his mother's and his older brother's lives. I cautiously asked if he'd ever wondered whether Grey was his father.

'Oh yes,' he replied blithely. 'After Mother's book came out, a friend saw the photograph of Grey and immediately asked if he was my father. We asked Mother, and she said that no, Leo was my father.' I asked whether he'd consider doing a DNA test, but Ian was adamantly against it: 'Now I just want to let sleeping dogs lie.'

The Zinovieffs liked quoting a saying about Catherine the Great's descendants along the (illegitimate) Bobrinsky line: 'It's the tradition from father to son that the son is never the son of his father.' Sofka was thus just fulfilling her disreputable genealogical destiny. Even more shocking, according to Aunt Elena, was that Sofka then abandoned her three-month-old infant at Mornington Avenue to run off with Grey. Sofka's account is different: she writes that she found a maisonette in Pond Place, Chelsea, for herself and the children. There was a 'nice, jovial Irish nanny' who took the boys and Chip out to the park every afternoon, and Sofka claimed that she 'always made a point of being back by 5 pm at the latest for our playtime hour', when she helped Peter learn to read from the same book Miss King had used for her. Tony, the Oliviers' boisterous lemur, later joined the household, leaping from curtain to table, entertaining the children and adopting Sofka as his mother and her bed as his nest.

Leo moved into a large serviced room near Sloane Square, and despite the wrench of breaking up, he and Sofka remained on friendly terms, dining together every night for the first week and then meeting up frequently. Leo's open-hearted nature was apparent both in his agreeing to separate and in a letter he wrote to Grey in early 1936. It reveals that while Leo's family was seething with hurt indignation at Sofka ('It cost him very dear, getting married to Sofia Petrovna,' was Manya's unforgiving, head-shaking refrain for the following decades), Leo was sad but calm.

Dear Grey
This is a letter which I have been meaning to write you for some time . . .
. . . I fully realise the force of circumstances that brought

things to a head and even had you not been there, the issue,
I suppose, would have still materially been the same . . .

. . . I would like to assure you from the bottom of my
heart that I hold no grudge against you in any way
whatsoever and my only regret is that owing to the
awkwardness of the situation just now, I have lost in you for
the time being a pleasant companion and something more
than just an ordinary friend.

Divorce and scandal were in the air in 1936–7. The Prince of
Wales was involved with an American divorcee, and Olivier fell
in love with Vivien Leigh, who like him was married (he later
starred in a film that publicists called 'Vaguely risqué! Slightly
scandalous!' – *The Divorce of Lady X*).

One evening at the Hungaria (a favourite haunt of Mrs
Simpson), the band stopped playing and Sofka and Grey heard
the announcement of King George V's death; it was a long time
since he and Queen Mary 'came to meet her' at Victoria Station
in 1919. After the coronation and subsequent abdication, the
public became fanatically divided about the rights and wrongs of
the glamorous new king giving up his kingdom for love; Sofka
and Grey were among the many who found it absurd. They also
identified with the pain involved; Grey's mother was so
horrified by her son's entanglement that she refused even to
acknowledge the woman who had ruined her son's prospects
(shades of Granny Olga with Sofka's gypsy-singer stepmother).

The whole preposterous palaver of getting divorced had been
recently exposed and ridiculed in a popular novel, *Holy
Deadlock*, by A. P. Herbert, and Sofka and Grey read the book
for tips. It must have been a bitter laughter though, to learn what
was expected of a divorcing couple: 'One of you must commit
intimacy – not both,' explains a solicitor to the dumbfounded

husband, who wants a divorce. 'And you must not consult together which one it is to be: for that would be collusion.' Collusion condemned the guilty couple to remain united in 'unholy matrimony', when even persistent cruelty was not enough reason for divorce. 'As the law insists, the one thing that matters is the physical act of love.' Though Leo offered to do the gentlemanly thing and provide the required 'evidence', Sofka refused to allow this hypocrisy when she was the 'guilty' one. Even so, the enterprise proved as complicated and ludicrous as Herbert's book suggested, and it took two attempts to arrange a visit to a hotel before they could be 'surprised' by a junior clerk, with Sofka as adulterous wife and Grey as disreputable co-respondent.

Sofka was clear that Grey was her future and convinced that unhappy unions were worse than divorce for everyone concerned, but this didn't erase her sense of culpability. She had destroyed her marriage and the break was harder than she expected – Leo's impeccably generous behaviour must have made her even more aware of how she had hurt him. Nevertheless, letters from the time suggest that he might not have been entirely blameless for the split. Just before the divorce was finalized, Leo moved into a house in Markham Square, off the King's Road. He wrote affectionately from there to Sofka, 'my ownest dear thing', sending a signet ring as a present and 'the last letter I'll ever address to you as my wife . . .': 'I took you too much for granted and did not realise until too late what I had been given in you. Girl dear will you please accept now my most profound apologies and regrets and do forgive me if you can for all that in which I know I failed and hurt you and sometimes hurt you horribly badly I know also. There are certain things which I will never forgive myself for – God knows!'

It is not clear why Leo was apologizing (was it about Oggi, or a more general neglect?), but Grey also mentioned to his future mother-in-law that although Sofka had remained 'best of friends' with Leo, the latter's behaviour had not been perfect: 'I won't refrain from saying that as a husband, he is the most "God-damned" selfish man I have ever known. In fact he might be 100% English – but that will soon be passed with all its consequences and leave us the pleasure of the friendship of one of the most charming men one can meet.'

When Olivier left Jill and their young son, Tarquin, for Vivien Leigh in 1937, Sofka felt almost as anguished as she had over her own separation. It was as though the world which had sustained and inspired her for so long was crumbling. In his memoir, Olivier writes that his love for Leigh 'sometimes felt almost like an illness, but the remedy was unthinkable . . .' Sofka recognized only too well the actor's emotional turmoil.

She was impressed by Leigh's breathtaking beauty, but didn't warm to her, finding her petulant and difficult. Though she continued to work for Olivier, Sofka's loyalty stayed clearly with Jill, who remained a lifelong friend. After the split, neither of the Oliviers could face staying on at their marital home in Cheyne Walk, and when they left Sofka and Grey moved in. It must have been strange for them, living in film-star surroundings and sleeping in Jill and Larry's enormous seven-foot-square bed. A replica of this symbol of marital love had already been ordered by the Oliviers as a wedding present for Sofka and was being made at Heal's, with linen and blankets to fit. Grey was now working as a salesman for Vent-Axia – 'the world's first electrically-operated window fans'. He went about in an elderly Alfa Romeo and would often drive Sofka up to the Old Vic for rehearsals. Olivier's fans now assembled in crowds out-side the stage door; it was one of the actor's greatest years, with memorable performances in *Hamlet*, *Twelfth Night* and *Henry V*, all of which imbued Sofka with an undying ardour for Shakespeare. Later, imprisoned during the war, she said that Olivier's voice declaiming Shakespeare was one of the things she missed most.

Pip and Tiny (as Peter and Ian were known) moved in with Leo for the summer (unless Sofka was lying and they were already there), and meanwhile the divorce came through. Two days later, Sofka became Mrs Skipwith at Chelsea Register Office on the King's Road. 'Mr Skipwith, aged 25, is son and heir of Sir Grey Skipwith, Bart,' wrote the press report. 'The bride, who is 29, wore a cerise coloured satin summer costume with a white blouse, and a turban hat. A spray of orchids was pinned to her coat.' The journalist was surprised to see only two witnesses: '"We do not know who is coming," Mr Skipwith said. "Our wedding was arranged so hurriedly that we have not given our guests time to reply."'

They dashed off to France for a month's honeymoon in the 'baby Simca' – a comically diminutive white convertible that they bought themselves as a wedding present to replace Grey's expensive and ailing sports car. Sofka's description of that trip has the aura of true romance – a golden time of unequivocal happiness and eroticism. In Nice, they swam far out to sea together and sunbathed naked and then drove down through Italy in their swimming costumes, stopping for cheese and wine along the way and getting sunburned.

The honeymooners drove back up through France, arriving in high spirits though penniless in Dieppe, where they had to pawn jewellery (including the engagement ring, which itself had been bought for £3 in a pawnbroker's) to pay their hotel bill and food. They returned to Cheyne Walk and started house-hunting. Having decided to leave London, they eventually found Dean

The Baby Simca was the ideal honeymoon car. Bought as a wedding present to themselves, Grey and Sofka drove it down to the Mediterranean in July 1937 for a month of blissful happiness.

Cottage, in Cookham Dean, a village near Maidenhead. Sofka wrote that they decided on country life as being good for Peter and Ian, but that when they moved, 'Leo begged to keep the children. He enjoyed having them and it made a home for him instead of life alone in rooms; Peter was doing well at his nursery school and couldn't I agree for them to live with him and come to me for holidays? Obviously I could not refuse.'

Some doubt has been cast on this narrative, but after so long it is complicated to untie all the knots which entangle Sofka's attitude to her sons and what really happened after the divorce. While she declared that she was awarded custody of the boys, Aunt Elena told me this was most definitely not true ('I'd cut my head off about that!'), and that as Sofka was the guilty party the children were automatically given to Leo. Uncle Kyril added that Leo would not let his children go to such an appalling mother as Sofka and wanted to protect them. Sofka's reputation as a 'bad mother' clung to her like a nasty smell. It is true that in her memoirs remarkably little space is devoted to her sons; far more detail is given to the playful ways of the Oliviers' lemur, for instance. But I suspect that she imagined people didn't want to read about other people's offspring, perhaps believing Disraeli's statement that 'the author who speaks about his own books is almost as bad as a mother who talks about her own children'. It is also true that she didn't hesitate to leave her sons when something more exciting cropped up. But while I saw that her offspring had never been the central pivot of her life, I wasn't convinced that she was much worse than countless parents of her generation: for many of her contemporaries who could afford it, it was usual for parents to live quite separately from children, who were handed over to nannies in nurseries, sent on separate holidays and deposited from an early age in boarding schools. Sofka's own upbringing had only been an extreme example of the easy negligence of wealthy parents.

I tried to unearth information about who won custody of the children, hoping secretly that Sofka had not been lying in her book; in today's emotional climate, the crime of being a bad mother is viewed as particularly heinous. I didn't want Sofka to be tarnished with more disgrace on this front than was necessary – after all, she wasn't beating or abusing her sons, but merely finding that life offered so much else to absorb her. In the end, I wasn't able to pour cold water over the accusations. Her Majesty's Courts Service came up with a copy of the decree nisi, but after countless letters and phone calls to the Registry of the Family Division nothing emerged – the records had probably been destroyed. I was interested though to come across a letter from Grey to Sofka's mother, from before the divorce, implying that the children were central to his and Sofka's existence. And though this could have been a gloss, it doesn't have the ring of a lie: 'Sofka sincerely wants one thing in life, and that is a home in the fullest sense of the word – not just a roof to keep off the rain: but a place where she can feel more or less secure and devote some of her time to bringing up her children.' Grey admits that he had been worried about taking on Peter, who 'strongly resented all semblance of authority', but added that 'he is growing up a really adorable child and seems to regard me as a very essential part of his life . . . As for Ian, that is quite in order because his life starts under my protection, both in fact, and as a god-child.'

* * *

Dean Cottage sounded like a rural love-nest, sitting in a large, sloping garden with apple trees, rough grass and a vegetable plot. It was 'within an hour's drive of Chelsea', but Sofka and Grey were happy to settle into village life. Instead of London parties, they planted tulips and got tipsy on ginger wine at the local pub. Grey received a small allowance from his father, which they supplemented by working as freelance translators, copy editors and readers for several publishing houses. For the first year, Sofka also continued to work from home for Olivier. The children, who were cared for by a German nurse in London, came for holidays. My father remembered some visits and he agreed to go with me to see if the house still existed. On the drive from London, he told me about new discoveries in epigenetics: how physical and emotional experiences in life can make molecular changes which actually affect the genes and continue through following generations. A poor diet during pregnancy can lead to the baby developing adult diabetes, and baby rats which were not licked by their mothers grow up to cope badly with stress. 'You are literally carrying the sins of your fathers . . . And mothers,' said my father without elaborating.

To my surprise, Cookham Dean had not been absorbed into some anonymous commuter belt but was a pristine chocolate-box village, with renovated cottages, tidy gardens and lots of expensive cars: it had obviously gone up in the world. We found the pub by the village green. It was still as picturesque as Sofka described, with old beams, scrubbed wooden tables and a large walnut tree in the garden. After asking around the village we eventually located Dean Cottage, which now had a big electric gate and was owned by a TV weathergirl turned celebrity. We wandered about, peering up at the manicured garden, now tamed with decking and with absurdly tall conifers to protect the owner's privacy. I looked up at the wooden balcony and bedroom windows – all identifiable from old photographs, though smartened up almost unrecognizably. That was where Sofka and Grey slept in the enormous Heal's bed given to them by the Oliviers. They loved it so much that their idea of a perfect Sunday was to bring everything they needed within reach (food, drink, cigarettes, books) and stay there all day. They were so attuned that often they'd wake up in the morning and know just what the other was thinking: a picnic; rowing on the river at Marlow; a trip to the sea in the Simca. This was also where Sofka's next child was conceived; within six months of moving, she was pregnant again.

My father tried to locate where the apple trees and children's sandpit had been. And what about the outside lavatory? He remembered being taken there by Grey, and being told he couldn't leave until he'd 'been'. 'It was my first memory of injustice,' he said, smiling, 'because it disappeared around the bend and Grey didn't believe me.' Nothing compares to children's capacity to prick the bubble of adults' romance; poor Grey, trying to be a dutiful stepfather.

It must have been around the time Sofka got pregnant that their resident chef moved out. They'd met him in Nice during their honeymoon – a Russian gourmet, who was unwell and sleeping rough. Having paid his ticket to England and helped with his medical treatment, they offered him a home in exchange for him cooking wonderful meals. It was hardly surprising, however, that he left, as he spoke no English and cut an eccentric, lonely figure in the little village. Sofka and Grey on the other hand had created a world for themselves, complete with secret jokes and nicknames – she was Ducca and he Puppadog, after the Dog and Duck, a pub near Maidenhead.

But they were not so cocooned in their pastoral idyll that they didn't notice developments in the world outside; like many people, their concern was growing. In addition to the translating work, which Sofka and Grey passed across to each other for correction or editing, they started to read quantities of political literature. Both had become strongly anti-Fascist and were appalled by the ground gained by Mosley's Blackshirts, who marched aggressively through London's East End. Once, Sofka and Grey walked out of a London party in support of a Jewish friend who refused to stay after an official from the German Embassy arrived; it was the first time that the implications of Nazism touched them personally.

Together Sofka and Grey read Marx, bravely tackled books on capitalism, materialism and empire criticism, and ordered anything that came out on the Soviet Union from the *Times* Library. The left was fashionable: an older generation of writers like Wells, Shaw and Mann had endorsed the Soviet regime; younger idealists had fought against Fascism in the Spanish Civil War; intellectuals were contributing to the *Left Review*;

thousands of readers subscribed to the Left Book Club; and Walter Greenwood's novel *Love on the Dole* had been hugely successful as a play. Even Virginia Woolf wrote for the *Daily Worker*. But Sofka and Grey were not tempted to become Communists. This was not only because they were worried by reports coming out of Russia of the Moscow Trials, of mass executions, of labour camps and exile (it was hard to know what to believe and what to dismiss as propaganda), but also because they didn't know any Communists. 'Our idea of Communism,' wrote Sofka, 'was that it was a world-wide conspiratorial organization to overthrow authority. Once you joined it, it ruled your life. Like the Mafia, there was no escape . . . We had never met any Communists and it seemed a pity that such a frightening organization should have the monopoly of aims that appeared so sensible. I had read the Communist Manifesto and could see nothing to disagree with.'

Patrick was born 'quickly and easily' at Dean Cottage, in the giant bed on 1 September 1938. Photographs show the new mother looking sensuously dishevelled, with cascades of unbrushed black Medusa locks falling over her nightdress, and the baby lying next to her, tiny and dark-haired in the rumpled sheets. A 'monthly nurse' moved in to help (it was what everyone they knew did then), and Sofka seemed proud that only a few days after giving birth she and Grey went off to Reading to see a display of Cossack riders. Sofka chatted with the riders in Russian after their show, asking a few of them over to Cookham Dean, but she was almost as surprised as the local villagers when two large vans appeared and out jumped twelve Cossacks. Photographs reveal 'that peculiar Cossack foppishness' (described by Tolstoy), with their astrakhan hats, high boots, breeches and tight tunics. They barbecued quantities of lamb *shashlik* in the garden, chewed raw onions and garlic, downed bottles of vodka and terrified the poor nurse by sweeping up the baby and dancing around with him like warriors in their shirtsleeves, doubtless shouting their ancient cry, 'All for one and one for all!' By the end of the day, Sofka was so pleased (and/or drunk) with these argumentative, affectionate dare-devils that she packed up a tent and sleeping bags, waved goodbye to the traumatized nurse clasping the infant, and she and Grey went off with the Cossacks for their show in the next county.

Grey was happy to be swept out of his tight, inhibited English upbringing and into Sofka's wild, foreign ways. They both planned that their son should be brought up trilingual in Russian, French and English, and Grey liked the fact that Patrick was baptized into the Russian Orthodox Church. Like Sofka, Grey was reckless with money; it was more fun to be extravagant and buy some champagne or books, or go for dinner at the Hungaria, than to penny-pinch and worry, even when funds had dwindled precariously. Sofka retained this trait, and though she never had much money she always believed that she'd get by somehow (she did), and encouraged others that money is for spending not saving. It was entirely characteristic of their spontaneity that on a trip to Paris the couple decided that it was not only cheaper but more pleasant in France and they should move there. How much thought they gave to practicalities or the children is unclear; the priority was grasping what they could from life. Nobody could ignore the rumblings of approaching war, but they overflowed with optimistic plans.

Less cheerful were 'the parents' (Sophy and Pierre), with whom Sofka and Grey stayed in Paris over Easter 1939. They had moved into a gloomy apartment near the river at Porte St Cloud – all dark furniture, dusty curtains and what relics of Pierre's past had not been sold off. Sophy, now fifty, was working as a secretary in the mornings and then retreated into her room, emerging many hours later in her pale dressing gown with a distant, glazed look. Sofka didn't know that her mother had already been to a clinic to treat her morphine addiction. It was only later that Sophy described the unbearable agony – the burning throat and excruciating sensation of insects crawling over her body – which sent her back to the wonderful, blurring mercy of injections. Pierre, meanwhile, was obsessed with money worries (he would anxiously, almost obsessively, count the centimes in his wallet) and had retreated into religious piety and tortuous translation jobs, which Sofka and Grey tried to help him with.

In spite of their elders' torments, Sofka and Grey were delighted by Paris. Years later, in an unpublished short story, Sofka described the city as 'the quintessence of delicacy, in colouring, in its approach to life, in the ethereal lightness of its avenues, its cafes and its skies. Paris, the loved, the unpredictable, the bitch among cities – beautiful and hideous and tender and uncaring.' Paris must have looked like a new start for them both, and by the time they left the city they had found a small house and garden by the river at Sèvres. They made an arrangement with the elderly owners to pay a *rente viagère* – a monthly sum for the rest of the old couple's lives, after which the house would become theirs. A return trip was planned for September to finalize the documents and the move would be in October. It sounds so full of promise: Sofka must often have fantasized later about what their life would have been like had they moved. Would they have stayed for good? Would they have continued so happy? What if . . .?

By the summer war looked unavoidable, the lease was up on Dean Cottage and Sofka and Grey had agreed to go on tour with the Cossacks, managing their British shows. After spending July dismantling their life in Cookham Dean and looking after all three boys, a few treasured things (including books and The Bed) were stored with friends in London, and Peter and Ian were returned to Leo. Patrick was sent to a village near Bracknell to stay with Mrs Butler, a widow with six grown-up daughters. Mrs Butler was the mother-in-law of the Cookham Dean milkman, and she had already looked after Patrick on various occasions when his parents were away. One of Mrs Butler's daughters, Phyllis, remembers that Patrick was nine months old when he came (which would have made his arrival earlier that summer). She thought Grey 'a very nice, kind father and very gentle', but had the impression that Sofka was a careless mother – 'rather fly-by-night, if you know what I mean? Not very wholesome.'

Sitting in front of the tulips at Cookham Dean, Sofka looks unaccustomed to being surrounded by all three sons. Peter (left) looks suspiciously at baby Patrick, while Ian appears more open-minded about his young half-brother.

The summer of 1939 was spent touring with the Cossacks. Sofka and Grey had given up Dean Cottage and their only home was now this white canvas tent. Chip, the dog, sits outside, as does the Baby Simca. Everyone was worrying about the impending war.

There is little doubt that Sofka's mind was not on her children. Perhaps there was also a sense of seizing what she could before the deluge that many believed was coming. Everyone was preparing for hostilities to begin. Still, Sofka and Grey look cheery in photographs of that summer, peeping out from their white tent with Chip the black terrier and the little Simca parked near by. They travelled all the way up to northern Scotland and back with the Cossacks, sorting out venues, stabling for the horses, posters and ticket sales, and consuming endless barbecued lamb and vodka. At night they snuggled down inside their modest canvas home (they had no other now) and Sofka would lick Grey's ears – something he loved so much that she later recommended it to daughters-in-law in times of marital trouble.

When war looked unavoidable, the Cossacks packed up early to go home to France and Sofka and Grey returned to Cookham Dean, setting up camp under the walnut tree in the garden of the pub. They had already been issued with regulation rubber gas-masks and they kept up with the disquieting Home Service news broadcasts thanks to Laurence Olivier, who had given Sofka an unusual present on his recent return from Hollywood: a new, portable radio, which was only the size of a briefcase and ran on 'dry batteries'. He owned one himself, and heard the declaration of war on a yacht off the Californian coast. Sofka and Grey listened to the grim announcement in Cookham Dean. They were overdrawn, unemployed and homeless, and a September chill was creeping into the tent.

CHAPTER 7

THE PRISONER

To-day that seems so long, so strange, so bitter,
Will soon be some forgotten yesterday.
— Sarojini Naidu

'I wonder, by my troth, what thou and I
Did till we loved.'
    Life did not exist till then, my pet . . .
    . . . Darling you must never die or let anything happen to
you, 'cos I know I would go mad. That is not just words: I
have realized so much during this enforced isolation. It is
only the hope of seeing you soon that makes the minutes
pass.

Grey wrote long love letters from his cramped cabin on a coastal
patrol boat. He had left Sofka in a furnished room in Oakley
Street, Chelsea, volunteered and left for duties on the south
coast. His letters are full of intimate endearments, thoughts
about baby Patrick (Ba), quotes from John Donne and other
favourite poets, and small sketches. Sometimes he is cheery
enough to put in little jokes and riddles:

How odd
of God
To choose
The Jews

But not so odd
As those who choose
A Jewish God,
Yet spurn the Jews.

Mostly, though, Grey's letters mourn the life he and Sofka have both lost: 'Now it has all gone – all my pretty world of dreams and I want to howl and howl and I can't 'cos Hiscock is in the room. I'm writing curled up on bunk, so have turned to wall as long silent tears are dripping and I can't let him see. Think I'll soon burst if I don't howl it off, but that is impossible shut up on a ship.' He breaks off to go on watch and takes up his pen again in the desolate, wintry pre-dawn.

Pet Lambkin,
What is there ever to say except that I love you more than any words can say? So how can I possibly tell you about it?
. . . You brought poetry into my life . . . [and] I'm finding rest in a new bed of your creation – a comfort for a tired mind caused by jagged nerves.
I hope I soon hear from you and get the number of the photo of you and our precious little Ba who brought so much into our lives. O, I love him so, and you – and you, and you.
. . . I know that if I tell you how much I love you, you'll probably cry – yet you would rather be loved than anything – and now I can only love you by telling you. Will

there be enough life left to us afterwards to make up for all this and to do all the things we want to do?

Monday 1.20 am

Still love you – glad? Tonight I swapped watches so get double the quantity of sleep. It makes me feel quite lazy after the recent exertions. Darlingest, I do hate night-work – Puppadoggies were made to be kept warm in a nice cosy bed by a most adorable, cuggly, snugly duccalin. And duccalins?

'Ducca' was despondent. The plan to move to Paris with Grey and Patrick was obviously scotched and it was proving hard to obtain enough translating work. Despite the ration cards, blackout curtains, gas-masks and anxiety, there was no real war. Patrick was still in the country with Mrs Butler and life had lapsed into a nervous, uneasy limbo. To add to her worries, it became impossible to send money to her mother in Paris and Sofka decided to go over to help. This was no simple task, but Sophy's old Foreign Office friend, Jock Balfour, smoothed out the paperwork and located a troopship.

By March, Ducca and Puppadog were back together in Oakley Street. Grey had been accepted by the RAF for training, having decided that the queasy claustrophobia of patrol boats was beyond his endurance, and it wasn't long before Sofka saw him off at the rainy station. She was so plunged into depression that she could barely get out of bed and admitted drinking red wine in the mornings to dull the pain. Once again, life was showing her that she was not mistress of her own destiny.

Forcing herself into action, Sofka spent some weeks learning Czech, passed the Foreign Office exams for translators and was promised work in the coming months. Leo (who was living conveniently near by in Markham Square with Peter and Ian) had apparently agreed that she should take all three boys and go to live somewhere 'deep in the country', out of harm's way, until the war ended. Meanwhile, according to Sofka's memoirs, her mother wrote asking for more financial help. So, with Leo agreeing to find a cottage while she was away, Sofka once more boarded a troopship for France in late April. This version of events is possibly true, but it seems doubtful that Sophy was the reason for Sofka's departure. Passport stamps show that Sofka had already been in France for almost four months (from early December until late March) and it was surely too soon for another cry for help, especially given the risky circumstances. My suspicion is that her mother was an excuse; Paris provided an escape. With her bevy of Russian friends and admirers, Sofka was distracted from the gnawing worry about Grey and the bleak loneliness of long evenings in the London bedsit. While I had always understood from family stories that Patrick was left with the milkman's mother-in-law so Sofka could go briefly to Paris, the truth is that by the time she went there for the second time he had already been with Mrs Butler for almost a year. Few mothers would have gone abroad at this stage in the war but, given her mood and her character, the prospect of full-time rural motherhood with three young children, rationing and tense, sleepless nights would scarcely have appealed. She didn't choose to go and get trapped in Paris, but she did put herself at risk. In times of crisis, Sofka had always moved; fleeing had become almost second nature.

I returned to Sofka's war diary, which looked different after all my scouring through her life. I could now make connections and was slightly suspicious of all the admirers as her diary entries veer from pitiful, lonely wife to vampish man eater:

9 September
Am seeing Kolia. He's being a perfect brick. Bek is a daily
occurrence, as well as Misha and the Beast. They, being
rivals for my favours, glare at each other and snarl politely.
Great fun.

6 November
Added another specimen to my menagerie – Michel
Kychenkov from the Russian consulate. Apart from twice
feeding me nobly, he presented me with a piece of (illeg)
soap and a flask of Chanel No 5, to say nothing of an alarm
clock . . . Otherwise have run round from house to pub
with Kolia, Misha, Bek and Yuri.

Yuri appears on every other page, taking Sofka out, helping
find food and providing daily support – the same man she
devastated with their '*affaire*' in the early years of marriage to
Leo. She now described him using Casanova's term, *cavaliere
servante*, to imply his devotion and her lack of it, and evidently
enjoyed his attentions and care. 'Beast' provided entrecôte,
melon and other rare delicacies in occupied Paris, and I found
him mentioned in letters after the war as an occasional lover; his
true identity was untraceable. I found myself hoping that there
had not been a sexual element to these friendships and looking
for evidence; I wanted to disprove Uncle Kyril's theory that
Sofka was sleeping around even when she was with Grey. But
ultimately I could reach no conclusion after all these years.
Perhaps Sofka *was* able to separate sex from the emotions of
love, as Uncle Kyril suggested: 'Like a man.' What is clear is that
she was pining for Grey as much as he was for her. I was no
longer troubled by Uncle Kyril's suggestion that Grey was so
unhappily married with Sofka that he'd joined the RAF as a form

of suicide. Nor was Aunt Elena's story plausible – that Sofka had gone to France in order to be sent to an internment camp, which 'were very nice places – all free and with food'.

At 2 Boulevard de la République, Sofka spent many of her long, curfewed evenings playing cards with the only other people remaining in the building – the Roches, a Russian-Jewish family who lived on the fifth floor. Before the war there had been no contact between them and the Volkonskys – 'the two worlds, even in emigration, were too far apart'. But now, through the Roches, Sofka became aware of the terrifying decrees which were continually being made against the Jews; it is unlikely that they survived the war and she never mentioned them again.

One mystery from this era remained. In a 1974 Granada television documentary I'd unearthed from the archives, a sixty-seven-year-old Sofka is interviewed about her life. She states that the last time she saw Grey was during his first RAF leave, when he managed to come to Paris. 'That was terrific,' she said. 'It was much more free and easy [than England] – we'd go dancing. He was there for five or six days. Our last fling.' There is no mention of this final meeting in her memoirs or in the diary, which began on 19 May. Would Grey have had leave so soon after joining air-force training in April? Could it have been a dream, or wishful thinking?

* * *

A dividing line in Sofka's life is marked by the French gendarme knocking on her door early on the morning of 9 December 1940, though she could not know that yet. In fact, a spark of hope was struck from his order to bring things for twenty-four hours. Perhaps she would soon be back and could still make her planned escape? At the local police station she was put in a large room which gradually filled with women. As officials sifted, signed and stamped their documents, it became clear that all the detainees were holders of British passports. Late in the afternoon some German soldiers hurried in noisily and herded the bewildered women with their small overnight bags out into the icy air and on to open trucks. Sofka was glad of her fur coat as they drove past snowy bombed-out buildings and across the darkening city to the Gare de l'Est. Nobody explained what was happening or where they were going as several hundred females of all ages were locked into third-class, wooden-seated carriages on a long train. Someone was ill, another prayed, some wept and many offered improvised and far-fetched theories about their possible fate. A baby wailed. Eventually the train left and moved eastwards, dawdling and halting frequently. Food was given: black bread and tins of sinister, foul-smelling meat that people called 'Monkey' and threw out of the windows in disgust. It was three days before they arrived at Besançon.

Stepping from the train on to the snowy platform, Sofka heard her name called with a long, Russian-intoned O: 'So-ofka!' It was Ellinka Bobrinsky, her twenty-one-year-old cousin. Like many other detainees, she had never even been to England, but had some tenuous, bureaucratic connection. Having been born in Malta, *en route* to exile from Crimea in 1919, Ellinka was endowed with a British passport, which was now an albatross around her neck. Sofka was pleased to see her young relation, but what she later recalled as being particularly significant was that Ellinka had brought *War and Peace* with her, which could be swapped for her own hastily packed *Brothers Karamazov*. Tolstoy and Dostoevsky were better companions than almost any others. Perhaps these were not her initial thoughts though, as the women were marched, shivering and disorientated, by impatient German soldiers through the snow-filled streets to the town's seventeenth-century Vauban barracks, now renamed Frontstalag 142.

The gates closed behind them and the entirely female crowd was ordered to find places inside the solid, three-storey buildings that stood before them. Sofka and Ellinka scurried about, checking the large, stone-floored, high-ceilinged rooms in search of corner beds. Many had already been taken, but they eventually located two on the top floor and sat on them, waiting for the rest of the forty straw-stuffed mattresses to be occupied. Gradually, dormitory 29 filled up with an odd collection of women, including a frail English Lady and her daughter, a half-Russian governess and a raucous, hardy group of middle-aged fishwives from Brittany who had enjoyed brief marriages with British soldiers during the First World War.

Like each of the four thousand women in the barracks, Sofka was issued with a pale-blue French Army coat (man-sized), wooden clogs (Parisian shoes fared badly in the snow), food tickets and a tin plate and cutlery. The long, scratchy coats were rarely removed, acting as an extra blanket in bed, and the clogs clacked noisily up and down the draughty stone staircases from morning till night. Rations were based on a weekly loaf – flat, grey, stamped with a long-gone date and often blooming with green mould. Eating it produced violent stomach cramps, but inmates learned to slice it and dry pieces on the dormitory stove to make it more digestible. There was a daily helping of disgusting soup, often made from mangel-wurzel or cattle beet, which was collected from huge, iron cauldrons in the kitchens. One prisoner noted the rats 'as large as rabbits' tearing open sacks of dried vegetables, and horse carcasses lying around in the filth. There were no bathrooms – just a large, iced-up trough where inmates could wash in freezing water, overlooked by guards. Understandably, few availed themselves of this opportunity, so the odour of massed unwashed bodies soon hung heavily in the dormitories. Visits to the lavatory were even more challenging; with only one open hole per six hundred people, there were constant queues in the muddy snow for the reeking, roofless, outdoor cubicles. When dysentery broke out, half the population was crippled with horrendous diarrhoea and vomiting. It was rumoured that several hundred women died.

Privacy was one of the first victims of camp life – available only in sleep and perhaps books (plenty of opportunity now to ruminate on Sophy's old demand to compare and contrast Tolstoy and Dostoevsky). Some people took to their beds, weeping and moaning, and everyone was appalled by the crowded quarters, the disgusting food, the lack of sanitation and the population of bugs which crawled down the walls each night. In Sofka's room, some people swore they could recognize individuals amongst the regular six-legged visitors and named the largest one Billy. Most women had only the clothes they left home in, and when these were washed they had to wait in bed while they dried on lines around the dormitory. Perhaps it was Sofka's independent spirit that led her room-mates to elect her *chef de chambre*, in charge of fuel and rations. She attributed this vote to her tendency to ignore the ubiquitous arguments, but her natural authority surely played a part – ever since her bossy teenage days with Rome's Russian youth she had realized that if you led, others followed. Her thirty-nine companions must have felt vindicated in their choice when she proved herself quick-witted enough to pocket extra coal-ration cards on a visit to the Commandant's office. The inefficient, smoking dormitory stove needed all the help it could get.

Sofka's most heartfelt complaint about camp life concerned the lack of bathing facilities; when she discovered that the French soldiers were periodically taking hot showers, she fought determinedly until inmates were given that privilege too. It was she who quelled the ensuing stampede by taking up paper and pencil to enforce a list and rota, and subsequently held the privileged post of 'chief of bathing'. She never forgot the feeling of 'infinite bliss' provoked by the steaming water; bathing was always a top priority in her life. (It was also Sophy's preferred indulgence – she too had suffered badly from the lack of bathing during hard times in Bolshevik Russia – and this predilection evidently passed along the generations; my father's weakness for bath essences and preference for being boiled alive is matched only by mine and my older daughter's.)

Sofka might have appeared practical and down-to-earth but she was also tormented and afraid. Putting on a good front was a matter of pride – a point of honour equivalent to not crying in front of the adults when she was a child. Her poems reflected her private despair.

> *... And all the while*
> *The voices, voices hem us all around ...*
> *... And on my lips a smile,*
> *A vapid smile, all meaningless, to keep*
> *My terror to myself ...*

Over the subsequent months, things gradually improved: indoor toilets and wooden bunks were constructed and the population halved to two thousand. The old, mothers with young children and the sick were released and some prisoners escaped – the mostly black French Army guards obligingly cleaned the dustbins which would carry them out. Once, in an ultimately foiled attempt, Sofka helped a Spanish woman over the wall and then distracted the guards. Best of all was the spring day when the Red Cross parcels arrived. The prisoners were as excited as children at Christmas, opening the sturdy, cardboard boxes with pale-blue interiors and falling ecstatically upon tins of Klim (Canadian dried milk), cheese, jam, powdered eggs, cigarettes, soap, the ubiquitous dry 'dog biscuits' and even luxuries like salmon and chocolate. Later, some books and clothes arrived. People ran from bed to bed, comparing and swapping contents and laughing from joy. Only the nuns were quiet – sworn to silence, they slept in a separate dormitory and exercised outside in mute, veiled circles.

In May, the two thousand internees were told they were leaving Besançon. Rumour had it that complaints from the Red Cross and threats of British retaliation to German internees were bringing a favourable change. One rosy summer dawn, all inmates were ordered to strip and have their clothes disinfected. Blank shots were fired to persuade the more stubborn or prudish types who initially refused. Many hours later, they were herded on to a train – a strange collection of women in clothes all now a worn shade of 'Vauban grey', wearing heavy, sweltering army coats and carrying strings of tins, pots, clogs and other assorted prisoners' oddments collected over six months. It took two nights to cover 150 miles northward, munching on dry 'dog biscuits', singing songs, dozing and speculating wildly about their next destination.

* * *

The spa at Vittel had been famous before the war as an exclusive resort for the rich and unhealthy. Its waters were thought to be therapeutic for kidney problems, arthritis and obesity; and its casino and theatre attracted famous and wealthy visitors including playboys, actresses, dancers and even foreign royalty, in addition to the frail and ailing. It was just the kind of place Granny Olga might have favoured and understandably M. Raspail, the hotel's French manager, was horrified at what looked like an invasion of madwomen. The Germans, however, took advantage of the photo-opportunity. As the women entered the camp, photographers were ready to snap evidence for the papers of 'British internees arriving at the Grand Hotel'. Surrounded by three barbed-wire perimeter fences, the old spa buildings, with their flowerbeds, lake and tennis courts, now comprised a 'model' camp – a highly convenient retort to accusations of Nazi cruelty and impropriety in other camps. Little did anyone suspect that later, it would also provide a picturesque front for more sinister activities involving Jewish detainees.

Sofka's closest friend at Vittel was Madeleine White, always known as Rabbit. Although they were strikingly dissimilar in temperament and character (Rabbit is careful, tidy, restrained, reliable, quiet and sparrow-like), they remained remarkably close, visiting and writing constantly over five decades until Sofka's death. Since then, Rabbit and I had corresponded regularly.

'For her I was always "Rabbit",' she confided, 'with long ears and no nose, who ran into a rabbit hole when things did not turn out as it wished: then she would call me "stupid Ra" or "Rabbit Stew".' Now, she had promised to take me to see the place where they'd been imprisoned and I went to Paris to meet her. I visited Rabbit at her apartment on the tenth floor of a vast 1960s block in the fifteenth *arrondissement*. Although she is over eighty, she looks much as she does in photographs in the 1940s: a small, girlish figure, with a round face, feline eyes and an orderly bob, once dark and now grey. She dresses like an obedient schoolgirl in grey V-neck pullover (neatly darned), grey woollen skirt, thick grey tights and sensible lace-ups. No trace of frivolity, jewellery or make-up; perhaps because there are too many tragic and important things in life to worry about. She is concerned about world events and French youth and still gives free lessons to young immigrants.

Her serious face only lit up when we spoke of Sofka. 'We were very happy together, very close. During the war we read everything together, from the Bible to Lenin – whatever you can think of. She taught me *everything* – she knew about different countries, other ways of life . . . she was a remarkable woman. And you know that her memory was so perfect she could recite poetry for hours. She was even afraid to read bad poetry in case she accidentally learned it by heart.' As she spoke, I noticed certain expressions that Sofka used to make, particularly a quick, grimacing, lips-only smile to accompany the telling of something unpleasant, which sometimes extended into an ironic, rapid, machine-gun laugh. Rabbit's bookshelves were laden with row after row of Holocaust books: her French scientist husband is an Auschwitz survivor and she spent years working for a Jewish Holocaust magazine. 'It's all in the past,' she replied, when I asked her about the emotional cost of all she had been through.

Carrying our overnight knapsacks (hers with a small black rabbit drawn on the label), Rabbit and I took the Metro to the Gare de l'Est. She showed me the plaques to Jews and others who were taken away from here to Nazi camps: seventy-seven thousand French Jews were deported to their deaths, with the willing cooperation of French officials. Eleven thousand were children. At the station bar, I bought some biscuits and bottled water.

'Don't buy Vittel,' Rabbit joked wryly. 'They say it rots your teeth!'

Our smooth, fast train journey eastward echoed all those terrible departures during the war, and it was perhaps these haunting thoughts that made me nauseous. I sat very still, listening to Rabbit's low, dry, perfect English, with only a hint of French intonation, as she told me her story. How her orphan mother was brought up by Catholic nuns and was so malnourished that she barely grew beyond childhood. How her father, an unpleasant Englishman, ran off soon after his marriage, leaving his daughter to be teased at school for being 'a bastard'. They were very poor. And then, in February 1941, they were interned in Besançon for having British papers. It was after the transfer to Vittel that Rabbit met Sofka.

Vittel's camp housed a bizarre mix of people – forty-eight different nationalities of all ages from newborn to sixty. There were nuns from a variety of orders, dancers (including several 'Bluebell Girls' who later escaped), artists, writers, musicians, teachers, governesses, students and nurses. There were pleasure-seeking ex-pats and Quakers; Catholics and Christian Scientists; and Jews who hadn't gone straight to concentration camps for one chancy reason or another. There was a group of old men, who were cared for by nuns and who knew how to construct all kinds of pots, pans and jugs out of emptied Red Cross tins, putting handles, lids and spouts on them. Despite their age, they were keen visitors to a madam from Boulogne, who was accompanied by two of her girls. 'Vite! Vite!' the ageing procuress would urge when an elderly saucepan maker left the ad hoc brothel. 'Go and fetch another client!' Later, more men arrived, including jockeys and stable-boys from the race-tracks, and in time there were even married quarters, after some husbands were brought in from Saint-Denis men's internment camp and some fortunate couples were reunited.

The hotel buildings were somewhat shabby (previous occupants had included Italian soldiers, who left graffiti all over the place), but after Besançon it was wonderful. 'I shared a room with my mother and another friend,' said Rabbit. 'There were real beds with proper sheets and pillows, and although there wasn't much water, we even had a bathroom. We found some linen cupboards and broke them open as we had hardly any clothes – no underwear even. An elderly Russian lady, Mme Barto, was a wonderful seamstress and she made us underpants and even bras out of old sheets.'

Sofka had initially shared quarters with Ellinka and another Russian woman, but she hated the enforced intimacy; paradoxically, two room-mates were harder than thirty-nine and she longed for a room of her own. Searching throughout the different hotel buildings, she eventually forced her way up a barricaded spiral staircase to the attics and found a small garret. There was a single round window, some broken furniture and no heating, but it was empty – a small lair where she could be alone and lick her wounds in peace.

'We couldn't stand all the "nice people" in the camp,' said Rabbit. 'They were the awful English women who moaned about everything and were very critical. They were always forming committees and rushing around being bossy.' Once Red Cross supplies became regular (after some months' delay), survival was no longer under threat and it became vital to fill the vast empty spread of time that confronted internees each day. 'Boredom is the one torment of hell that Dante forgot,' wrote Albert Speer in his account of Spandau jail. Much later, Sofka quoted the former Nazi in a letter, explaining to a friend how much this applies to the prisoner's predicament: 'Gradually,' she wrote, 'the outside world fades . . . And everything closes into a tiny microcosm.'

Certain women just waited for years on end, knitting, drinking ersatz coffee, cooking on little stoves and gossiping, but most instigated activities to combat *ennui* and pessimism. A library was established and anybody who could teach something did, from cooking, dancing, Bridge, gymnastics and gardening to painting, languages, music and literature. German movies were shown on Sundays at the Casino, though Sofka and other inmates boycotted screenings with strong Nazi propaganda, such as the horrifyingly anti-Semitic film version of *Jud Süss*, made in 1940 under Goebbels' supervision. Sofka started a dramatic society and gave lectures on Russian poetry. Soon she had requisitioned the Casino's theatre, and over the next years utilized the skills she had gained working for Olivier at the Old Vic. She enlisted inmates into performing a variety of plays from Shakespeare (*Twelfth Night, Hamlet, Julius Caesar*) and Chekhov (*A Marriage Proposal*) to dramatized A. A. Milne poems for children and *Ali Baba*, featuring Sofka as the blacked-up, leopardskin-wearing Chief Eunuch. Official cast photographs remain, giving the impression of cheerful, orderly creativity; nothing shows of the prisoners' underlying torment.

'I was Ophelia in *Hamlet*,' said Rabbit, laughing. '"Get thee to a nunnery!" But I actually met Sofka earlier, when I put a notice on the board for an intellectual to help me with my university lessons in English literature. I was nineteen and I needed to prepare for my exams and I was told of "a Russian lady who knows all about Shakespeare and the poets and who writes poetry". We immediately became close friends. Later, we started to learn Russian too. She taught me everything about life and literature. She was completely different to the English women who moped and wept and were indignant that the Germans arrested them. I'd been through a lot of unpleasant things – just before I was interned, my fiancé killed himself because our families were against the marriage. I was very shy – I'd run away from people. But Sofka helped me through my tragedy. She was never tired and I could work with books from eight in the morning till eight at night.'

It was a bright, chilly spring morning when Rabbit and I arrived at Vittel. The whole place was now a Club Méditerranée complex, with golf courses, swimming pools and a jazz band

Rabbit was only nineteen when she met Sofka in Vittel. Her older fellow internee became her mentor and remained her closest friend for decades: 'Sofka taught me everything.'

playing at an open-air café. There were lots of healthy-looking French families and polite employees, who smiled *'Bonjour, mesdames'* as we walked around the grounds. We were an unlikely pair. I sometimes wondered if Rabbit thought I was bourgeois, a word she used to criticize or send up all number of things, from our comfortable hotel to the 'nice people' in camp.

We walked along the driveway, past the Casino and through the gardens. If internees picked flowers, a crackly tannoy would spew out threatened punishment. Later, German inmates (British-passport holders), who worked for the Commandant, would suddenly appear at the culprit's room for an inspection. Inside the Grand Hotel lobby, Rabbit remembered the marble columns, mosaic floor and mirrors from her day, although it was much scruffier then. It was here that the mail was sorted and prisoners gathered to play Chess. There were some little shops where inmates could buy wooden shoes, needles, thread, old-fashioned dresses from the 1920s, brooches and boxes inscribed SOUVENIR DE VITTEL. A noticeboard was used for bartering, with cigarettes as the currency and the room number given for identification: *I offer pilchards for 15 cigarettes, corned-beef for 20 cigarettes.* Or *Wanted, pair of shoes, size 5, 320 cigarettes.*

Internees were allowed two letters a month and they'd call out names in alphabetical order. It was overwhelmingly exciting to receive news from the outside world, even if it had already been read by others. Grey's letters to Sofka arrived on the regulation Prisoner of War Post paper, to Prisoner of War number G.H.30, Mme Skipwith. Instructions stated: 'Write very clearly within the lines to avoid delay in censorship,' and the front was stamped PASSED.

My darling, darling girl,
. . . How are the white hairs progressing? But don't let anything worry you because I'm quite safe and certain to be waiting. I'm loving you more for everything.
Adore you.
Puppa

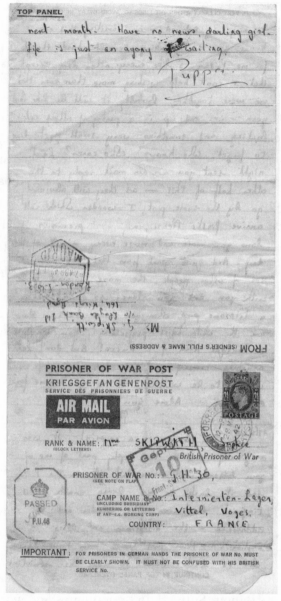

Grey's letters to Sofka had to be written on special Prisoner of War Post paper and were checked by a censor, but they were as exciting to her as any love letter. They both missed each other desperately and Sofka was terribly worried now that Grey was a gunner in the RAF.

231

Of course, Grey was far from safe. Being a gunner was notoriously dangerous; a rear gunner's terrifyingly small, isolated turret at the back of the plane was the first place the enemy attacked. One RAF gunner's memoirs describe how he'd seen people 'swilling out of a turret all the bits of meat and bones' after the damaged plane managed to land. Did Grey wish he was back on the cramped patrol boats?, I wonder.

Rabbit told me about how she felt back in this place, sixty years later. I imagined it must provoke powerful emotions. 'It's all history now,' she said, unwilling perhaps to wallow sentimentally or to give me a conveniently touching soundbite. We sat down, and I mentally transformed the French golf players in pastel pullovers into 1940s Englishwomen and the uniformed receptionists into Nazi guards. I asked Rabbit about how the days passed.

'I'd get up at about seven,' she said, 'and fetch hot water from the cauldron in the basement and carry it up in a Red Cross tin for tea and "dog biscuits" with my mother. I'd read some Shakespeare and then get more water and take it up to Sofka's room. If she'd been playing cards – usually Preference – with other Russians until midnight, she'd be fast asleep. You know how she was. I used to put our broom around her room, as she didn't care, and later, when she got a stove, I'd bring dry leaves and wood into the secret store across the corridor, using an empty Red Cross box.' Sofka, dressed in her thick, brown cotton nightdress (Mme Barto's construction, using army-coat lining), would drink tea in bed while talking to Rabbit. The room got terribly cold during the first winter as there was no heating, but according to Rabbit, Sofka didn't complain: 'She wore her fur coat all day and then slept under it at night. We'd sit under it sometimes while we read together.'

'The only thing she minded about was not bathing,' said Rabbit. 'Normally she'd wash in a bucket of warm water, which we'd bring up, but an old Russian widow called Mrs Hicks let us use her bathroom when there was hot water. She'd shout up the stairs: '*Goriachaya voda!* Hot water!' and we'd leave everything and run downstairs. I'd have the first bath and then Sofka would stay in for ages, soaking. Sometimes I'd wash her hair for her and then we'd wash our clothes.'

There were some morning duties – young people had to take turns on the potato-peeling rota – but afterwards, Rabbit and Sofka would settle down to study. 'We'd do English all morning,' continued Rabbit, 'but by lunchtime, my mother would be getting annoyed, so I'd have lunch with her. I'd go to the kitchen to get the awful soup, but it was rarely edible and could make you ill. There'd be old meat and bones and you'd find things swimming in it – a cork, or once a rat – so we didn't eat much for some months. Later, we planted things like lettuce and radishes, a little shop sold a few vegetables and they started to send the Red Cross provisions again. Then, people cooked all sorts of things.' Mme Barto had been a marvellous cook, making cakes for people's birthdays (using ground-up 'dog biscuits', dried egg and cocoa) and *tyanushki*, a type of Russian fudge, in which she substituted condensed milk for cream. Some internees, like Miss Bayliss, hoarded with friends to create feasts. Her unpublished memoirs of the camp record her close friends' menu for Christmas 1941, which announced ambitiously: '*Soupe à la Vittel, Saumon à sauce blanche, Cornbeef de l'espoir, Tarte de la victoire, café de triomphe, cigarettes de rêve et de l'oubli.*'

'In the afternoons, I'd go back up to Sofka for Russian,' said Rabbit, pointing out of the window to indicate where they went in the summer to read Tolstoy, Lermontov and Dostoevsky. 'We'd take a rug under the trees, and the "nice people" would stare at us,' she said happily. 'They weren't intellectuals and they couldn't understand us reading all the time. They thought we should be playing tennis. The English women disapproved of Sofka because she did what she wanted. She stayed in bed if she felt like it or stayed up late with the Russians playing cards, and she didn't join their committees or go to their gymnastic classes. Later, they suspected her of helping prisoners escape.'

Although life in Vittel was riddled with tragedy, there was also something inherently comical. The backdrop was war and broken families, but the daily female dramas were often storms in teacups and the preoccupations petty. There was a plucky, jolly-hockey-sticks, pull-your-socks-up, buckle-down approach, which kept people going. Even when all the pet dogs were killed by the guards, to huge outcry and grief, some women still managed to keep stray kittens, one had a rabbit on a string, another a hen in her room, and three Scottish sisters smuggled puppies into their bathroom. When the USA entered the war in December 1941, a batch of smart, hat-wearing American women joined the camp, allegedly transferred from their temporary incarceration in Paris's zoo. They received superior Red Cross parcels (including highly desirable Spam) and the intellectuals gathered around Sylvia Beach, the founder of the famous Paris bookshop Shakespeare & Co. By then, an element of competitiveness had emerged, with wealthier internees in fine clothes managing to get money and belongings sent in. There was a strange contrast between those dressed in patched, grey rags, with stolen sheets for underwear, and those who wore jewels and flowery cocktail dresses to Bridge parties.

Some of these contradictions were captured in a 1944 British film based on Vittel. When Sofka saw *Two Thousand Women* after the war, she was horrified by the unrealistically perfect hairdos and luxurious hotel rooms, but notwithstanding the actresses' shining platinum waves and satin negligées (and the film's intrinsic morale-boosting duty) the hothouse environment of quarrels, collusion, camaraderie, deceit and rumour are well portrayed. Naturally, there were many aspects of camp life not referred to in the film. One of these was the number of love affairs between women. Some of the inmates were already established lesbians; Parisian tolerance of Sapphic love had long provided a haven for numerous women from more strait-laced countries such as Britain and America. Various established couples were known throughout the camp: one hefty Englishwoman, nicknamed 'Monsieur Huntley-Walker' (sporting man's haircut and coat and carrying a whip), took up with the feminine Lady Bradley; the aggressive Miss Ehe made violent jealous scenes over gorgeous, enigmatic Bébé; and 'the Peewits' were a quiet, music-loving pair who kept to themselves but were much loved.

Sofka dropped into her memoirs that 'it was obvious that confined proximity over a number of years would give rise to lesbianism. Even I had tried it, briefly, but being definitely "hetero" was never tempted again!' I broached the subject with Rabbit, wondering secretly whether she might have been Sofka's lover; the intensity of their feelings was clear. However, she made it evident that she hated lesbians and had no clues to her mentor's indiscretion: 'You'd find those ladies, especially the awful Monsieur Huntley-Walker, waiting in the dark corridor. "Come, we'll give you cigarettes or cakes . . ." they'd say. I'd kick them hard in the thigh and they understood very well.'

Later, on another visit to Paris, I met some other former internees and uncovered more. Shula was now an octogenarian, but she still had the attractive, youthful energy which drew so many to her in camp when she was a beautiful, vivacious, French-Jewish girl of seventeen with a British passport. She clearly remembered meeting Sofka, some weeks after their arrival at Besançon, when Shula was still in shock. Like many women, her periods stopped from malnutrition and she was anxious about her mother, who was in hiding, and her father, who ended up in Auschwitz. It was New Year's Eve 1940 and Shula was in the small dormitory she shared with a group of other young women. Just after midnight, Sofka burst in. 'She was completely naked,' said Shula, laughing. 'Her long black hair was all loose and she was reciting Pushkin in Russian. She held a glass of wine in her hand! I don't know where she got the wine or the glass from, but she was Bacchanalian. She had a natural, pagan wildness about her.' Shula, a budding artist, got out her paints and dashed off a watercolour of the extraordinary visitor who brought in 1941 so memorably.

This unrestrained, Slavic reveller sounded quite a different character to the authoritative, efficient procurer of baths and coal chits. I asked Shula about Sofka's female lover and she admitted that many others in Vittel believed that Sofka and Rabbit were a couple.

'Little Rabbit,' smiled Shula. 'She was so beautiful when she was young – very supple, slim and rounded, like a wood carving. But so puritanical and ascetic; like a nun. Really, she was Sofka's disciple. If Sofka had an affair, it was with Stanley. They were friends even before Rabbit came along – in Besançon.' Shula had brought some photographs and one showed Sofka lying tangled in a heap of six laughing women sprawled around a bed (no sign of Rabbit). Lying with her bare leg in the air, leaning heavily on a beaming Sofka, is Stanley. 'Stanley was a gym teacher,' explained Shula. 'She was a nice, healthy English girl, with a boyish look – a bit like a Boy Scout – and a beautiful smile. She had short, light-brown hair and wonderful legs – she always wore shorts. Stanley adored Sofka and followed her everywhere.'

Shula had a daring glint to her remarkable blue-brown eyes as she showed me the sketches and paintings of camp life she

Shula was only seventeen when she met Sofka at midnight on New Year's Eve, 1940. She quickly got out her watercolours and painted this picture of Sofka, who had come into the room naked, drinking wine and reciting Pushkin in Russian.

Sofka looks happy, lying among members of la Petite Famille. *Sprawled on top of her is Stanley, a gym teacher, with whom she was having an affair. Shula is clutching Stanley's foot and Lopi (a dedicated Communist known as 'the Marvel of the Marvels') is reading a book. The large, enamelled pitcher was their 'teapot'.*

had brought from her home in Brittany (there were several of Sofka, including that first nude, in bold black and yellow). She had lived an artist's life, marrying Morley, the English prisoner of war who was sent in 1944 to give art lessons in Vittel.

Later, re-reading Sofka's memoirs, I unearthed a brief, non-committal reference to Stanley: 'Stanley was a PT teacher and very soon had us and most of the younger members of the camp doing morning exercises, forming teams for volley-ball and netball, running tennis and table-tennis tournaments. She was a vividly energetic person with a brilliant smile and very soon became the object of hero-worship for our youngsters.' There is no hint of Sofka's sexual experimentation, though somehow I couldn't imagine her willingly doing morning exercises if there hadn't been another motive.

There was not much love lost between Rabbit and Stanley – something which heightened my conviction: 'Stanley was upset with me for not going to gym. She said I was a bloody foreigner,' said Rabbit, trying to pour cold water on the theory of Stanley as girlfriend. 'Anyway, if she was with Sofka, it can't have been for long because she and I were working eight to ten hours a day and I'd wake her at eight a.m. with tea.' It emerged that Stanley was expelled from Vittel only months after their arrival, apparently for complaining to the Red Cross inspectors about Germans stealing cigarettes from prisoners' parcels. She was banished to Libenau, another camp, and though the youth of Vittel petitioned for their gym teacher's return she was never heard of again. Stanley's departure indicates that her involvement with Sofka was probably during the summer of 1941. It was therefore one clear case of infidelity to Grey, though I suspect that Sofka didn't view it in that light at all . . .

I was puzzled as to why Rabbit had been controlling what information I was given, when it was clear that she had affectionately adopted me as Sofka's namesake and spiritual heir and showed me a remarkable degree of generosity. She wrote, rang, handed over original documents and even gave me some beautiful ivory opera glasses, still in their silk-lined St Petersburg case, which she had inherited from old Mme Barto. But as 'disciple', I guessed that Rabbit was also tidying up Sofka's precious relics for public display. Subconsciously or deliberately, she wanted *her* version of Sofka to prevail. It took two years of conversations before Rabbit told me something less appealing about Sofka's behaviour in camp.

'She'd take things – books, objects – if she wanted them,' she admitted. 'Often from the older Russian women, who didn't realize what had happened. I never said anything to her.' Rabbit didn't comment on this anti-social, unprincipled side to her cultured, inspirational teacher. Yet again, though, I was struck at how odd it was that this innocent, shy, deeply serious student should have become the strongest ally of an uninhibited, gregarious older woman, whose sexuality was so manifest.

If Sofka's friendship with Rabbit sounded exclusive, it wasn't. Both belonged to la Petite Famille, a politically motivated substitute family, in which Sofka was the oldest but not necessarily the leader of the eight-odd members (though I suspect she devised the animal nicknames: she was Dog, Shula was Lion, Morley Snail). Two of the English members, Frida (Stewart, later Knight) and Lopey (Penelope Brierly), were both already Party members – the first Communists Sofka had met. Lopey was extremely clever, had travelled and studied at Oxford, and was known by the younger Family members as 'the Marvel of the Marvels'.

Also known as the 'Cat Family', members would miaow for identification when they knocked on each other's doors. Their evenings discussing the forbidden subject of Marxism 'at last seemed to answer those questions about the inequality of society that had so disturbed me all my life', wrote Sofka. 'I felt that here was an ideology that could provide an equitable existence for humanity.' It was at this time that Sofka joined the underground Communist Party, along with Rabbit. As prisoners, they had nothing to lose but their chains, and these beliefs and newfound commitment certainly helped fill the vacuum left by the absence of home, husband, children, faith and future. But it was no passing fancy. Sofka never let go of the inspiration she found in these hidden, female conversations. Even later, when many of her associates abandoned the Communist Party in disgust, she retorted that just as Torquemada did not represent the true concept of Christianity, Stalin's evil-doing could not be said to detract from the basic idea of socialism.

The 'Little Family' established links with the Resistance, largely through local men who regularly entered the camp as plumbers, electricians and maintenance workers; much day-to-day resistance was carried out by ordinary people camouflaged by regular jobs. These villagers would whisper news, supply wire cutters and other useful tools and pass out messages, or sometimes inmates, to a local 'passeur' who handed them across the frontier to the Allies. As a Party member, Sofka paid her membership fee through the Resistance and she stopped smoking so she could donate her cigarettes to help their cause. She even contributed food from her Red Cross parcels. She, Rabbit and Lopey made up a Communist 'cell'. More experienced in these matters, it was Lopey who listened to the BBC news on a hidden radio and reported back to the other two.

A number of Vittel's inmates managed to escape, and two members of Sofka's Family used the rehearsals for Ali Baba to remain in the Casino overnight and break out. Frida took with her a secret message for De Gaulle rolled inside a cigarette and made it back to London, where she worked for the Free French. Rabbit and Sofka made sure that the escapees' room looked normal and that post and messages didn't pile up behind the door, and it was several weeks before the two women were reported missing. The Family were now known as 'bad internees' and were put overnight in the soldiers' lock-up as punishment for their suspected involvement. Sofka maintained that she dismissed thoughts of escaping herself because she feared possible German retribution on her mother and stepfather; it was another matter for those with no relations.

Among the stories that both Sofka and Rabbit liked telling was the intrigue with the wire cutters. The tool was wonderful for cutting the perimeter fence, but had to be kept somewhere. Sofka's remote attic room was as good as anywhere and she stored it under her mattress. Rabbit was in Sofka's eyrie when they heard the unusual but unmistakable sound of German guards stomping up the spiral steps. Perhaps there had been a tip-off; certain inmates received privileges for helping the *Kommandantur* and spying was rife. It was widely rumoured that Sofka had Communist leanings and helped with escapes and her claims of White Russian natural antipathy to socialism didn't convince the authorities. Rabbit smiled at the memory of Sofka's cool head and fine acting over the next anguished minutes. The two women raced around, trying to think of a better hiding-place, and just as the guards reached the door Sofka whipped the cutters on to her chair, sat on them and opened a book: 'Come in!' She was only in her early thirties, but Sofka could act the imperious *grande dame* when she cared to. The Nazis stripped the bed, rummaged through books and clothes and confiscated the forbidden electric ring that was so handy for making tea. Sofka remained seated, adding helpful comments – 'You haven't checked on top of the wardrobe yet' – until they tramped off in annoyance.

'The Germans were stupid,' said Rabbit gleefully.

If Sofka's appearance showed that she was coping positively with internment, her poems at the time reveal how hard it was:

> *Oh, let the whole world go*
> *And smash itself to atoms,*
> *Burn and slay,*
> *Let rivers run of blood and men turn clay –*
> *What do I care . . .*
> *When every nerve cries out in me in pain,*
> *When every thought that writhes within my brain,*

When every prayer
That surges upward, driven by despair,
Is that the end should come
And that this end
May not, for you and me, love,
Be too late.

But the end was too late.

* * *

It was early June 1942 when Sofka heard two sets of female footsteps climbing the stairs to her room. She was alone; Rabbit had gone off to Paris in handcuffs, accompanied by a German guard, to take her university exams. Voices mumbled outside the door before knocking and Sofka opened to find two inmates – senior members of the German-appointed committee. One held a notification from the Red Cross. Had she imagined this moment? Did time slow down or speed up and disappear? The words said that Flying Officer Grey Skipwith was announced missing after operations on 30 May.

Sofka's memoirs are strangely muddled on what ensued. She describes an unpleasant period of waiting and managing to 'keep going' until Grey's death was confirmed in September; the announcement came with horrible synchronicity on the day of her mother's only visit. Although Sofka believed that this was when she collapsed, Shula and Rabbit both recall the more likely scenario that Sofka's breakdown began soon after learning that Grey was missing; the 'killed in action' was an unpleasant but expected formality. A long, rambling letter written to Rabbit while she was away in Paris in June (and an Air Ministry confirmation of Grey's death dated 26 June) seems to verify this version. Sofka describes her drugged lethargy after the doctor ordered sleeping pills (and cod-liver oil): sleep became reality 'while this side is merely the nightmare'. Sofka pictured Grey wounded inside a plane that was falling and twisting over and over. 'Rabbit, it's not fair,' she wrote. 'There must be some limit to hurting . . . Fate is the dirtiest player of the game of life!'

Rabbit returned to find Sofka in a terrible state. Unable to put up a front to her distress, she had taken to her bed – turning her back on the world was the only way of fleeing disaster; this time there was nowhere else to run. There came a point where she decided to die. 'It is fairly easy in the early stages,' Sofka wrote in her autobiography. 'You somehow retire from life, you lose interest, you do not want to eat or sleep, not even to read. You are retreating.' Rabbit brought up tea and her mother's soup, but to no avail.

It must have been during this time that Grey's last two letters arrived, sent soon before his final flight. There was also a small present from beyond the grave for Puppadog's imprisoned Ducca – a brooch in the shape of a dog's head. Grey quoted Swinburne's 'The Oblation', ending:

> Mine is the heart at your feet,
> Here, that must love you to live.

The poem later became a favourite of Rabbit's. When I visited her in Paris she showed me her French translation, which took sixteen attempts to perfect; Sofka's life had become hers.

After a week or so Sofka was admitted to the camp's hospital by Dr Levy. A delicately framed, French-Jewish prisoner of war, the doctor's exceptional character and kind, quiet intelligence were just what she needed. He sat talking gently, telling her about his own life: as a Jew, he lived under constant threat (it was only his medical skills that had kept him from deportation) and he feared terribly for his wife and child, who were in hiding. Sofka already knew that he was supporting the Resistance, but they didn't speak of these things; until now, la Petite Famille had deliberately avoided contact with him. Gradually Sofka realized that she was not going to die. She began to eat. After several weeks, she returned to her attic room, visiting the hospital for a daily glass of milk. Other internees were surprised to see the energetic, laughing woman they knew transformed into a pale, thin, listless creature, but it was now that Rabbit dragged Sofka back to life. With tireless energy, she kept on at Russian grammar and literary exercises all day, until both were dropping from exhaustion. At night, the younger woman would try to soothe the older, when the growling drone of Allied planes flying over drove Sofka to distraction. 'We were on a direct line for British bombers to Germany,' explained Rabbit. 'Most people were happy to hear them – we knew they were bombing railway lines in France too. But Sofka would hear them and go mad – crying under the sheets, unable to go to sleep all night. I was helpless.'

One day, they found a tortoise in the park. 'It said, "Eeugh,"' said Rabbit, 'and Sofka liked it. We kept it in her room.'

Sofka was back playing cards with the noisy old Russian ladies after a few months, but she knew that nothing would ever be the same. She never went into the details about Grey's end (perhaps she suffered too much imagining it) but her poems and letters show that it was the nadir of her existence; she was in pain for years. Even as an old woman, her face clenched when she spoke about becoming widowed and she soon changed the subject. As I delved deeper into the story, I felt very affected by her catastrophe. I even had the sort of dreams I imagine she had, of the couple's blissful reunion after the war, only to wake with the sour flavour of desolation. In reaction, I tried to find out more about Grey's life and death in the RAF and with help from my Uncle Patrick (as next of kin) wrote to RAF archives, telephoned squadron associations, obtained his old operational records and learned of his last hours. A correspondence with a charming old squadron contemporary of Grey's called 'Bluey' Mottershead revealed that all sorts of people were still mourning for men killed on the night of 30–31 May 1942. It was Bomber Harris's daring plan to make 'the greatest bomb raid in history' – the first 'thousand-bomber raid'. Novices were plucked from their training courses and thrust into the flimsy-looking fabric-covered planes to make up the vast numbers required for this 'bomber stream' to devastate German cities.

Under the full moon, on a clear, spring night, Grey's plane took off from Driffield, Yorkshire, at 23:37, joining a vast swarm of a thousand planes heading for Cologne. Grey was listed as Front Gunner, along with four other crew members under Captain O'Brien. His plane 'reached its objective', so they dropped their deadly load and saw the German city in flames, the snaking Rhine glistening red, anti-aircraft lights and guns sweeping the skies and aeroplanes exploding. It is horrible to think of the savage fear Grey must have felt in his tiny turret; I just hope it all happened quickly after they were hit. They were heading for home when they crashed at Meiderich, outside Duisburg. His body was recovered along with the rest of the crew and they ended up buried in Reichswald Forest Cemetery at Düsseldorf. Sofka never went there; tombstones meant nothing to her. Grey's Mark II Wellington was one of forty-one planes that went down that night. The 3.9 per cent rate of casualties was considered 'high but acceptable'; Churchill had said he'd be prepared to lose a hundred aircraft. The loves of other people's lives are dispensable.

After Grey died, Patrick was taken away from the Butlers. Mrs Butler's daughter, Phyllis, told me how 'one day, at the cottage, along comes a taxi, and a person who calls herself Lady Skipwith.

She had a most demanding voice and thought she was the cat's whiskers. She was very snobbish and said, "I want Patrick. He has no business here." She grabbed him under her arm, and Patrick was put into the back of the taxi, screaming and crying and scratching like a tiger. He had a terrible temper – he'd scream until his face went blue.' Grey's mother didn't even say thank you to the people who had been Patrick's family for almost three years.

It sounded odd to me that Patrick never stayed with his grandfather, Sir Grey, during or after the war. Sofka's memoirs state that her father-in-law had written warmly after Grey's death, promising to continue Patrick's allowance. But then, after his hated ex-wife had taken Patrick he cut off all contact and financial assistance, apparently believing it had been with Sofka's approval. This theory didn't sound quite right, especially given Sofka's absence in Vittel, and I contacted Grey's half-brother Egerton (Sir Grey's son from his second marriage), to see what he knew. He wrote back explaining that his father had never accepted Patrick as his grandson. This was quite a surprise to me, but Egie (as he signed his letters) traced the story back to his mother (Grey's stepmother). She had claimed that Grey had made a terrible, private confession to her, shortly before his death: 'When I've gone, please tell my father that my marriage is over.' Patrick was not his son, Grey allegedly announced. He and Sofka had been separated at the time of Patrick's conception, which happened 'when Sofka was with the Don Cossacks'. This all sounded absurd: the evidence allowed little doubt about Grey's love for his son and wife or about the chronology of the Cossack encounters (which began when Patrick was newborn). I was very intrigued by these stories, however, and gratefully accepted Egie's invitation to stay in Dorset.

The Old Rectory was surrounded by well-kept grounds and filled with Skipwith heirlooms and memorabilia, which had been handed down from baronet to baronet, but not to Patrick. Portraits of proudly wigged Skipwiths in frills and red coats peered from the walls, accompanied by spaniels, similar to those which roamed the house. Egie showed me his father's shooting album which contained long lists of what Sir Grey bagged over the years in Scotland, Ireland and Egypt. Pictures reveal a grouchy-looking, tweedy man dripping with dead grouse. His entry for 1940–41 complains of the lack of beaters: 'War still raging . . . which is ruining what should be the best shooting season for many years.' Sitting by the fire (elegant Georgian furniture, comfortable chintz, pot pourri), I listened to Egie's stories. 'Sofka was seen as a corrupter,' he said, and I could imagine how this penniless, unconventional foreigner with such palpable sex appeal must have seemed explosively dangerous to the Skipwiths.

Egie's mother once visited Sofka and Grey in London and reported back that Sofka liked to dress in black 'because it doesn't show the dirt'. There was also 'a Chinese lodger, by whom Sofka had a child'. This last story made me laugh, but I was also shocked at how the deceptive rumours about Patrick had held sway for over half a century. My guess was that it all came down to Egie's mother's fondness for titles: she had married a gruff, much older, divorced man with a baronetcy; it must have been maddening to think that the title would head off in the direction of a scruffy little Russian boy, rather than to her eldest son. How easy then, after Grey's death, to circulate a few stories . . .

One person's life ultimately consists of as many differing storylines as there are witnesses. It was not just Sofka's two sets of disapproving in-laws, but even her closest friends and relatives who created their own narratives. It was hard enough for Sofka herself to get her story straight and this seems to be particularly true in relation to her children. Perhaps she felt guilty, although she never expressed it. In her defence, while she was interned she did write to them (Grey mentioned them receiving her letters), she knitted woollen toys for Patrick and she told Rabbit of nightmares in which 'the kids were being bombed'. She also believed that her offspring were at least safe, fed and cared-for – far more than what many children in Europe had. Perhaps it is just as well that she didn't know the details of how traumatized her three sons were by the war.

Patrick's bad-tempered grandmother soon passed him on to some distant Skipwith cousins in Cornwall. They remembered a disturbed little boy, who screamed and cried and didn't fit in. Peter and Ian, too, were removed from the dangers of London and delivered to the Visitation Convent in Bridport, Dorset. Leo had joined the army and his parents had moved to Guildford, but nobody could tell me why Catholic nuns were favoured as guardians for two Russian Orthodox boys of seven and four. Perhaps it was cheap and the nuns seemed friendly; the reality was more like a prison camp. Each boy's name was removed and he was known as a number – Peter was number 9. At mealtimes they sat in numerical order, and through the compulsory silence came the chewing and gagging noises of children forcing down lumpy porridge at breakfast and sickening tripe at lunch. The nuns' apparently limitless capacity for cruelty included beating Peter every day and leaving him locked in the upstairs dormitory during air raids. He understood that this was a punishment for not being Catholic. By the time the Zinovieff brothers were removed in 1944, Ian was so malnourished that he was dangerously underweight for his age; Peter was left with psychological scars which haunted him over a lifetime.

* * *

249

It was early in 1943 when about 280 unusual prisoners arrived at Vittel in two batches. Sofka noticed immediately that these people appeared particularly anguished and thin. They were all housed in Hotel Providence on the far side of the camp, which could only be reached via a temporary wooden bridge, identical to that erected by the Nazis at the Warsaw Ghetto. The bridge can only have been an awful reminder: the ghetto was now completely destroyed, and these inmates were the last, traumatized remnants of its once overcrowded population, who by chance, determination, influence or 'Aryan appearance' had escaped the round-ups.

Sofka and Rabbit took up the cause of these Polish Jews, realizing that their situation was extremely precarious. They quickly started giving lessons in English and French, to help them should they escape. These new arrivals were very different from the grumbling 'nice people' or the card-playing Russians. Some of the women arrived in fox-furs and velvet hats, but they wept a lot. About half the group were strangely quiet, painfully emaciated children. They drew pictures of shootings and Nazis throwing people out of tall buildings. The young men crept furtively in and out of lessons, often through the windows, looking over their shoulders.

'For the first time we heard the dread names: Auschwitz, Belsen, Dachau . . . the Final Solution,' wrote Sofka. 'We heard of deaths by torture, by starvation, the floggings, the humiliations.' There was a baby who was said to have miraculously escaped death at Treblinka. His mother and a trainload of deportees had been sent straight from the train to the gas chamber, but some were not quite dead when they were thrown into a pit and covered with earth. Someone had pushed the baby up to the surface and a passing Polish peasant heard its cries. It still had a travelling-label around its neck and it was sent back to its address in Warsaw. Somehow, the infant ended up in Vittel.

Among the Jews in Hotel Providence was the well-known Yiddish and Hebrew poet Itzhak Katzenelson, whose wife and two younger sons had already been killed by the Nazis at Treblinka. Arriving in Vittel with his remaining son, Zvi, he was shocked by the comfort and apparent normality. It was like a wonderful, peaceful dream, soured by doubts and dread. Hearing a young Jewish girl playing the violin noisily outside his window, Katzenelson wrote furiously in his diary: 'If the murderers of my wife and sons will not kill me, this violin will.' Over the next months, he poured his agony and anger into (among other things) an epic poem, *The Song of the Murdered Jewish People*. He rolled up his writings in bottles and buried them under the trees in Vittel. *The Song* became one of Sofka's treasured poems, which she repeatedly copied out and distributed.

> *They are no more.*
> *Do not ask anything, anywhere the world over.*
> *All is empty*
> *They are no more.*

Increasingly Sofka stayed over on the other side of the camp, teaching, comforting, and trying to help. 'I never knew where she was any more,' said Rabbit. 'She'd come back late, not having eaten. I was afraid she'd get trapped there after curfew.' Sofka was desperate to find a way of helping these terrified people, many of whom held dubious papers for Latin American countries or were awaiting certificates from Zionist organizations to travel to Palestine. Using her Resistance contacts, she copied all their names on to cigarette papers, learning new skills with a mapping pen and magnifying glass. She then rolled the papers into toothpaste tubes or capsules (which could be swallowed if necessary) and gave them to a *passeur*.

Rabbit showed me the Hotel Providence and its plaque to the inmates she knew. She explained where the hated wooden bridge crossed the road, and gave me related articles and Katzenelson's poem. But she didn't tell me about Darling. It was later that his name cropped up, as I read through letters Sofka wrote to Jack in the late 1950s. She was explaining her deepest anxieties – how her association with loving someone was now 'fear of loss'. It was like Pavlov's dogs, she said.

> When a letter did come it left one sobbing and shattered, and when it did not come, panic seized one so that one had to clutch hard for control. Then 'Missing' – three months when panic had its way. The 'Killed in action' when there was nothing more to live for and I very nearly succeeded in dying. A year later came Izio – a very different affection, the clinging of two people lost – and with the fear again of the extermination camps, the fear that turned again into uncontrolled panic and ended with the death in me (as I hoped) of any feeling.

Who was Izio? Why had nobody told me? I rang up Shula, and then Rabbit in France. Shula sounded mystified at first, then realized who I meant. 'We always called him "Darling",' she said. 'He was a very beautiful young man of about thirty, with lovely blue eyes – very, very sad eyes – and dark hair. He was boyish and warm, but everything in his body was sad: he had lost everything except his little daughter, Visia.' I trawled through Sofka's writings, eventually locating some brief, desiccated references in her book. He was from Lodz. He had walked all the way to Warsaw with his mother, his four-year-old daughter and his wife, who had died during the journey. As in many shattered families, another woman was brought along in his dead wife's place, covered by their Honduran visas. The affair is barely hinted at: 'There were film-shows regularly on Saturdays and Sundays at the Casino, to which I usually went with Izidor Skossowski.' No more.

Rabbit didn't discuss why she edited Darling out, but admitted that he and Sofka had been inseparable: 'They clung to each other.' I pictured them clinging literally: a bodily expression of the terrible things they had suffered; a defiance of death by making love. 'I think he'd studied architecture,' said Rabbit. 'He was very kind and sweet. He'd offer to make tea and was helpful. He and Sofka never asked each other any questions – they each just accepted what the other had been through. And he was a good father. He always cared for his daughter before anything else. He'd even miss seeing Sofka if there wasn't someone Visia knew to care for her, though sometimes I looked after her.' The couple spoke in a mix of languages, as Sofka picked up Polish and she taught Darling English. They went for long walks in the park, where the British internees gave disapproving looks.

After our conversation Rabbit recommended a book to me without saying why – Abraham Shulman's *The Case of Hotel Polski*. I imagined that it would be yet another harrowing litany of Holocaust death and destruction – the kind of thing that Sofka had regularly passed on to me from a tender age – but in fact it revealed some extraordinary details about Darling and his fellow Poles in Vittel. By 1943, Warsaw's ghetto was in ruins and the city was declared officially *judenrein* – Jew-free. However, some Jews had survived, in hiding, disguised as Gentiles, or because they were rich, influential or persuasive enough. Darling's brother Lolek was at the centre of a strange story which made the modest Hotel Polski the focus of these last Jews' lingering hopes. Lolek and his friends were known collaborators with the Gestapo but they were also apparently running a system to help Jews leave the city. Some accused Lolek of taking gold, diamonds and cash in exchange for false *promesas* from Chile, Venezuela, Paraguay and Honduras as part of a Gestapo trick to 'catch' rich Jews. Others said that he tried to save Jewish lives by organizing the trains to Vittel. After all, he even sent his brother, mother and niece off on one. Letters arrived back from the first shipment to Vittel, talking of life in comfortable hotels in a famous European spa where nuns were teaching their children. To these exhausted, panic-stricken, starving people, who had crawled through sewers and seen unimaginable horrors, it sounded like paradise. One of these survivors, Adolf Ruknicki, later wrote a fictional account: 'People were being burned alive . . . and there was Vittel. We had constant expectations of death . . . and there was Vittel. We were in perpetual fear of blackmail, of suspicious landladies . . . And there was Vittel.'

Among the Polish children who arrived in Vittel via Hotel Polski was Stephan Schorr-Kon, whose mother and grandmother made a great impression on Sofka. His grandmother, Tamara Schorr, was the widow of Warsaw's Grand Rabbi, and her daughter, Felicja Kon, was strikingly tall, elegant and cultured (Rabbit described her as very beautiful and grand – 'a bit like Sofka'). Stephan was to see Sofka again over forty years later, after I became friends with him and his young family while an undergraduate at Cambridge. It was some time before his story emerged, the strange coincidence was revealed and I put him in touch with Sofka. For Stephan, meeting Sofka was an extraordinary opportunity to learn more about the harrowing episodes his mother had wrapped in silence and refused to discuss to her dying day (decades later after a successful life in New York). Sofka described how his grandmother's courageous dignity and piled, snowy hair had reminded her of her own grandmother, Olga. She remembered giving chocolate to the five-year-old Stephan and his brother, who were both very talkative and dressed in little sheepskin coats. She didn't tell the adult Stephan about Darling. Perhaps her private pain seemed insignificant compared to the inconceivably huge horror against which it was set.

When trains with boarded windows arrived in Vittel in April 1944, most internees paid no notice. The Poles in Hotel Providence, however, understood their significance immediately. Felicja, Stephan's mother, was prepared; a quick death was preferable to deportation and she had carefully stored cyanide capsules. I wonder what Felicja said before she helped her mother take the poison; harder still to imagine the revulsion when, like so much during the war, the cyanide turned out to be ersatz. Mme Schorr was in great pain, but did not die. In desperation Felicja handed over her own pill and, having witnessed her mother's death, opened the fifth-floor window and jumped. Rabbit was outside and saw Felicja hit the ground. Sixteen others also tried to commit suicide, cutting their wrists or drinking corrosive. Three people died, but astonishingly Felicja was not among them. The earth was soft following rain, and she was not even badly injured. Dr Levy bandaged her up and whispered some advice on how to act. He then informed the Germans that she was completely paralysed and could not be moved.

By the luck of the draw, Darling was not taken away, but everyone was now terrorized. Who knows what the children – Stephan, Visia and dozens of others – understood? They already knew far too much. The local Resistance offered to take twelve of the Polish children into safe-keeping, but it was a dreadful decision for the parents. If caught outside the camp, they would certainly end up dead. And maybe there wouldn't be another deportation? Maybe they would get to South America or Palestine? Darling could not face giving up Visia. (Only one man, Professor Eck, sent his eleven-year-old daughter out, and miraculously found her later, having himself escaped from a train. They both made it to Israel.) Sofka redoubled her efforts at alerting the world to the atrocities. She wrote several letters to her mother's old friend at the Foreign Office, Jock Balfour, hoping that as he had helped her over to France, he might aid these desperate people. She tried putting every argument, stressing the case as 'a matter of the gravest importance': 'They are eye-witnesses of all the unbelievable horrors that have been perpetrated on their race. Their lives are important from a documentary as well as from a humanitarian point of view. Their danger is only too real and I cannot sufficiently stress the need for rapid action. Their nerves are at cracking point.' The signet ring that Leo had given Sofka before her wedding to Grey went to pay for two *passeurs* who took these letters out to Switzerland and eventually to other addresses including the Red Cross and London's Board of Jews.

When the second windowless train arrived a month later, no one was in any doubt. Apart that is, from the 'nice people', who preferred to believe the comfortable stories put about by the Commandant, that the Jews were merely being transferred. 'Nothing to worry about.' Sofka found Visia and hurried her over to the hospital, which was already providing a discreet haven for Stephan and his brother. She told Darling that 'should anything happen' she would take care of his daughter. The night passed. Did anyone sleep? The next morning, the far side of the camp where the Poles were housed was closed off. Threatening SS officers strode around – quite different to the mostly older, war-weary German guards, who would sometimes exchange a cigarette or a quiet word with internees. Sofka sat waiting on a bench near the Commandant's house – Rabbit showed me the quaint chalet, still bearing the inapt sign LES FEES – The Fairies. It was May and the park was at its most beautiful; a thousand shades of green and lilac in bloom. Suddenly, Darling appeared in front of Sofka. He had asked the guards if he could go to the toilet and miraculously just walked away. Sofka begged him to come up to the attic where he could stay in a secret store-room until they could help him escape. Some of his compatriots had already found hiding-places in the Casino cellars. There was still a last chance of life . . . But it was an unenviable choice: what kind of life could Darling have if he left his daughter and mother to their fate?

Before he went, Darling gave Sofka a list signed by fifty Jews, certifying that his brother Lolek had helped them escape the Nazis. Darling didn't want to die with a brother remembered as a collaborator; whatever Lolek himself had believed, it looked certain that those he had 'helped' at Hotel Polski were now doomed. They said goodbye in front of Les Fées and Sofka watched him walk back to the wooden bridge past the still-tended hotel flowerbeds.

After he had gone, Sofka and Rabbit ran to the hospital in search of Visia and arrived in time to see the child being carried out to a waiting van. Beside her were those who had just tried to kill themselves; this time there was no clemency even for them – stretchers bore those with roughly bandaged wrists on to the blind trains. Sofka described this point in her memoirs, and though she didn't admit her love for Darling, she recalled how every glimmer of hope was gone:

'It was over. Madeleine [Rabbit] and I felt emptied of all thought and feeling, drained of all energy. Our efforts had come to nothing.'

It took time for Sofka's deadening grief to turn to fury about the Holocaust and the Allies' lack of response. Years passed before she learned details about how Darling and the others died, though rumours of Auschwitz quickly returned through the Resistance grapevine. Thirty-five people avoided deportation: two men escaped and reached Switzerland; Stephan, his brother and his mother Felicja remained in the hospital with some others who were gravely ill; and a number hid themselves around the camp buildings until the Americans liberated Vittel some four months later. One man survived in the bathroom of Miss Tilney, an old, devoutly Protestant English spinster, who was so annoying that he was almost driven to give himself up.

Over the summer, Sofka and Rabbit took turns letting frightened men spend nights in their rooms and took tins of food to others in the depths of the Casino. They also managed to smuggle out a baby. The infant boy had been born just before the second deportation and was overlooked when his mother was taken away. Dr Levy gave him a sedative, swaddled him in blankets inside a Red Cross box and gave him to Sofka and Rabbit.

'We had often helped people through the fence,' explained Rabbit, taking me to see the place where they cut the barbed wire in advance and then replaced it loosely. 'We'd hide them in the small shop, which sold notebooks, matches, thread and sometimes some vegetables.' Rabbit and I walked through the shady arcade where Club Med tourists were sipping Vittel's curative water from the source and along to where the shop had been. 'We'd wait until about four a.m. and then meet up with the lorry. I knew all about the timing of when the guards went past.'

They all also knew how the Commandant, Captain Landhauser, and his officers went out at night, hunting down and executing saboteurs. It was no game.

The barbed wire was gone and it was a bright spring day, but we both stood looking at the scrubby area where they had gathered in the dark, listening for sounds, hoping the baby would not wake, hearts beating, a tree rustling . . . As the smaller of the two, it was Rabbit who squeezed through the gap in the fence and handed over the precious package to a village woman. The orphan was kept near by until after the war, when he was sent to a kibbutz in Israel. 'We never found out where, but we felt that we had done something,' said Rabbit.

As a war widow with children, Sofka had already been offered repatriation in late 1943, but had turned down the opportunity to return home to her sons. 'It was felt by the Party that I should stay and carry on the work of trying to save the Poles,' Sofka wrote later. Presumably, beyond duty and principles, the love and hope she shared with Darling also kept her there. Now, with everything gone, she and Rabbit put themselves down on the list to be repatriated. Rumours seeped through about Allied successes: the Normandy landings; heavy bombardments in Germany; Soviet forces pushing the Nazis back. In mid-July the camp's loudspeakers echoed through the baking hot grounds with nine hundred names of those who were going home. Sofka was to leave first, followed by Rabbit and the rest of the Little Family a week later, and they began packing: forty kilos allowed but no paper; strip-searches would see to that. They hid names and addresses of relatives of the Poles inside coat hems and powder compacts and handed them over to other, less suspect internees (they were already in trouble – Sofka had been confined to her building for a month after the second deportation for 'meddling' in matters which did not concern her).

It was a long, hot, uncomfortable train journey, winding, halting and doubling back across France, taking three weeks to reach Lisbon. They passed Lyons, where the whole station had been destroyed by bombs: engines stood upended in craters like toys; and emaciated Russian PoWs were digging and repairing the tracks, watched by Nazis holding whips. Once, when the Resistance presumed the unmarked train contained German troops, they stopped just before hitting explosives on the rails. Later, they were attacked by US fighter planes. Everyone ran to hide in a ditch and then returned to help put out the fire in the rear carriages. At other times, when the stiflingly hot train was stationary, the passengers wandered off and lay in nearby fields until the whistle blew for their return. Once, in the Camargue, Sofka and Della, her Turkish travelling companion, were resting under some almond trees when several horsemen galloped up. After learning who they were, the men invited them to join the Resistance; the women would be helpful and might end up home even sooner, they argued, at the rate the war was going. Sofka was very tempted. Had it not been for her children, she said later, she would not have hesitated.

The most baffling aspect of the journey was the attention given to Sofka and Della by the Gestapo officers: they transferred the two women to first-class carriages, organized the best-available food in the restaurant for them, and produced magazines and books for the trip. Neither woman understood, though they didn't refuse these welcome privileges either. Their fellow internees already disapproved of Sofka (as a camp trouble maker) and now became convinced that they had two collaborators in their midst. Both women were given black looks and sent to Coventry. The puzzle was eventually solved when the Nazis invited Sofka and Della to join them for coffee and brandy after dinner. Radio Berlin needed assistance with its propaganda programme and the women were invited to help (neither knew yet of P. G. Wodehouse's notorious Berlin broadcasts as a prisoner of war). The Gestapo assumed that as a White Russian, Sofka might well support the German cause as opposed to the Soviet one and that neither she nor Della (as a Turk) owed any loyalty to Britain. Admittedly, the officers said, the Germans were undergoing a setback in the war, but there was no doubt that things would eventually go their way. Sofka and Della would have to proceed to Lisbon to make up the correct exchange numbers with a group of German internees from South Africa, but then they would be transferred straight to Berlin.

The two women left to discuss the matter. Despite the threats from other prisoners to report them to the British authorities, they decided to play the Germans' game; perhaps they'd learn something useful to pass on to the authorities themselves. Over celebratory champagne, Sofka and Della agreed that they would go the Lisbon address, and from there to Madrid and by plane to Berlin. The street number and secret knock were learned and Hitler was toasted ('and his damnation', Sofka remembered adding secretly). The next day, when the Germans left the train at a station just before the Spanish border, Sofka's relief was immense; she'd been terrified that the plan could have backfired badly, ending up with her in Germany.

Once in Spain, the train took speed towards Portugal with its cargo of hot, dirty women. They were tired and their ankles were puffed up from weeks of sitting still, but they couldn't fail to feel an anxious excitement welling. Three years after the Nazis arrived in France and following their strange imprisonment, nobody could imagine what freedom would mean.

CHAPTER 8

THE COMMUNIST

All reasonable men accept the status quo.
Therefore all progress is made by unreasonable men.
— George Bernard Shaw

It was not unusual to see bewildered, unwashed foreigners arriving in Lisbon in the summer of 1944. As a neutral oasis in a brutalized, war-bruised Europe, its blisteringly hot streets were already bustling with refugees, exiles, other nations' royalty, spies and all sorts from both Allied and Axis countries. Jews and other vulnerable people escaping from Vichy France often made straight for the Portuguese capital, continuing by boat to America or waiting, stranded, for family, visas, money or peace. Sofka and her companions stepped gingerly off the train; their legs were painfully swollen and they were exhausted. There, on the platform, officials from the British Embassy were waiting, and following instructions from Jock Balfour, her friend at the Foreign Office, Sofka was whisked away in a car with her friend Della.

Installed in a smart hotel, Sofka's first act of freedom was to take refuge in a bath, letting water work its cleansing, soothing magic on three weeks of grime, aching limbs and fearful anticipation. The two women then visited a hairdresser (who couldn't believe the filthy state of their hair), and went out for dinner. After thirty months of internment, they found the busy city overwhelmingly noisy and crowded, but exciting too. Savouring the first fish they had eaten since 1941, Sofka and Della devoured lobster then two helpings of sole each in a restaurant. It was a wonderful renunciation of mouldy German bread and austere portions from Red Cross tins.

The ten days in Lisbon gave a taste of liberty, but it was hardly home. There were debriefings by embassy staff, who recorded Sofka's messages from Vittel's local Resistance groups and were delighted to learn of the Gestapo's Lisbon address and secret knocks. One evening, Sofka encountered one of the German officers from the train in a nightclub, who glared balefully while she and Della laughed at his reproaches for not having shown up as promised. She spent her days writing numerous letters and also visited the US Embassy and the Polish legation to give news of the recent deportation of Vittel's Poles. There is no record of her private grief for Darling, which was surely still acute.

In early August the Vittel women were taken to a Swedish boat bound for England, where they were joined by a second trainload of internees, among them Rabbit and the remaining members of the Little Family. Sofka was hugely relieved to see them again; there was nobody she was closer to than Rabbit, and the others had become like real family. It took five days to reach Liverpool, where Immigration officials greeted them with a stinging insult Sofka never forgot: 'Well, it's an end to being lazy and easy living. You'll be made to do some work now that you've decided to come back.' The Red Cross issued raincoats and thirty shillings to each woman and when they had proved they had somewhere to go, they all headed off in different directions – Rabbit to an aunt in Leamington Spa and Sofka by train to London.

Sofka arrived in the blackout; the war was far from over. This was the 'doodlebug summer', in which thousands of Londoners were killed by V1 'flying bombs' and many more had abandoned the city. Sirens wailed and crowds were already bedding down in the underground stations for the night. When she arrived at the house of some friends, she was taken to sleep in the basement. It's when the sinister rasping drone of the engine cut out that you have to worry, they explained. Then you have fifteen seconds to hope that it drops somewhere else.

Over the next days, Sofka tried to organize some practical details: the bank; ration cards; new clothes from Peter Jones. She hadn't expected a warm welcome from Grey's mother in Park Lane, but still she was dazed by Lady Skipwith's anti-Semitic remarks and complaints about the standard of white bread. She became more aware than ever of the gulf between those who had experienced the horrors and humiliations of Nazi occupation and those who only knew what she described as the more physical, straightforward fear of bombing.

Sofka's disorientation at being back in England was not just the confusion of the caged animal let loose. She made an effort to adjust, visiting friends and dropping in for drinks at her favourite old haunt, Jack's Club, but realized she was returning to a life that lacked its very centre. She had no family to go to, no home and no job; without Grey, London was bleak and desolate. Her bruised, thin-skinned emotions manifested themselves physically: her teeth wobbled in their gums; she felt exhausted; and her skin was so sensitive that even a vigorous handshake could leave violet smudges on the back of her hand. After a friend lent her an empty flat in the Fulham Road, she went in search of the people who had been caring for her and

Grey's belongings – their furniture (including the huge bed), books and letters. Instead of their house, she found a gap in the street – a common enough sight throughout London now. She claimed not to have fretted too much; a few precious photograph albums were still at the pub in Cookham Dean and if life had taught her one thing, it was that material possessions were the least important element. At least she had a clean start, she reasoned.

The world suddenly looked brighter when she was invited by Laurence Olivier to take up a position as secretary of the regrouped Old Vic theatre company. On receiving the telegram, she went straight over to their latest premises at the New Theatre in St Martin's Lane. Walking in on a rehearsal of *Peer Gynt* was a thrilling moment. On stage with Ralph Richardson was Olivier, speaking in the unforgettable voice that Sofka had thought of so often in Vittel. Afterwards she took a taxi with Vivien and Larry for a celebratory lunch at Claridge's, where they drank a lot and ate from the fashionable *smorgasbord*, defying rationing. The glamorous pair of actors had lost none of their witty, urbane, sexy panache – they seemed just as before – whilst Sofka felt she had emerged out of the longest, darkest tunnel a different person. Hard to even begin to tell them what she had been through.

It was another week or so before Sofka took two days off work to travel down to Cornwall to see her youngest son. Patrick was living with some Skipwith cousins, who invited Sofka to stay. There is no evidence that she longed to be reunited and close to her children, but it is clear that she wanted to make sure they were safe. Sofka described the 'extraordinary sensation' of meeting 'a six-year-old son whom one had last seen as an eighteen-month-old toddler'. Unlike his father, Grey, who would now remain a youthful thirty-one for ever, Patrick had leaped, unseen, through time to an utterly different age. What

Sofka didn't mention in her memoirs was the shock and pain she felt on recognizing something of Grey in Patrick. It was only in a poem that she confessed how merely seeing the young boy's smile and the familiar turn of his head felt like 'dulled blows falling on the half-healed scar'.

Sofka surprised her hosts by leaving for London again the next day, not having even considered the possibility of taking her son with her. One of the household's young daughters, Tina, remembered how the grown-ups were all very disapproving of this 'Russian adventurer', who they believed had 'snapped up poor Grey'. Taking morning tea up to Sofka in her bedroom, Tina found her 'very exotic'. She was still in bed, 'with acres of dark hair lying around all over the place'.

The next weekend it was Peter and Ian's turn, and Sofka took the train to Guildford, where they were living with their Zinovieff grandparents. 'I met my mother aged eight on Guildford Station,' Ian told me. He remembered being walked down to the station by Manya, the Russian cook, and waiting at the barrier. If it was bewildering to meet an unknown mother, it must have been just as awkward to see two large, unfamiliar, wary boys who were your own. Manya was holding a letter in Russian for 'Sofia Petrovna' from the grandparents; Sofka was not welcome to come to the house, it announced, and future visits must be arranged so that she did not knock at the door.

'Sofka was not received by my family,' Uncle Kyril had once told me, using their way of phrasing the rejection. There was to be no compromising over the Zinovieffs' feelings of hurt and offence. It is not clear how soon they discovered her new-found faith in Communism, but this surely sealed her fate. 'Now it looks like a historical phenomenon, then it was like treason,' explained Uncle Kyril.

Peter remembered how, for a twelve-year-old, it was rather exciting to have a mother who was so despised. 'My grandparents made her seem quite fascinating with their hatred and I remember being terribly excited when she came to visit,' he said. 'She used to take us on outings, on trains and buses and rowing on the river. She'd bring a picnic and sometimes we'd go mushroom-hunting in the woods at Guildford. Once we found an unexploded doodlebug and went to tell the police and another time we put out a fire on the railway line. After the cocooned life with my grandparents and the abuse in the convent, she was great fun. Every memory of her is a good one; it's the things she didn't do . . .'

Sunday picnics every once in a while were apparently the sort of mothering that Sofka could manage and that suited her, and she was shaken when, in December, the Skipwith cousins asked her to take back Patrick. Although the Skipwiths deny this version, I can't believe she would have wanted him at this stage – her existence was hardly one into which a child could easily be fitted. Her long hours at the Old Vic often started early in the morning, helping Olivier with his lines, then continued through afternoon rehearsals and frequently included evening performances (the shows went on even during bombing). And naturally, there was the subsequent round of parties and drinking. 'One was apt to find oneself in many beds with unexpected companions,' Sofka confessed. She was not alone in finding alcohol and passing encounters an answer to the seemingly endless war, with its daily threat of bombs and bereavement. Her heart was now 'an empty gourd', she wrote in one of several poems expressing her continued longing for Grey; it seemed that nothing would replace him. Sex was a pleasurable distraction, but she didn't want and wasn't capable of giving love.

She had taken some insalubrious furnished ground-floor rooms in Sydney Street, Chelsea, an area which had been badly battered by the war and abandoned by many of its old inhabitants, who had not yet returned. Next-door was missing (the neighbour had woken up in bed in the garden) and Sofka's house had no roof.

It was nearly Christmas, during the coldest winter for years, when Sofka collected Patrick at Harrods' toy department. He remembered clutching on to someone's skirts in fear . . . They belonged to the Skipwith nanny, who had brought him up to London and who watched as Sofka picked up the screaming child and walked away. 'I remember being taken off,' said Patrick. 'I was terrified and bawling my head off.'

'Poor Patrick did not appreciate being reunited with his parent,' wrote Sofka, admitting that her own first reaction, too, was a panic-stricken call for help. There was only one person she could really trust – Rabbit – and the twenty-three-year-old left her aunt and rushed to London. They were a strange little family now, in the freezing, leaky flat.

'Sofka wasn't a good housewife,' admitted Rabbit, with characteristic understatement. '"Life's too short for cleaning," she used to say. She'd leave all her washing until there was nothing to wear. So I did all the cleaning and washing up. We were very hard-up, but the butcher would give us bones, and we'd use them to make soup in a big pot on the fireplace. We'd filch coal and wood from down near the river.'

During the night, Sofka and Rabbit would take turns to accompany Patrick down to the air-raid shelter when the sirens went off, while the other stayed sleeping, too tired to care. In the day, the new and murderously silent V2 missiles plunged without warning from the stratosphere. 'One day,' said Rabbit, 'Sofka and I were in Woolworths in the King's Road when a V2 bomb exploded. We never saw it, but we were lifted up and thrown in different directions. Luckily, we weren't hurt.'

After Christmas the threesome was evicted by the landlady, who didn't like children. Patrick was sent off to a weekly-boarding prep school and Sofka rented a basement flat at 20 Oakley Street – the very road where she had last lived with Grey. It must have provoked terrible nostalgia, seeing the places where they had been together and following their old tracks – along the Embankment, with its peeling plane trees, and past Cheyne Walk where they had stayed in the Oliviers' house. Sofka's new flat was owned by a fellow Communist whom she had recently met in the Chelsea branch. Later, she recalled with amusement how she sidled up to someone on the street selling *Russia Today*, and hissed conspiratorially that she would like to contact the Party. After all the danger and secrecy of her endeavours in Vittel, she was shocked at how easy and simple it was to join up. There was no better time for supporting the policies of the Soviet Union: Uncle Joe was in fashion and the Russians were allies, beating off Hitler's forces with tremendous bravery. Russia was also suffering appalling losses; by the end of the war, twenty-five million people had died, nineteen million of whom were civilians. Sofka was quickly absorbed into the Party, and was soon selling *Daily Workers* and canvassing for Russian soldiers on the streets at weekends. Along with the collection of artists, journalists, writers, doctors and the odd 'worker' who constituted the eccentric, 'intellectual' Chelsea branch, she too furiously debated the future of the world. On Sunday mornings they'd go to the Soviet Embassy and watch scratchy old Russian films.

When the end of the war in Europe was declared, on 8 May 1945, there was dancing and jubilation in the streets, but for many, like Sofka, there was a sense that it had come 'too late'. With whom could she now share the joy and freedom? However, she knew about keeping busy and putting on a good front; people didn't see her internal anguish. Two weeks after VE Day, the Old Vic Company was assigned to ENSA, the Entertainments National Service Association (known by some of the servicemen and women who saw the performances around the world as Every Night Something Awful). They were given uniforms, and on 25 May, headed by Olivier and Richardson, they left for a seven-week victory tour of Europe to show *Richard III* and Shaw's *Arms and the Man*. Strangest of all was the visit to Hamburg – still a horrifying collection of ruins and rubble covering hundreds of thousands of decomposing corpses. Even worse was Belsen. The company was not allowed into the camp due to an outbreak of typhus, but Sofka described her view of the place: the huts; the crematoria; the skeletal inmates, who still hadn't left. It was only a year since Darling and the Poles had died in a place like this and Sofka experienced what she called 'a crying jag' afterwards. Everybody was drinking heavily to combat the depressing environment, but even with the theatrical camaraderie and constant parties (often in smart villas of former Nazis), it was agony to confront the war's dreadful legacy.

The happiest part of the trip was undoubtedly Paris, where the Old Vic performed at the Comédie Française. Sofka stayed in her old room, which had remained locked ever since her arrest in December 1940 – remarkably, the police had kept the key. On 14 July, the first Bastille Day after France's liberation, Sofka finally celebrated the end of war with several of her old Russian friends, including Nikolai, who had planned her escape, and his cousin Yuri, her old *cavaliere servante*. They danced and sang in the streets with the crowds all through the summer night – an epiphany, during which Sofka felt true optimism about the future of a socialist world, which would emerge out of the ashes. 'We were still young enough to join in the building of a universe,' she wrote. 'The wine we stopped to drink at the still open cafes, the night, our high hopes, all combined to arouse in us an intoxicated exaltation I have never since experienced.'

* * *

Sofka confessed that, like many at the time, she didn't pay too much attention when two far-off cities in Japan were reduced to noxious vapour. The names 'Hiroshima' and 'Nagasaki' meant little and at least their destruction brought an end to the war. Life in London was no longer dangerous but nor was it easy, especially as Rabbit had now returned to France. Sofka was struggling to care for Patrick, while working hard and trying to establish her own life. Patrick remembered different men at Oakley Street each weekend when he came home from school. And under his mother's bed he discovered a horrible-looking pink rubber balloon with a spout, which he sensed was somehow linked to sex, though he knew nothing about vaginal douches. I was curious as to who these myriad lovers might have been and asked Rabbit about whether she remembered any of them, but she said she didn't know, though 'whoever they were they'd have been Communists'. But she did tell me about Dutch caps, which were all the rage then. Sofka certainly used one, and Rabbit even organized special trips to bring over French women to be fitted by a doctor friend of Sofka's, as caps were unavailable in France.

Again it was Shula, the same person who had first told me about Darling and about Sofka's lesbian affair, who let drop that Sofka had lived with someone after the war. We were sitting in Rabbit's apartment.

'David. David Rocheman,' said Shula. 'He was an officer in the British Army. Very nice-looking: blond, blue-eyed and well-made. They lived together for a long time.' I could barely believe what I was hearing. Why had nobody ever mentioned this man?

Rabbit entered the conversation at this point. 'It was a scandal because he was the brother of Raymonde – one of the members of our *Petite Famille* in Vittel. He was much younger than Sofka.'

'And what happened to him?' I asked.

'He's still alive,' replied Shula, glancing anxiously at Rabbit.

'Where is he?' I was trying to remain calm.

'He's here in Paris,' said Shula.

I felt nervous ringing David Rocheman's bell in Boulogne-Billancourt, but as the door opened I quickly understood there was no need. Now in his early eighties, David looked much younger and was still remarkably attractive, with enquiring, intelligent eyes. As I entered the airy, modern apartment, he introduced me to his wife, Marjorie. Both were warmly curious to see Sofka's granddaughter and spoke with the careful, courteous diction of people who fear (needlessly) that their perfect English might have gone rusty.

'I lived with Sofka from the end of 1945 for three years,' said David, explaining how he'd met her through his sister, who was living near by in Chelsea. Both David and his sister had been born in England but were brought up in France by their Jewish parents. After the Nazi occupation of France, David escaped to England, while his sister was interned, his father was deported and his mother went into hiding. He was only sixteen, but he joined the British Army when he was eighteen and soon became an officer.

'I was twenty-two when I met Sofka,' said David. 'And she was thirty-eight. Though she lied and said she was thirty-seven! Some people looked at us strangely when we went out together, because of the age difference, but I didn't care. We were interested in the same things – Shakespeare, the theatre . . . and she made me read. She always looked fantastic. She dressed well, though she didn't follow fashion. And it was very interesting to be with an older woman. I proposed to her, but she told me not to be silly – "You'll meet someone your age," she said. In my mind it wasn't silly though; I was in love with her. And she loved me. My memory is that we were completely attuned.'

After the war David became an instructor at Sandhurst and then got a job as a bank clerk in the City. Each day, Sofka set off for the Old Vic and he'd take the number 11 bus in to work. Naturally it wasn't long before Sofka took him along to a 'meeting'. 'I wasn't politically minded,' said David. 'I didn't take sides by nature, but I soon joined the Communist Party. I even gave speeches on the King's Road, though the only people listening were three chaps from the Party and a policeman who wanted to have my name. On Sunday mornings, we'd sell *Daily Workers* at World's End.'

I had spoken with enough old Communists and friends of Sofka's to realize that belonging to the Party at this time was almost like joining a cult. Although Sofka remained privately sceptical about some aspects of Communism, it would have been hard to live with a non-believer. 'It was all based on belief,' said a former Party member. 'There was an enormous *élan* around Communism at that time, and belonging brought such an exciting, heady feeling of oneness, in all believing in the same thing. You were a political creature. You were on the side of the angels, without believing in angels.'

'Wherever you went in the world, if you met another CP-er, you trusted each other completely,' said an old comrade. 'It made you part of a family.' Sofka had given herself whole-heartedly to this family; she didn't really have another, and the Party was delighted to have her. 'She was shown off by the leadership,' remembered one friend and colleague. '"Comrade Sofka – our Communist princess!" they'd say.'

For many years, Sofka's belief in socialism was the most significant element in her life. All her passion was thrown into promoting the only political system that seemed to address not only her long-standing unease at social injustice, but also the pain she had suffered during the war. The personal desolation provoked by Grey's death and then Darling's were confronted in her battle to change the world; Communism brought comfort in the promise of a better future.

In 1947, Sofka and David started up a magazine with two friends, the journalist and writer Maurice Rosenbaum and his wife Eve, who lived near by. David searched through his papers until he unearthed a copy of their monthly publication, *Front Page*. Boldly black and red, the cover was a patchwork of newspaper front pages; inside, national and international newspapers from all political viewpoints were raided to provide the 'full story' on foreign affairs (slanted leftwards, naturally). But by now Communism and the Soviet Union were going out of fashion again. Who would give funding for such a venture when an iron curtain was 'descending across the continent' (as Churchill put it) and the chill of a cold war was already in the air? 'We only had two issues before we ran out of money. It was a dismal failure,' David admitted, smiling.

I had noticed a small reference to this short-lived publication in Sofka's memoirs, but there was nothing to hint that David was more than an acquaintance. I wondered why she left these gaps; it certainly wasn't prudery. Later, after talking to others, I sensed that Sofka probably hadn't felt as deeply about her young man as he had about her. When David eventually fell in love with someone his own age – Marjo – Sofka showed little dismay. 'She said, "*C'est magnifique, Marjo!*"' said Marjo, explaining how she had known Sofka a little from before, as she too had been interned in Vittel. 'Sofka was a person who dominated problems. She was very, very strong.'

Among his papers, David also found his old passport from 1946. Wearing army uniform, he has the film-star good looks of a young, Gallic David Niven. One eyebrow is slightly raised, giving him a quizzical gaze. I could quite see why Sofka would have snapped him up. But apart from what must have been at least a sensuous diversion, David shared other things with Sofka too. Thanks to his sister, he was automatically an honorary member of la Petite Famille, and as a Jew he was someone in whom she was now naturally interested – she also made numerous other Jewish friends after the war. In an environment where the Holocaust was still not widely discussed, David was a direct link to Sofka's war experiences. His father (plus grandfather and uncles), like Darling, had been killed at Auschwitz and his family had lost everything, including their home. As a Jew, David probably also shared Sofka's sense of being an outsider; neither could really belong in England. Perhaps he also reminded her of Grey, who had been around the same age when she met him a decade previously; another honourable, sensitive, intelligent, adoring younger man, but what seemed a lifetime later.

I asked David about Sofka's sons; it seemed so odd that none of them ever realized their mother was living with him.

'Peter and Ian didn't come to London often, and I'd keep out of the way then,' explained David. As to Patrick, 'he looked like a child who wanted his mother's affection but didn't get what he was hoping for. She loved her children, but they were a nuisance.' The three sons confirmed this. Peter and Ian remembered disliking their occasional visits to the gloomy, cave-like flat in Oakley Street, where piles of clothes and unwashed plates lay unattended. They preferred the forays into Soho,

Nobody in Sofka's family knew that she lived with David Rocheman in London for three years after the war. He was sixteen years younger than her but remembered that they were 'completely attuned'. When I met him in Paris, he revealed that he had asked her to marry him and she had told him not to be silly.

learning to eat with chopsticks at cheap Chinese cafés, or trips to the theatre and then dingy, smoky Jack's Club.

Although Patrick was around most, he recalled barely seeing his mother. 'I was rather afraid of her,' he admitted. 'She was very practical, but not loving. She taught me Latin. And Kipling's *Just So Stories* were my Bible. But there were no hugs. She and my father wanted me – I was their love child . . . but she left me in England, and then didn't see me for another four years. By then it was too late. She never spoke about my father and I never asked.' Patrick spent much of his time with an Irish family called the Devlins, whose garden backed on to 20 Oakley Street's outside lavatory. Sofka had been happy that Patrick was cared for by these working-class, Communist neighbours with countless children, but Patrick's memories sound almost like those of an orphan: wandering the streets; playing in the rubble of Chelsea's blitzed ruins; eating fat Mrs Devlin's bread, margarine and sugar; and being beaten with a broomstick, like the rest of her offspring.

It must have been an extraordinary contrast for Patrick when in 1947 he was suddenly smartened up, put in a chauffeur-driven car with his mother and transported to a film studio. Vivien Leigh was acting the title role in *Anna Karenina* and Alexander Korda had been unable to find a boy to play her son, Sergei. Olivier came up with Sofka's son, and with his dark hair, soulful eyes and the Russian good looks which Grey had so appreciated, Patrick turned out perfect for the part. His rendition of a fearful child yearning for maternal love was only too realistic, as Vivien Leigh tucked him up in bed in front of the cameras. Sofka saw the matter in more practical terms; the ten guineas a day plus chaperone's fee was just what was needed to buy Patrick clothes and equipment for school, as money was very short. It was only with help from the RAF Benevolent Fund that she was able to pay for Patrick's schooling, as his Skipwith grandfather never relented, despite requests from Sofka for help with his heir's education.

'Sofka's Saturday Soups' began as a cheap way of producing nourishing food at the end of the war and developed when a few friends came to share it, bringing their own bread, plates and spoons. Eventually it became a well-known Chelsea institution, where writers, poets, actors, journalists, doctors, divorcees, Communists, homosexuals and bohemians of every shade regularly made their way down the scruffy outside steps to Sofka's crowded, inelegant basement and took pot luck from her cauldron. Visitors to the animated court included Dylan Thomas and his wife Caitlin, who lived around the corner, and the actress Peggy Ashcroft. A fellow Communist *habitué* recalled how 'the only thing the crowd at Sofka's Saturday Soups had in common was an interest in the arts and anything that required active work of the brain. None were conservative, but many of them weren't interested in politics. And they all admired and adored Sofka. She was a very beautiful woman, though she didn't behave as though she was. She had a sort of devil-may-care attitude to life.'

Sofka delighted in telling how she regularly fed her unsuspecting guests *pot-au-feu* using horsemeat, as quantities could be bought cheaply and she had nothing against the concept, having lived in France. But food was only incidental to the drinking and talking, talking, talking. Sometimes they'd listen to music or end up dancing and what Sofka described as 'necking'. Beer was fetched in buckets from the Pier pub on the corner of Oakley Street and the Embankment, and sometimes the entire company would walk over the bridge to Battersea, where the pubs stayed open half an hour longer. Dinner was often at midnight, with most guests sitting on the floor or on cushions.

'Sofka had a "soul as open as a shirt" – *dusha na raspashku*,' said a Russian friend of hers from the Chelsea days. 'She had an enormous physical strength,' said another friend. 'She'd do arm-wrestling with men and was stronger than many of them. And she was great fun. Very exciting.'

'She had a Russian temperament,' remembered David's sister, Raymonde. 'I loved that. She could drink a lot, but didn't get drunk. She was a sensualist – she loved food, wine and all that side of things. And she was fascinating, intelligent, poetic, extraordinary . . .'

Everyone remembered Sofka as happy – 'the life and soul of the party', which was usually hers. Now I had discovered that she was also living with a charming, handsome young man who cherished her. They sound like marvellous times: interesting work, political commitment and sexual excitement. And yet she wasn't happy. Her poems show she still desperately missed Grey:

I woke to find the room dark and alone
And life as empty as the empty room,
Without your voice . . .

Her letters later admitted that she had given up on ever finding love again. She didn't really care that she was now regarded as a class traitor and rejected by her former friends and relatives on account of her Communism, but she felt an emptiness which was not filled by all the noise and movement in her life. There was nobody (not even David) who guessed.

* * *

It was while pondering these hidden elements in Sofka's existence that I wondered about Britain's secret services. If she was sad when she looked happy, lived with a man when she supposedly had dozens of different passing lovers, and felt she'd never love again when she was believed to be in love, why shouldn't there be other secrets? Especially the sort that might be hidden away in official buildings where Communists were considered enemies of the people. In 1946 Sofka had given up working for the Old Vic, unable to balance all her activities and feeling too exhausted to cope. She continued as a reader for Olivier, went back to freelancing for Universal Aunts (as a 'have-typewriter-will-travel secretary') and threw herself more keenly into the Party. She quickly took over as branch secretary in Chelsea, and worked in both the Local Government Department and the Propaganda Department. She gave Russian lessons, translated Party documents from Russian and was secretary of the British Soviet Friendship Society. She always suspected that she was being watched and it was with this in mind that I wrote to the enquiries desk at MI5, asking whether they had any record of Sofka Skipwith.

It was only after a second request that I received a reply, on smart dove-grey paper, with a PO Box address and a coat-of-arms saying REGNUM DEFENDE. There *were* records, it emerged. Some of them (up to fifty years ago) would soon be available under the Freedom of Information Act, but 'it might be possible for you to see the papers ahead of release under certain conditions'. Following a wonderfully cloak-and-dagger phone call, where the receptionist claimed there was no such person as the name signed on the letter, I was put through to a suave male voice, which instructed me to come to the 'imposing front door' on Millbank at a specified time and date. On the day, I turned up a bit early and took a couple of photographs outside, until a pair of chummy policemen advised me not to. After I explained I had an appointment inside, one of them added, 'Well, they'll be watching you through cameras! There's a man in there with a whip and a cane!'

Giving up my camera and mobile phone at the front desk, I was handed a security tag and taken up to the fifth floor by a kindly woman. I was strangely fearful as I entered a small, windowless room, where a tall, smiling, strawberry-blond man in a pink shirt, whom I guessed to be in his sixties, introduced himself. He told me his real name, as opposed to the one he had signed on the letters, and I looked around the anonymous, sightless room with dull, sound-proofed acoustics, wondering whether there were hidden cameras. Mr Sutcliffe spoke about Communists and spying after the war.

'The Communist Party was used as a stalking horse for Soviet agents right from the start,' he said, 'whereas the number of people we were employing would hardly have made a team on a rugby field. But they knew they were being bugged at CP headquarters – Blunt had told them from 1941.' I found it slightly hard to concentrate. My gaze kept wandering down to the low table, where two fat, beige files sat waiting, tempting as treasure. PF 93749/V2 SKIPWITH, MRS, SOPHIE. Mr Sutcliffe explained that he would sit with me while I looked. He had a book to read (on spies, naturally) and brought us mugs of Nescafé and chocolate biscuits.

There was a mass of papers: press cuttings, police reports, 'telechecks' (phone-tap records), photographs of letters from Sofka (with envelopes), and page after page of 'extracts' – snippets of gossip, rumour, impressions and information. Some of the extracts were labelled TOP SECRET, some were torn and yellowing, patched up with tape, and many were marked casually in the margins in biro and green pencil, giving references to other people's files. Various pages had been removed for security reasons, possibly because of references to the Soviet Embassy, and some had been censored with white patches. The bundles were both fascinating and repulsive; like witnessing somebody else's dirty secrets and not quite turning away; I was peeping at the peeping Tom. The opening entry was a glamorous 1931 *Evening Standard* photo of Princess Sophie Dolgorouky, posing in fox-furs with a pair of dogs, in what must have been the Duchess of Hamilton's drawing room. I flicked through at random and my eye was caught by the wildly contrasting comments during the mid-1940s.

Metropolitan police report: 'Born 1907, height 5 ft 4 [she was actually five foot seven], medium build, hair dark brown, eyes brown, complexion pale, oval face, usually smartly dressed.'

Extract: 'A Ukrainian woman, apparently married to a British Subject . . . This rather flamboyant creature, in her early thirties, who wears rather outré clothes and looks a typical Chelsea bohemian type, works at the District office with Jack WODDIS'.

Extract: 'This woman is outstandingly intelligent, courageous and active. She is a brilliant linguist with vast contacts in all spheres . . . She is an invaluable recruit for the Communist Party and should be watched.'

Extract: 'BRIT [an MI5 agent] has known this woman for many years and considers her quite unreliable. She is over sexed and this had led to her having many affairs.'

Working my way through the files, I followed Sofka's activities, documented with fastidious detail (unlike the Party's own notoriously patchy records). Meetings in the Chelsea Town Hall with titles like 'Russia – Friend or Foe?'; campaigns for road safety in World's End; articles for the local press (the police comment is mocking – 'invariably taking upon herself the role of "people's champion"'); helping to organize squats for homeless families; protesting about Mosley's freedom to promote Fascism in Britain; and tiny banal details from phone conversations (meeting someone for a film show, or arranging travel plans). It all seemed innocent enough, but it was from a perspective I hadn't imagined I'd gain on her life.

Several reports mentioned Sofka's move to Paris in December 1948, though none explained quite why she suddenly abandoned London. Sofka's own memoirs cite homesickness for Paris, plus the fact that all three of her sons were now in boarding school, but these sound like excuses, especially as there was no work to lure her (Olivier wrote her a reference letter: 'To Whom It May Concern, I have known Sofka Skipwith, man and boy, for fifteen years. She has been private secretary, company secretary, play-reader and present help in time of trouble . . .'). Her transfer coincided with the exact time that David left her for Marjo, but her ex-boyfriend's presence in Paris seems an improbable attraction. This is reinforced by an MI5 extract that describes Sofka as having 'plenty of boyfriends' before she left London for Paris – something that adds weight to the idea that David was not always at the centre of her existence.

More significant was that Sofka still pined for Grey, and London was a reminder of their life together. She couldn't get back to normal, as without him there wasn't a 'normal'. On New Year's Day 1949 she wrote a mournful, lonely poem in the little Paris attic, which she had kept on all this time:

> *. . . Because you lived once – must I love no longer?*
> *Because I loved – can I no longer live?*

It hardly sounds as if Paris was a new start, however much it was Sofka's well-trodden escape route. The city still had fresh memories of the war, despite having regained some of its old elegance. Dior's New Look already had the women stylish and wasp-waisted, but bunches of flowers lay on pavements beneath plaques marking where citizens had died. La Petite Famille was one of the significant attractions of Paris for Sofka. Its members understood only too well her heartache and terrors; many of them were plagued by nightmares, depression and guilt and were still grieving their own dead. Sofka could be herself with these people, who empathized with her inner turmoil and saw past the gregarious, fun-loving creator of Saturday Soups. She described this internal contradiction years later, in a letter to Jack: 'I have seen Belsen a month after it was liberated. And however much I talk nonsense and go mad at parties, it is there as a sort of gaunt background – a reminder of things we must fight with every bit of energy. It's not only war, it is human cruelty . . . I can't accept that an act can be a "crime" if done by a German and a "mistake" if under Stalin. The one desperate conviction I have now is the need for truth – for each one first of all.'

Now forty-one, her dark hair streaked with grey, she found herself looking backwards as well as forwards. Sofka was pleased to return to the people she had known and loved in her youth. She liked 'being among people who speak Russian, who recognize the same quotations, are amused by the same family stories', as she explained in a letter to Peter. All this was evidently more significant than being close to her children, and she did little soul-searching about leaving them; it was good enough that a friend agreed to put Patrick on the train to Paris at school holidays. Twenty years later, Sofka felt sufficiently guiltless to sermonize in her autobiography on motherhood: 'The mother must remain a person with her own life and interests, so as not to resent the children growing up and leading their own lives, so as not to be left with nothing to do but, vampire-like, batten on her own offspring. But having insufficient time to give the child is even worse.'

In the spring of 1949, Sofka worked as an interpreter at the World Peace Congress and then (sometimes single-handedly) on a journal called *In Defence of Peace*. It was a focus on peace that, paradoxically perhaps, preserved war as a central preoccupation. Rabbit, too, kept her own candle burning for the war, reinforced by her recent marriage to Jean-Louis, a young Jewish scientist who had survived Auschwitz, but lost his family there.

Sofka, on the other hand, had turned for love to Russians. Her first fling in Paris was with Yuri, her old *cavaliere servante*, whom she now called 'my everlasting'. He had escaped from a forced-labour camp, joined the Resistance and survived the war in hiding, but he didn't last long with Sofka (he was 'very interesting, but unlivable', she confessed).

It was Yuri's cousin Nikolai who replaced him. Nicky, as Sofka called him, was tall and rangy, with an animated, witty manner and affable ways. Before the war he had been a Chess champion and worked in a bank, but he joined the Foreign Legion and was wounded in the head when his boat was mined in the Mediterranean. That he had been the organizer of Sofka's thwarted wartime escape from Paris is an indication of his versatile intelligence and his social contacts as well as his affection for Sofka. In her memoirs she declared that Nicky 'had always been gaily attentive whenever we met in Paris, as gaily forgetting my existence the moment I left'. Still suffering repercussions from his injury, he was now working for a company that made ballet shoes. Two years younger than Sofka, he not only came from the same sort of White Russian background as her but shared her political leanings. MI5 reports from the early 1950s describe Nicholas Ratkoff-Rojnoff erroneously as Sofka's husband:

Born 3.2.1909, grandson of a Russian Admiral . . . formerly deported from the UK for undesirable activities . . . living in France since 1934 . . . a fanatical Communist, believed to be a member of the Russian CP . . .

Sofka Radkoff

This woman, whose real name is Sofka Skipwith, acted as the Russian–English translater [*sic*] at the Paris World Congress for Peace.

She is at present living with a Russian named Radkoff.

She is described as a fanatical Communist, but intelligent, attractive and charming. 19 September 1949

Sofka's file reveals that she was 'under constant surveillance by the French authorities', and a photographed letter (sinister in white-on-black negative) indicates her plans: 'Nicky has come into a little cash and we are going South,' she confided to a Party colleague, 'to try and buy a house on the sea, where we shall let rooms to comrades only and hope all will come and spend holidays.' While there appears to have been no grand passion (at least on Sofka's part), Nicky evidently seemed the right person to provide not only familiar warmth and Russian liveliness (they knew all the same émigrés in Paris) but also the enticing prospect of a stable home.

Since her return to Paris, Sofka had seen little of her mother, who was habitually in bed 'with a headache' when she visited her apartment. She knew little of how Sophy's long-standing drug habit had turned her into a semi-invalid, and how she only rarely emerged from her squalid, dusty room in a pale old dressing gown. Sophy had shrewdly obtained prescriptions for laudanum from nine different doctors around Paris, also visiting various chemists for the opiate, but the crisis came when she stopped going out and asked Pierre to get the medicines for her. Police inspections of a local pharmacy's drug register uncovered an abnormal number of entries for Sophy Volkonsky and she was questioned at home. She was advised to attend a clinic for treatment while awaiting her appearance in court, and Pierre was forced to reveal all to Sofka when he asked her to help with payment. It was also Sofka's task to help clear out Sophy's room in preparation for her return home. Nobody had been allowed into it for years and she was appalled by what she found: piles of clothes filled with mice nests; untouched copies of the *Times Literary Supplement* covered with spider-webs; unopened letters; congealed coffee in cups; empty medicine bottles; and old hypodermic needles. It was horrifying to discover that this strong, intelligent woman who had been a surgeon and a pilot, who had rescued Pierre from a Bolshevik prison and who was a natural fighter, had been defeated by the pitiful escapism of drugs.

Sophy's decision to kill herself was quite rational. In the clinic she was discovered hoarding sleeping pills and then rescued by nurses when she tried to hang herself, but Princess Volkonsky was nothing if not determined. She was predictably furious with Sofka and Pierre for having entered her room, perhaps because they'd witnessed evidence of what she had become. On the first evening back, deprived of her key, she hammered the door shut with nails. Unknown to anyone, Sophy had hidden four bottles of Veronal – a medication for 'insomnia induced by nervous excitability'. Removing them from under a loose brick, she took dose after dose until she fell asleep with the glass in her hand. In the morning, Pierre was unable to open the door and rushed up to Sofka's attic to fetch her. Sofka later said that she took her time in coming down, understanding quite well what had happened and considering it cruel to try and revive her mother. The fifty-seven-year-old had long dreamed of finding a way of visiting Russia and taking a last look at the Neva, but now that appeared impossible. She could no longer face her Parisian exile, let alone a drugs trial.

Eventually they broke down the door and found Sophy

unconscious but breathing. An ambulance took her to a nursing home and Sofka and Pierre took turns to sit by her bedside. But the prognosis was not good. On the seventh day, Sophy seemed to be waking and, encouraged by the nurse, Sofka spoke to her:

'Moppy, can you hear me? Moppy, come back.'

Sophy's head moved suddenly and she moaned, 'No . . . o . . . o . . . o.' It sounded like a rejection of life. The following day she died.

Given the depressing, sordid details of Sophy's end, I was better able to understand what Rabbit had already told me about how Sofka removed all her mother's papers and burned them. It was a terrible pity for history and for understanding Sophy's extraordinary life, but for an angry, grieving daughter it removed evidence of unhappiness, drugs and chaos – a purification. Perhaps also there was an element of revenge on her cold, severe mother. Could certain papers have even revealed Sophy's disappointment and disapproval of what she saw as her hedonistic, under-achieving daughter? The fire was another instance of Sofka starting again with nothing, as she had now done so many times since childhood. (She must have kept a few documents, as she quoted Sophy's poems and writings in some of her own later work, but the originals have not survived.)

Sofka's dreams of peace and quiet in the Mediterranean with Nicky were displaced by the offer of a job with Progressive Tours – a new Communist travel agency. 'The idea was to create opportunities for the working people of Britain to meet the ordinary people of other countries – surely the best way to overcome prejudice and intolerance, to counter the threat of another war,' wrote Sofka optimistically. 'We proposed arranging group tours for workers – bus drivers, journalists, bakers, engineers and their families at the lowest possible cost.' Their logo was TRAVEL–FRIENDSHIP–PEACE and featured a dove speeding to earth, carrying an olive sprig in its beak and a little suitcase in its claws.

The first trips were to Paris for Bastille Day (advertisements in the *Daily Worker* brought one thousand people), and Sofka seemed ideally placed to take charge. The directors of the firm (Lou Kenton, a Jew from the East End, and his wife Rafa) were Party friends. They told me how Sofka 'feared nobody' and 'didn't care what people thought', bulldozing her way past officious bureaucrats, pushing hotel prices down and even, on occasion, persuading a train driver to delay his departure for her group or to drive backwards (in Bulgaria) to fetch a forgotten passenger. Once, when there were not enough tickets to cover all the children in the party, she sneaked the children from carriage to carriage during the ticket inspections and gleefully outwitted the inspectors. It must have felt like child's play after the dangerous deceptions she had organized during the war. Sofka showed her tourists the famed delights of Paris but also took them to meet trade unionists and to the Maison des Enfants des Fusillés – an institution for war orphans, where many regular visitors 'adopted' a young friend and brought presents or food. When Prog T (as the company was known) started trips to Eastern Europe, it was, for several years, the only agency to break through the ice which had set in between East and West.

The MI5 files contained numerous records of tapped phone calls and intercepted letters going between the Kentons and Sofka. 'We had a person in Progressive Tours,' admitted Mr Sutcliffe, when I asked how certain photographs and other pieces of evidence had turned up. Several police reports describe Sofka's trips between London and Paris: 'A discreet search of her baggage (flight from Paris AF 520) by HM Customs did not reveal anything of interest.'

When I spoke to the elderly Kenton couple, they were

amazed: 'Imagine having a "mole" in Prog T!' said Rafa. 'And all those hours spent listening to our domestic conversations . . . But they didn't manage to go and catch the real spies! What is funny is how MI5 showed a complete lack of understanding of what we were doing. They were so convinced that something funny was going on, that there was some sort of clandestine activity. But as far as we were concerned Prog T meant working very self-sacrificingly to raise every penny we could. Lou, Sof and I all worked for "Party wages" – the absolute minimum, to run an efficient business. And Prog T was the only branch of the Party which made money!'

Although Sofka spent part of the year preparing trips and another part as a tour guide, there were still quiet periods. Having abandoned the move south, she and Nicky decided to move into the countryside outside Paris. Nicky's war injury had left him plagued by headaches and he was becoming increasingly weak, while she longed to settle down in a real home with a garden as she had had with Grey in Cookham Dean. The dream cottage was a small, two-storey building on a plateau above the village of Gif-sur-Yvette, about half an hour south of Paris by train. Sofka loved it and was soon keeping rabbits and chickens, growing vegetables, bottling fruit and learning from the village women how to make *marc*. They acquired a black kitten which they named Chort (Russian for devil) and friends from Paris visited at weekends, including la Petite Famille, various Russians and assorted intellectuals, actors and artists. At Easter, the neighbours gave them a kid from their herd of goats to barbecue in the garden. For a while, David and Marjo moved in with their young child, until they eventually built their own house around the corner; Sofka firmly believed in keeping lovers as friends if possible, enjoying the closeness 'with the madness forgotten'. Patrick was duly put

MI5 files described Nicky as 'a fanatical Communist' and erroneously, as Sofka's husband. This picture shows him looking well, with little sign of the head injury from the war that would bring such horrific problems. Sofka's three sons appear cheerful as they pose with him in Paris (from L: Peter, Patrick, Ian).

on the train from London each holiday, and Peter and Ian made regular visits.

Sofka's letters from this era indicate her delight at 'doing fairly little' after being so busy for the last twenty years, though her journeys, criss-crossing Eastern Europe by train, were filled with all the discomforts of cheap travel compounded by sleepless nights, awkward officials and ignorant tourists.

'The tourist job I grouse at but enjoy – travelling is always fun,' she wrote to the teenage Peter. 'And to be mistress of one's own time for six months of the year is such bliss that I wouldn't exchange it for the highest salary.' With her and Nicky's income, they could live simply but comfortably; there was even enough for a few extravagances and Sofka developed a lasting fondness for the flowery perfume Quadrille, made by the fashionable Spanish designer Balenciaga. In another letter to Peter, she described the luxury of staying in bed on a stormy day ('sounds disgusting, doesn't it?'), getting up only for 'an excursion to the kitchen to produce a wonderful omelette with almonds and served burning with brandy like a plum pudding. The pleasures of the table should not be despised, as the flesh is ours, why not extract from it the maximum pleasure?' Somewhat later, when Peter was a student at Oxford, Sofka explained why she had moved in with Nicky. Evidently she was not in love, but she was content:

> I've known Nicky for over 20 years and have always liked
> him a lot, while he invariably fell in love with me every
> time we met . . . You see after Grey was killed it was awful
> in London. A job is all very well, but I've had jobs from the
> age of 17 and one gets tired of having jobs! Also after one
> has become used to the married state it is very difficult to
> live alone. I don't mean physically – there were always

plenty of volunteers to remedy that deficiency and I confess I permitted them to remedy – but purely from the point of view of sharing the unexciting daily round. My contention is that (as one gets older) it is more important to have someone to help with the laundry than someone writing sonnets to your eyebrows.

It wasn't only laundry. Sofka and Nicky shared not only the same friends, but the same attitudes. While both believed in building a socialist future, they lived their life determinedly in the present. As a couple, they were keen party-goers (he was what she called 'gay') and brave drinkers and they never tried to save any money. If Nicky had any spare cash, he'd blow it on taking Sofka out to a wonderful dinner or buying something extravagant. And she was the same. Both knew that life was too fragile to take anything beyond today for granted.

Sofka became increasingly interested in her sons; she delighted in discussing books with them – her reading-lists were wide-ranging and well planned – and her affectionate letters were full of advice and plans, but eschewed maternal tones in favour of the teasingly friendly. As they grew older, the teenage boys appreciated the visits to France: Peter remembered busking with an accordion in Paris; riding a Mobylette; and discovering Sartre and 'unsuitable' authors like Henry Miller among the burgeoning collection of books that swamped Sofka's tiny sitting room. He also persuaded his mother to explain the facts of life; sex was still an opaque mystery to him. However, ordinary life was lived far apart and Sofka was often away. According to Ian, 'Mother would send postcards saying "Do write!" but with no address.'

When Grey's father died in 1950, twelve-year-old Patrick inherited the baronetcy. This produced great hilarity amongst

Sofka's Party comrades. More controversial perhaps was Sofka's decision to send Patrick to Harrow, taking advantage of its generous terms to sons of Old Harrovians killed in the war. She confessed in her memoirs that she went against her better judgement, fearing that it would be held against her if she prevented it, but also worrying that he would suffer there from a lack of money and a conventional home. And indeed, young Sir Patrick hated Harrow: 'Socially, I was like a little London street urchin,' he said. 'I spoke with a cockney accent. That and a baronetcy didn't go together. I felt caught between two social levels, belonging to neither.' His journeys back and forth to France were lonely and frightening and often badly planned: once, aged thirteen, Patrick slept the night in Waterloo Station and was picked up by a man who raped him. Later, he was expelled from Harrow for stealing. With his mother often away, he spent many holidays back with family members of Mrs Butler, who had cared for him during the war. Although Sofka would periodically rush to England to help one of her sons (her intervention saved Peter from being sent down from Oxford for rowdy behaviour), unknowingly – or perhaps unavoidably – she had made her sons replicate the haphazard, motherless patterns of her own teen years.

Sofka's two Zinovieff sons were not having an easy time either. Their father had married the Duchess of Hamilton's eldest daughter, Jean, in 1947. Whilst Sofka's post-war, Communist life had made her *persona non grata*, Leo had replaced her as the Douglas-Hamiltons' close friend and, ultimately, relation. A divorced mother of four, Jean was narrow-minded and snobbish (she insisted on curtseying to the duke – her own brother – and was rude to the servants), but observers saw that she and Leo had at last found peace and calm with each other. They moved to a farm in Sussex, where Jean proved an archetypal wicked stepmother, favouring her own children over her two stepsons. She also persuaded Leo to uproot the Zinovieff boys from Guildford Royal Grammar and a stable home with their doting grandparents in order to send them to the 'right sort' of boarding school. Peter went miserably to Gordonstoun and Ian to Harrow, both returning to Sussex in the holidays.

The difficulties turned into tragedy when Leo was killed in a train crash in 1951. Jean refused to have anything more to do with Peter and Ian, banning them from their home. She wrote cruel letters: Peter was castigated for not making his father happier while he was alive, and she insulted her 'hysterical' Zinovieff in-laws for draping the death of their son 'with Russian drama' in their anguished – and ignored – pleas for burial rather than cremation. Ian was forced to leave school at sixteen, as Jean would not pay his fees, and she reported eighteen-year-old Peter to the police for 'stealing' some silver teaspoons from home and pawning them. An MI5 'telecheck' shows that Sofka did at least go over to England a week after Leo's death. 'Kenton (Lou) to Lady Jean Zinovieff. Unidentified woman. Peter comes to phone, arranges to meet at Eve Rosenbaum's flat tomorrow.' It was chilling to read of these dreadful times in this manner.

At MI5, I found a photograph of Sofka from around this time labelled 'Skipwith, Sophie Petrovna'. It didn't look like a spy picture, as she is smiling for the camera, but I wondered how it ended up here. Was some deception involved? She has put on weight rather majestically and is wearing a loud floral frock, a rope of dark beads and a jaunty turban hat, and is smoking with an extravagant bamboo cigarette holder. This cheery, theatrical exterior is belied by her eyes, which reveal something more of her troubles. Nicky had looked like a solution, but was now her main problem. His headaches had become so severe that he was

It is unclear where MI5 got hold of this photograph of Sofka. It was taken on a visit to her son Peter when he was at Oxford in the mid-1950s. Despite the jaunty exterior, her eyes reveal something of the dreadful problems she was having with Nicky.

spending weeks on end in bed and had stopped working. In 1952, the doctors recommended a leucotomy, admitting that he might be '*un peu diminué*', but that the pain would go. In an operation mainly used for helping patients with delusions and severe mental disorders, a sharp instrument was inserted through Nicky's tearducts, penetrated the bone and disconnected the brain's frontal lobes. Nicky came home without the headaches, but within months had become an imbecile. Sofka's three sons were appalled at witnessing the rapid disintegration, feeling embarrassed when Nicky picked cigarette ends out of the gutter or urinated in public. They didn't want to come and stay 'with a loony'. Friends, too, found it hard when Nicky turned up at their homes to beg for money, and most visitors to Gif gradually stopped coming, unable to cope with Nicky's drunkenness and unpredictability. To add to the problems, Sofka had to leave Nicky, often for weeks and months on end, while she travelled for Progressive Tours. There was now barely enough money on which to survive and certainly no surplus with which to pay a full-time nurse.

1956 was a year of troubles for many. The Suez crisis had raised fears of war, while the Soviet Union's brutal invasion of Hungary shocked many Communists into leaving the Party. What with Khrushchev's exposure of the appalling horrors of Stalin's rule, there seemed little left to inspire faith.

At a domestic level, Sofka was plagued by Nicky's deterioration. She normally left money with friends, to be handed out gradually to Nicky while she was away, and expected to find problems when she returned from abroad; she learned to hide precious belongings after Nicky sold her fur coat and her mother's last pieces of jewellery to buy wine, cigarettes and sweets. Nothing prepared her however for the discovery, on one homecoming, that Nicky had sold their house in Gif for a pittance. She located him in a slum near the Porte des Lilas. He had bought two rooms, former stables, without furniture or bathroom. A bare bulb hung from the ceiling. Water was collected from a trough in the building's courtyard (a photograph shows Nicky blithely bathing in it). The building was always noisy, and filled with unemployed men with nowhere to go. The only toilet was a stinking, communal, outdoor affair near the dustbins, reminiscent of the Besançon camp.

There seemed no escape from the nightmare. Sofka thought about suicide and even made some half-hearted attempts with the gas oven, but ultimately came to the same conclusion as one of her favourite poets, Dorothy Parker, whom she often quoted:

Sofka returned from her travels in 1956 to find that Nicky had sold their house and was living in two unfurnished slum rooms in Paris. Water was collected from a trough in the courtyard, where Nicky can be seen here bathing. He looks quite content and was probably unaware that Sofka was almost driven to suicide by the situation.

Razors pain you;
Rivers are damp;
Acids stain you;
And drugs cause cramp.
Guns aren't lawful;
Nooses give;
Gas smells awful;
You might as well live.

The getaway came later that year. Nicky's brother and father returned to Paris from Morocco, where they'd been living, and agreed to care for him. Plagued by guilt, disappointment and sadness, Sofka did what she always did in a crisis, and fled.

CHAPTER 9

THE OWL

Thou blind man's mark, thou fool's self-chosen snare
                                                    – Sir Philip Sidney, 'Desire'

When people asked Sofka where she was living during the late fifties, she quipped, 'In a train.' It wasn't far from the truth. She was now travelling for up to nine months of the year, taking in Yugoslavia, Czechoslovakia, Hungary, Bulgaria, Poland and Russia. At least the long, uncomfortable rail journeys were a distraction from the debilitating despondency she felt at abandoning Nicky. This peripatetic work was another version of running away, though there were times when she was so anguished that she wondered whether it would have been better to stay. The indomitable tour leader who bulldozed and beguiled her groups around Eastern Europe now became tearful over a laddered stocking or a delayed train. It was as if all the culpability she had never felt about leaving her children was condensed in this remorse, which gave her palpitations and heart pain. To add to her dejection, her faith in Communism was at a low point: 'And there was I, alone, of no use to man or beast, unable to fling myself back into party work because of a lack of conviction,' she wrote later. It wasn't what she had envisaged for her fiftieth year.

Train life was tough. Most destinations took a good two days to reach, though it was sixty-eight hours to Sofia and seventy-two to Moscow. With Progressive Tours' budget there was no question of sleepers, let alone flying; it just meant sitting up through the nights, second-class. When Sofka was tired she read thrillers, but her chief consolation during the tedious journeys was studying Shakespeare. Her notes on Shakespeare's life and works fill many exercise books and files and reveal a serious attempt at learning: annotated reading lists which indicate that she managed to read all the plays, sonnets and poems; pages of her thoughts (cross-referenced to other commentators') on the Bard's subject matters and style; and extensive analysis of the enigma of 'W.S's character and life'. Much of this work was done jolting along on uncomfortable trains, crossing and recrossing the Iron Curtain. Sometimes she was alone, other times with groups of tourists: border checks; luggage searches in the nightmarish small hours; dawn pacing along desolate platforms in the middle of nowhere; disagreeable breakfasts of cold water, hard-boiled eggs and stale bread.

Sofka really didn't have a home. Her belongings were stored with Rabbit in Paris, and when she returned there between trips, she slept on different friends' sofas and camp-beds. To add to the sense of being adrift, her sons were now grown-up: Peter was twenty-three and doing a D.Phil. in geology at Oxford, where he was known as a 'wild Russian' for his uncontrolled existence of parties and practical jokes. He was supposedly 'caring' for eighteen-year-old Patrick, who lived with him, attending a crammer before he went to university. While Sofka could easily comprehend excess as an escape from pain, Ian's progress was more of a mystery to his mother. Aged twenty-one, he left the navy and became a devout Presbyterian, even contemplating joining the ministry. In April 1957 he married a young woman he met through the Church. The three sons now barely knew where their mother was and it was often impossible to contact her. When they did meet, Sofka emphasized her work's inherent comedy: the herd-like stupidity of tourists in groups and their inflexible conservatism when confronted by foreign foods or unconventional toilets. Or she'd describe the ridiculously slothful Yugoslavian trains, whose drivers stopped their ancient engines in the middle of fields to pick up passengers and livestock waiting by the track, or to drink with friends.

Sometimes the routines turned into adventures. In February 1957, Sofka became the first Western travel agent to enter Albania, taking the maiden flight into the country from Belgrade. It was a tiny plane, complete with air hostess, and Sofka was the only passenger. There were dreadful storms, and it was hard for her to avoid picturing a terrible end on the dark, jagged peaks of Montenegro's mountains below, as the aeroplane was tossed about and crockery smashed in a cubby-hole. On landing, an Albanian official explained that it was a national holiday and they were expecting a state visit from Bulgaria. As Sofka's car approached Tirana, the waiting crowds assumed that this must be the Bulgarian dignitaries. Bands struck up, the people waved flags, and Sofka took full advantage: 'I waved my hand in acknowledgement, like royalty,' she wrote, 'grinning at the discomforted faces of those in charge now trying to silence the bands and crowds.'

In July of the same year, Sofka took a group of tourists to the Soviet Union for the second year running. Again, it was overwhelming to see Leningrad – both familiar and changed since her childhood. They stayed at the Astoria, where her father had so often dined out in its heyday before 1914. 'No matter how often I have been back to Leningrad,' Sofka wrote, 'I am each time as intoxicated by its beauty.' She was enchanted by her birthplace, noting what Pushkin called 'its severe and slender air' and what she described as its 'broad nature'. In a person, she explained, this particularly Russian compliment implies kindness, generosity, understanding and warmth – endearing qualities which she recognized in the city.

She revisited her old haunts. Her mother's place on the English Embankment had become a communal apartment and the old sitting room was now home to a whole family. But it was still recognizable from when Sofka had lain by the fire on a bear-rug, gazing at the walls lined with books stamped with D for Dolgorouky and at the skeleton in the corner. The grandeur of the vista across the Neva had barely changed; it was what her mother had always pined for. Talking to the inhabitants, Sofka discovered that the 'house superintendent' had been a maid in the flat below theirs before the Revolution. And yes, she remembered a little girl with long dark plaits. The two women embraced.

Once, at a group visit to Leningrad's 'House of the Veterans of the Stage', Sofka found herself talking to an attractive former actress in her late sixties. When the woman learned that Sofka was a Dolgorouky, she was overcome with emotion. 'Oh Petya! What a wonderful man he was,' she said, remembering Sofka's father, her eyes full of tears. 'I knew him very, very well indeed. So gay, so handsome.' She turned out to have been Petya's mistress before the First World War and was delighted to finally meet his daughter. From then on, whenever Sofka went to Leningrad, she always organized an outing to the retired actors.

Sofka also met up with Nina, an old émigrée friend from 1920s Paris, who was one of the very few to 'go home' in the fifties. She found Nina's example inspiring. Through her she met 'ordinary Russians', and spent countless evenings sitting around kitchen tables, drinking vodka and talking poetry and politics. Everyone was still discussing the previous year's astonishing revelations by Khrushchev about Stalin's atrocities. Younger people in particular were stunned to learn that their god had in fact been a monster. Sofka, like Nina, remained a critical supporter of the Soviet regime – the awful details of concentration camps and executions were not enough to throw her off course. However much she recognized the problems – the lack of human rights and of freedom of speech – she still believed that Russia offered something that was missing in the deeply unjust, materialistic West. She would not abandon her faith in the noble idealism of perfect socialism; it went without saying that there should be equal opportunities for everyone – her own experiences of both privilege and deprivation only confirmed that. Her excuse for Soviet oppression was that it had not begun under the Communist regime but was a continuation of what she called 'the historical, paranoid fear of dissent that has dogged Russian rulers through the centuries'. She liked to quote Tolstoy's remark about tsarist censorship in his time: 'It is not so much what I have written as what I might have written that is affected.' Far from being disappointed by Soviet reality, Sofka was enamoured enough with what she saw to fantasize about returning to live there one day.

Sofka must have surprised her group of English trade-union officials, factory workers and unfashionable idealists when she took them on an Intourist visit to the Bobrinsky Palace, now the Geography Department of Leningrad's university. This had been her grandparents' house, she announced, pointing out the huge stuffed bears which had been shot by her relations, the pens where the cubs had been kept, the garden where she had played as a child and the familiar furniture, much of which was still in place. It was quite right, she told them, that all this had been

*On her trips to Leningrad in the 1950s, Sofka sometimes
contemplated 'going home' and settling there. She was
'intoxicated by its beauty' and she loved being with Russians.
Even the revelations of Stalin's atrocities didn't make her abandon
her belief in the possibility of ideal socialism.*

taken from her family; far better that it should belong to the
nation and be used for educating young people.

Even more astounded were the Russians who learned of
Sofka's origins. Far from seeing her as a former enemy of the
people, Comrade Dolgorouky was warmly welcomed, kissed
and embraced. Once, she was picked up by an armed guard for
photographing the back of the Bobrinsky house from the street,
which happened to be in a sensitive military area. Sofka
enjoyed her subsequent interrogation at the nearby army
headquarters, pleading innocence as a British tourist guide. The
increasingly annoyed officer insisted on knowing her name.
'Skipwith,' she kept replying as he banged on the desk,
demanding her Russian name. It was then that she pulled rank,

moving over to the window and pointing to the Bobrinsky and Dolgorouky Mansions, which were both in view.

'Comrade,' she said, 'do you see that house? I lived there – it used to belong to my grandmother. And you see that house? I used to play there. It was my grandfather's.'

The officer insisted: 'WHAT IS YOUR NAME?'

'Dolgorouky.'

The officer walked to the door, opened it and saluted.

'I quite understand.'

In Moscow, too, she was fêted; there were banquets, speeches and endless vodka toasts, which Sofka described in a letter: 'Somehow am being greeted rather like my great-grand dad himself. Intourist has really put itself out: a whole deputation and photographer to meet ('Where is the Dolgorouky?').'

On the trip that summer was a small, watchful toolmaker from London called Jack King. A forty-year-old bachelor, Jack was active in the trade unions – elected to shop steward in Acton – and a long-standing though independent-minded Communist. Following the Soviet Union's suppression of Hungary in 1956, he had wanted to see for himself this vast country, which he read so much about in the *Daily Worker*. He was evidently intrigued by the ebullient, opinionated tour leader, who had already instructed him (and many others) in the art of proper Russian vodka-drinking: 'You swallow it in one gulp, throwing your head back to assist its passage. The vodka should barely touch the lips.' And then there were the toasts to accompany each glass: the second round is justified by saying, 'One leg is lame,' to be followed by 'God loves a trinity,' 'A house has four corners,' and 'the fifth wheel of the cart.'

It wasn't until the group reached Minsk that the unlikely liaison struck up. The Byelorussian capital was not exactly a romantic setting; Dzerzhinsky, the founder of the Soviet secret police, had been born near by and the whole place had been devastated by the war. Now, it was being turned into a model Soviet city and bristled with hideous architecture. I don't know which hotel they stayed in, but I imagine it as a large, anonymous block, still smelling of grey paint and wet cement, somewhere near the newly built Victory Square.

Sofka once told me the story of how she and Jack got together. 'There I was in bed in the hotel one morning,' she said, 'sleeping off a heavy drinking bout, when the phone rang. Half asleep, I answered. It was a colleague down in the hotel lobby, in a panic. One of the tourists was missing. A Mr King.' Sofka replied that she couldn't help and turned over in bed to nestle closer to Mr King, lying asleep beside her. I pictured them like a couple on a saucy seaside postcard – the large, heavy-bosomed woman about to squash the skinny little man – but that was imagining it over twenty years later. At the time, men still found Sofka's powerful body highly desirable.

Sofka liked Jack. He was intelligent and witty and perhaps she felt his patent differences from her were some kind of foil. Where she placed words (spoken and written) at the centre of her life, he was content to be silent. Where she had no home and no roots, he had been born, brought up and lived all his life in Shepherd's Bush. Where she was emotional and expressive, he was closed and independent – he seemed to need nobody. Jack's mother had died when he was seven, he had left school at fourteen and he had never had a serious, long-term relationship with a woman. His great passion was athletics: he still trained as a runner, entered numerous marathon races and coached younger athletes, and he had been a 'sponge carrier' for runners in the 1948 Olympic Games. His friends used to say, 'He'd make a lovely husband, but you've got to run fast to catch him.'

Sofka didn't take this kind of 'bedding', as she called it, too seriously and it didn't look like something that would go further. Quite apart from adventures with her tourists, she had admirers in many of her regular destinations, some of whom had become close friends, welcoming her on each visit. In fact, she had become notorious for her wild parties and casual flings. A top-secret MI5 document from 1955 noted a bugged conversation between two officials at Party headquarters in London: '. . . one of the Scottish Comrades who had been on the French trip had come in to complain about the immoral goings on. Apparently Sofka had been the prime instigator . . .' Later, Sofka proudly told Patrick that she'd had over a hundred lovers in her life.

* * *

It does not seem likely that Sofka's decision to move back to London that autumn was connected with Jack, but perhaps he was there, somewhere in the back of her mind. Certainly Paris was now unbearable, and she learned that Nicky had been sent to an institution after becoming violent. And so it was that, thirteen years after she had started from square one in London in 1944, she did the same thing again. True, this time she had a job, continuing her work with Prog T, but there was no home, no partner, and her sons were dispersed and living their own lives. She took a bedsit in Chelsea, at 18 Bramerton Street, where it was back to feeding the water heater with pennies when she wanted a bath and anaesthetizing herself with noise, drink and constant socializing. The men she found in her bed in the mornings were meaningless. She didn't care. 'It didn't matter what I did or who I was with,' she later admitted, declaring that 'not a quiver had pierced the surface of my emotions' since 1944, when Darling had been deported.

Nobody would have guessed her sadness and loneliness – 'the coldness', as she confessed in a letter to Jack, 'of not really being needed, or being part of anyone's life . . . and the utter futility of one's own'. Just as in the days of Sofka's Saturday Soups, she appeared to be the most enthusiastic guest at the numerous parties she attended. One Communist friend remembered her from that time as 'very big, laughing all the time and very happy. She was always eating something funny – half a chicken or maybe a melon . . .' Others described her cheerily haphazard way with clothes. Once, when her sandal strap came off just before a reception at the Soviet Embassy, she got a hammer and nail and nailed it back on, saying, 'Nobody notices your shoes.' She was also known to turn up in the Prog T office saying, 'I made a dress before breakfast today.' 'And it looked like it!' remembered a colleague. 'Even though she *could* look terrific, clothes didn't matter.'

In London, Jack was among Sofka's occasional bedfellows, but it took time before she admitted that this was more than something purely physical. Between meetings, she began to write him affectionate letters and cards (neither had a telephone) and as with almost anyone she had ever cared for, she invented animal names: he was Mongoose or Goose; she was Owl. 'How could I have guessed,' she wrote as she saw him more regularly, 'that what seemed merely pleasant bedding with a person I found very attractive would, as I gradually got to know you better, turn into what might be termed a "Mongoose way of life"?' What Jack made of her long, rambling missives, often scribbled at four in the morning and picked up again the next day, one can only guess. Her long analyses of French 'sentimental friendship' and the descriptions of her complicated life must have seemed terribly foreign. Jack, on the other hand, was known for his belief that 'if you say anything, it gets around'.

His replies were evidently few and brief; the complaints from Sofka that he hasn't written, that he 'mistrusts words' and instructions not to thank her for her letters all bear testament to that. In any case, his letters were never found; it is possible that he burned them after Sofka's death. Hers, on the other hand, give great insight into her character and feelings, as she teases, flatters, criticizes, quotes poems, debates Shakespeare, queries politics and makes confessions.

> A gypsy's life like mine is fun, and one makes it fun but underneath has always been such a hunger for roots of some kind. Strangely enough, this mad scramble over the surface of Europe has never been deliberate – always 'circumstances.' Whenever there's been a chance of staying put – I've seized it and stayed. Until for some reason I've been obliged to set off again. I'm sure you'll never believe me, but wait and see.

This was not quite accurate, as Sofka's move to France in 1948 *had* been chosen, but the emotion was true; she longed to settle down. And against all odds, her last statement was eventually vindicated, although initially Jack didn't look like the man who would be there to witness it. At weekends he was busy with his running and coaching with the Thames Valley Harriers and during the week they only had time for the odd evening out. His previous relationships had been exclusively light-hearted – weekly outings with young women from Shepherd's Bush. More, he believed, was unnecessary and would lead to boredom.

Reacting to Jack's moderation in love, Sofka's writing became ever more expressive ('darling, isn't it dangerous for me to take up a pen!'), and by the spring of 1958 bedsit life was definitely looking up.

> Listen, I like being with you because of you. Not just because you're a wonderful lover. And life is very, very short . . .

As you know, over these years I've gone to bed merrily with anyone who seemed pleasant and entertaining. It was an agreeable pastime, good exercise and meant a very little for a week or two, a day or two, an evening. Fizzy like champagne and flat as quickly. But no sooner does one's emotion become involved than physical attraction for anyone else disappears. I could no more at present go to bed with anyone else than jump into a cess pool.

A dedicated Communist and Trade Unionist, Jack wanted to see the Soviet Union for himself after the suppression of Hungary in 1956. His improbable relationship with Sofka began on one of her tours in 1957. Whereas her life was now lived mostly on trains, he had barely left his native Shepherd's Bush. Aged forty, he had never previously had a long-term relationship with a woman.

Sofka often described her aversion to conventionality: 'I am so convinced that in order to get the most out of life one must be ready to experience anything – and unafraid. That's where most people fail: afraid of what the neighbours will say, what people will think, afraid of losing a little comfort, of having to assume responsibility: Christ, the weak cowardice of humanity. Thank heavens that once in a while one comes across creatures like you.'

By the end of the summer of 1958, Jack was the still point at the centre of Sofka's life: 'You as a friend are one I treasure above all, you as a companion – a "life-sharer" – are so completely satisfying, that I am bored with anyone else, you as a lover lead me to the utter fulfilment of love . . . Your most unlawfully wedded (bedded?) Owl'. '. . . You know, the last time I was happy – like this, over a long period, I mean, was in 1938. That's a hell of a long time ago. So you can chalk it up in your life, because it is a terrific thing to achieve, to make another person happy.'

Although her existence was far from easy, she claimed to live 'entirely in the present' and not to want any more than she now had. 'And surely that, if anything, is the supreme gift of the little fishes,' she added, using one of her favourite expressions. Sofka often invoked the little fishes instead of a prayer, perhaps cocking a snook at Fate, which had been such a bully. They were not her invention, but came from the old saying 'Ye gods and little fishes', which James Joyce also quoted in *Ulysses*. Whether or not the little fishes had brought her Jack, Sofka's rediscovery of powerful emotions was a revelation; she even quoted the Swinburne poem that Grey had sent in his last letter, without revealing its connotations:

> *I that have love and no more*
> *Give you but love of you, sweet!*

But Jack did not always provoke tenderness:

Do you know why I write to you? It has suddenly dawned: because if I try and talk, you run away . . .

You, the cold and the reserved, should never have got mixed up with any Russian. But now you have – make the best of a bad job and enjoy it . . .

. . . Never have I had dealings with anyone who is so filled with complexes so self-conscious.

Occasionally, Sofka mentions her sons: 'A telegram has just come from Patrick [now studying geology at Trinity College, Dublin]: Send Sixty Crumpets Express Urgent. So off I go to buy and dispatch sixty crumpets. One joy of having offspring is that life is not dull for long – not with pups like Peter or Patrick . . .'

On another occasion, when Sofka explained that she would be seeing Peter instead of Jack one evening, she sounded apologetic: 'My offspring take the place in my life that athletics do in yours. See?' And if this remark sounds vaguely insulting to her sons, it was probably meant to indicate that they were as central to her life as Jack's training was to his. Whether this was really the case is another matter; Jack certainly spent more time running than she did with her 'pups'.

Sofka was nothing if not contradictory with respect to Jack. She would declare that she now wanted something more than a 'bed-partner' – 'if it's only that, frankly I'll try as quickly as possible to get you out of my system'. But she also claimed to appreciate the sense of freedom in 'our little love affair'. After all, she could never be heartbroken again, she argued, quoting a favourite Chinese proverb: 'He who has been drowned does not fear the sea.' Having requested Jack's photograph to take with her on her travels, she then teased: 'Any moment I feel at all sentimental I have only to take out one of your photos, gasp: "What? That?" And go cynical and tough.'

When abroad, Sofka bombarded Jack with cards, telegrams and letters, often complaining at his silence or moodiness and playing about with their animal names, transmogrifying his moods into bizarre cross-breeds, complete with little sketches:

A great thought struck me. Religion. Three in one and one in three. See how it works:
1. MONGOOSE – a nice beast, amusing and loveable
2. PIGGOOSE – horrible animal that grunts and snarls, has not bitten yet but will shortly
3. PORCUGOOSE – a wickedly mischievous creature that shoots barbed quills into one's skin when one comes near it.

Sofka herself is always Owl: 'Darling, I think I'm an owl: night bird . . . rather evil, but soft and oh so wise. Also it hoots.' She spent her free time, whether in Prague, Budapest, Sofia, Moscow or Warsaw, searching out owls of wood, metal, glass, stone or clay to bring back for Jack. Sofka became 'Your owl in every way and obviously your very private zoo'. The zoo was code for making love: 'I'll try and bring a spot of food from Vienna – otherwise we'll go out and eat. And think up something nice for Sunday evening – of course in the afternoon we'll go to the zoo . . .'

Sofka delighted in hamming up her traveller's tales, with their drinking bouts and flirtations: 'Superb lunch starting with a double martini, then beer, then schnapps, then whisky . . .' she wrote with a surprisingly steady hand. She evidently enjoyed describing the men she turned down: the Moscow 'boyfriend' who inevitably asks her to marry him ('Goose, I'm a vain bitch. I like being proposed to at the end of an evening – the yearly proposal! I purr . . . and refuse'); the hotel guests ('Have been amorously attacked by a large Czech living in the next room who embraced a most unwilling me in the passage'); and even an

Sofka's letters to Jack were playful and passionate. While she was Owl ('rather evil, but soft and oh so wise,'), he was Goose or Mongoose. Her little sketches of a Piggoose and a Porcugoose were one way she expressed her discontent after he had been bad-tempered or hurtful to her.

attempted rape on a train near the Finnish frontier ('I did a sort of wild cat struggle, slapped his face hard, bit a hand and achieved liberty with virginity untouched'). Occasionally she made a small confession – 'I admit to getting kissed in the taxi. Sorry – please goose. I do tell you everything.'

Sofka was completely open with Jack about Dog, a.k.a. Ladislav Zizka. She met him in Prague in 1954 and he had been her lover when things got really bad with Nicky; her 1955 small pocket diary imparts mysterious clues:

30 Aug. Prague/Evening dog lead/Evening dog kennel
29 Sept. Arrive Prague Dog/Golden Tiger shut/Nice Dog
Notes.   Dog/Everything on Shakespeare/Bible in Tibetan

Dog was an interpreter and an official on Czech railways who shared Sofka's obsession with language and above all Shakespeare: for over thirty years they compared notes, swapped books, and founded a 'Golden Tiger' club at the eponymous pub in Prague, where members had to steal a small pub tray and read one Shakespeare play a year to join. The pair was also linked by their traumatic memories of war. Dog had undergone dreadful horrors after being arrested by the Gestapo while he was working for the Resistance. He was only a teenager when he was sent to Auschwitz and then Buchenwald and by an extraordinary fluke managed to escape the gas chambers twice. Although Sofka often told Jack about the significance of her friendship with Dog (perhaps occasionally hoping to provoke a little jealousy), she was careful to mention that even Dog was now turned away when he arrived in her room at night: 'He felt he had prior claim to a bit of bedding than any mongoose, whatever I felt about it! But was duly persuaded to the contrary. You know, it's strangely nice being so unwaveringly faithful in spite of all invitations to the contrary. Goose, I'm sure you've never influenced a life as much as you have mine – and remained untouched in the process, damn you!'

Sofka admitted that, despite her other admirers, she suffered debilitating insecurity when Jack was out of touch: 'Rationally,

I do not think you've been squashed by a bus, whipped off into a gas oven, or crashed in a flaming aircraft. But until I establish contact – even by the sending of an express letter – the panic is that of a nightmare . . . It is a pathological reaction which no reason can control . . . [because] all periods of happiness have ended in such misery that I am afraid, afraid of being hurt.'

Sofka's letters were not only about love. Many touched on politics, and she sent Jack books on subjects like the loss of working-class consciousness in capitalist society and frequently analysed the British Communist Party:

> I think it is the lack of honesty, this double think and
> double talk that has for the past 12 years been steadily
> developing in all our propaganda, in the D.W. [*Daily
> Worker*], that has lost us far more influence even than
> capitalist pressure . . . When the Soviet Union is attacked –
> physically or verbally – it is the first duty of any communist
> to leap to its defence. But lies are not a defence . . . We
> want a new approach from the leadership – an admission
> that mistakes can be made, have been made, will be made
> again; honesty and integrity of thought and action . . . And
> we should talk about the things people want in the kind of
> language they use, avoiding charming expressions like
> 'imperialist warmongers.' We must stop being self-righteous
> and condescending . . .
> But how to get all this???

This clear-sighted scepticism was surprisingly lacking, however, whenever Sofka witnessed the pomp and ceremony of Moscow's May Day celebrations: 'I wished that you had been here! That terrific parade, the surge of excitement and pride that rises in one, the feeling of intoxication that one is really a part of it, a part of that impulse towards Justice and socialism that I am so sure will one day rule . . .'

It was this optimism that kept Sofka going, but she was increasingly exhausted by her endless travelling for Prog T. Once, passing through Austria, Sofka remembered this same trip from her teenage years, when her mother had dragged her away from love and scandal in Rome: 'I've done this stretch in heat waves and been snowed up on it. And I don't like Vienna and Budapest has all my life been a place I go to when I want to be somewhere else . . . ' And worse than the journeys were the tourists, or 'subhumans': 'People wanting to go to Budapest, to Sofia, people wanting berths on Turkish boats and sleepers to Warsaw. Why the hell can't they all stay at home?'

Almost as bad were the groups of Russians, who now came on trips to England and had to be herded around from Buckingham Palace to Marx's grave and the British Museum. 'Russians are nice but they have no sense of humour. All is very, very solemn. And they never sleep. You'd die. They ask questions well into the night and are ready for more at 7 am . . . Enough of this infernal and eternal racketing.'

Sofka was still living in a bedsit (she had moved to 31 Norland Square in Holland Park) but she longed to set up home with Jack: 'It will all work out in time, love, and I'll become a placid and docile owl making no horrible shrieks and night noises that shatter your peace'. The opportunity came in 1960, when Patrick was twenty-one and came into a small Skipwith inheritance. He bought his mother a house in Shepherd's Bush, close to where Jack had always lived, and as 94 Frithville Gardens was large enough to let some rooms, Sofka nursed hopes that she might retire: 'After all, I've been earning my living now for 33 years and will soon need to be put out to grass.'

Her letters to Patrick indicate that, even if it was usually from a distance, she loved him and worried about him when he was abroad: 'You monstrous horror, you anti-pup, you revolting hound – no answer to 2 letters, my maternal heart beating anxiously as my imagination envisages you eaten by camels, swallowed by octopuses, engulfed in earthquakes, buried by avalanches and what have. And all the time you are comfortably (or not) in London or presumably cuddling warmly with Doreen . . . '

It was that year that my parents met. Sofka informed Patrick by letter of his older brother's developments: 'Peter is in love. She is sweet 17 and called Victoria. He is jobless, moneyless and in love. On Wednesday he goes with Victoria and Mama to Greece for six weeks. Thinks of marrying in a year and a half or so.' In fact, my parents married only months later. My mother never forgot being introduced to her future mother-in-law, as her twenty-seven-year-old fiancé had warned that she must curtsey before a Russian princess. Sofka roared with laughter at her son's practical joke as the blushing teenager attempted the obeisance, but she was always kind and friendly and got on with her youthful daughter-in-law. Photographs from my parents' wedding reception at the Ritz (after a Russian Orthodox ceremony), show Sofka looking matronly and stern, standing next to an even sterner Uncle Kyril, whom she hadn't seen since before the war.

A year later, I was born. I don't imagine that Sofka was particularly interested, despite my being named after her; there were already two young grandchildren from Ian and there was no escaping the fact that other people's babies bored her. Later, she was a magnificent grandmother, but almost any worthwhile relationship had to be negotiated through books. My mother remembered how Sofka once visited them in London and was thrilled to find her daughter-in-law sprawled on her bed at

11 a.m., reading a book. 'Oh,' she exclaimed with surprised pleasure, 'I didn't think you were the sort of person who would be reading at this time in the morning!' It cemented Sofka's friendship with Victoria, and when my parents were about to separate a decade or so later she tried to help in her typically frank manner.

'So, how's sex?' she asked. When Victoria's reply was 'Not so good,' Sofka offered a solution: 'How about drinking half a bottle of vodka and seeing what happens?' It was a recipe she had evidently used to good effect (could she have tried it with Leo when they struggled to resurrect their marriage?), but apparently it didn't appeal to my parents.

Frithville Gardens was Sofka's first home since her exile in 1919 that was not rented: 'It's an incredibly pleasant feeling to have one's own front door,' she wrote gratefully to Patrick. Even more significant was that Jack had committed himself to joining her and she joyously began signing her letters 'Marital Owl': 'I need you so much just now – it's a new life we're starting together – a life I hope will be permanent. It means more than I can tell you to build a home for us.'

However, for many of Sofka and Jack's friends and relations their moving in together was the first intimation that the two were actually a couple. Jack was notoriously private and colleagues of Sofka's at Prog T recalled that she had previously made disparaging comments about Jack, along the lines of 'If that man King rings up, I'm not here'. Some had the impression that the association was merely a convenient friendship ('I know that Jack was very useful on trips with things like luggage,' said one); and to many it was surprising that as sophisticated a woman as Sofka would choose someone like Jack. A close friend from that era added somewhat ironically: 'Jack looked an inconspicuous little fellow, but . . . Sofka said that he always wore short Y-fronts, and you know he was a great athlete. So maybe he had hidden strengths . . . '

Sofka herself was known to make chilly remarks about Jack, such as: 'Well, you have to have someone to say good-morning to.' Even worse, a letter to Patrick gave a treacherously offhand, inaccurate and uncharacteristically snobbish-sounding description of her beloved Mongoose: 'Jack King (my devoted prole) has given me his furniture and his money to buy more . . . ' If it hadn't been for Sofka's love letters, I would have understood something entirely different about this improbable liaison. Like many others, I would have assumed that Jack had pursued Sofka and that she had eventually given in and agreed to comfortable companionship. The evidence in her fervently needy correspondence told another story.

There was a housewarming party at 'Frith', as they called their house, where guests surreptitiously wiped dirt and mould off their mugs while they lined up to be served from a huge pot of soup – Sofka's housekeeping skills remained as dubious as ever. The couple was happy together, but Sofka's health was deteriorating as she suffered blackouts, bouts of angina and thyroid troubles. She visited her doctor and old friend Rachel Pinney, whom she had met in the Party in the 1940s and had joined in Peace Movement activities. A well-known eccentric and ardent feminist, Dr Pinney protested against nuclear weapons and had vowed that 'until the Bomb was Banned' she would keep silent one day a week, passing notes across to her patients instead of talking. Her order to 'take things easy' was just what Sofka needed. She had been longing to give up Prog T and try once more to acquire peace and a country garden. It was almost too good to be true when Jack announced that he too wanted to leave London.

CHAPTER 10

THE LITTLE FISHES

If you want to be happy for one day, get drunk;
If you want to be happy for three days, get married;
If you want to be happy for ever, get a garden.

— Chinese proverb

The hunt for a cottage began in 1962. Initially Sofka and Jack favoured Berkshire, but armed only with Jack's savings of £2,000, there was nothing suitable within their price range. 'Frith' would not be sold, as it would provide rental income on which to live, and supplement Sofka's small war widow's pension; Jack never got another job. The story goes that they kept moving westwards until they found something they could afford – a primitive stone cottage in the middle of Bodmin Moor, whose nearest village was Blisland. It was an auspicious name. In early December they sent their belongings down by lorry and, clutching the mops and buckets they'd used to clean Frith, the two set off to Cornwall by train.

It was the coldest winter in two centuries and England was almost paralysed by a freeze which lasted until March. I imagine they splashed out on a taxi at Bodmin Station and, still bearing their mops like spears, were driven across the white expanse of snow-bound moor. The narrow, walled lanes wound down to the hamlet of Bradford and their small granite house. Everything was frozen, motionless and muffled by snow. Even the kitchen's one tap was iced up, and for the next three months Jack had to bring water from the river in buckets, waiting each morning for the local farmer's tractor to arrive and break the ice for the cattle. Inside, the hideous yellow paint on the walls trickled with water when they lit fires, there was no electricity, and trips to the outside lavatory involved negotiating tangles of ice-covered nettles. But they were happy. Sofka wrote to Patrick soon after their arrival: '. . . This place is heaven – real heaven! No matter that lots has to be done and at the moment we struggle with fires and pressure lamps . . . Now the next thing is to get builders and plumbers onto the question of drains – baths.'

They cooked eggs and sausages on an ancient iron stove fuelled with twigs, and ignited oil lamps using whisky. Their isolation was barely broken apart from old Nehemiah, the postman, trudging across the snowy fields, and the moor ponies who passed by to drink at the waterhole. They had no car or phone, and it was many years before they gave in to family pressure and the vulnerability of age and acquired a telephone. It was a whole-hearted retreat.

In the spring, Sofka started work on the neglected garden – the beginning of one of her greatest sources of joy. She described her delight in some memoir notes: the contentment of 'rediscovering that sense of deep communication with the soil that I used to know in the hills above Nice or on the Wiltshire downs so long, long ago, when I would lie motionless, scarcely breathing, feeling myself an integral part of the earth with the force of nature around me'. Eventually, she acquired a small greenhouse, filling it with seedlings and delicate plants which she nurtured with true tenderness. Friends were given cuttings – one of them recently gave me a cutting from her strange, purple-leafed Tradescantia or Wandering Jew, which she had grown from Sofka's plants. It was almost like meeting someone Sofka had loved – I was careful to tend it well.

Jack, too, took to Cornish life, and in a letter to Patrick, Sofka sounded proud of how he was 'turning into the true countryman – doing miracles with complex tools and putting curtain runners up on stone walls, chopping firewood and grappling with compost heaps and blocks of granite'. In the hope of making some money, they built a henhouse in the field and bought three hundred chickens, but the thousands of eggs they sold only made £12 profit in the first year and the enterprise gradually wound down. However, they were almost self-sufficient in vegetables, which were eaten, preserved and frozen, along with pounds of raspberries and rhubarb. Soon after they had settled in, Peter sent his mother two young silver-grey 'blue' whippets, which eventually had puppies. For the next thirteen years Bradford Cottage was dominated by the needs of five sleekly elegant, wildly spoiled dogs. It was not lost on Sofka that whippets had been the favourite animals of her ancestor Catherine the Great, but far more significant was the impact of these much-loved creatures on her new life. They accompanied Jack and Sofka for long walks on the moor, snuggled up on sofas by the fire as they read, and were fed, cosseted and nursed in ways that Sofka's children might have envied. After all these years, 'the little fishes' had finally rewarded her with what she had been longing for: peace, roots, and companionship. Gradually, she even lost the fear that it would be taken away.

The couple embraced their rural isolation and at their relatively young ages (Jack was forty-five, Sofka nine years his senior) they settled into the sort of comfortable routines that

*Sofka, Jack and their whippets on Bodmin Moor. Settled and
happy at last, Sofka gave the five dogs more stability and
attention than she had ever provided for her children.*

they would keep for the next three decades. Naturally, they were
more energetic when they first arrived, but I don't think that
their early years in Cornwall were markedly different in
atmosphere to when I started to visit in the 1970s and on into
the '80s and '90s. Best of all for Sofka was having the time to
read: 'There can really be no greater adventures than the delight
of books – far more enduring really than those of the flesh!' she
wrote to a friend in London. She was perfectly content when
Bodmin Moor was awash with its frequent rainstorms, as they
gave her the excuse to do nothing but read: 'The joy of old age
when you don't feel guilty at doing nothing but sit with a hot
water bottle reading "frivolity" [Harold Acton's biography of
Nancy Mitford] – it is like champagne for breakfast.'

The mobile library brought her regular supplies and she was happy to take piles of what she called 'penny dreadfuls' – thrillers to read herself to sleep with – as well as the latest publications from London. She was constantly hungry for more, as she revealed in a letter to a friend, written when she was in her seventies:

> If you imagine that retirement enables you to read all the things you have always intended – how wrong you are. There are all the new things of interest to take up one's time – the biographies of the people whose books you have read – new writers (or new to me) such as Paul Scott, Fowles . . . so the prefaces to Shaw's plays remain unread, as do the works of Dickens that wait patiently on a shelf in my room . . . As for things like *Decline and Fall* or Herodotus . . . well . . . Time narrows perceptibly until I suppose the moment when it ceases to exist.

Spatial horizons also narrowed after the decades of travel. Both she and Jack occasionally took the train to London (usually separately), but were invariably thankful to return home. In 1964, Sofka did her last job for Progressive Tours, accompanying a group of Russian Shakespearian actors and scholars on a tour that included a meeting with Laurence Olivier. But it was a relief to see the back of the company that had dominated her life for so long. Although both she and Jack were still nominally Communists, they retained minimal links with the Party and were not interested in local activities. There were a few exceptions, such as the first issue of a socialist magazine, *Albanian Life*, which Sofka edited in the late sixties ('The works of Enver Hoxha are a great treasury of Marxism-Leninism and a sharp weapon in the hands of the working people of our country . . . ').

There were times, however, when they were forced to confront repercussions from their political beliefs. In 1966, George Blake, the notorious double-agent, escaped from Wormwood Scrubs and the entire country was on alert. He had been serving a forty-two-year sentence for passing on British secrets to the Soviet authorities and newspapers quickly reported that the KGB had probably whisked him away in a helicopter or submarine. It was horribly shocking for Sofka and Jack when police invaded their peaceful existence and searched their cottage for signs of Blake. It only emerged much later that acquaintances of Sofka's from the Peace Movement had been behind Blake's escape, smuggling him out of England in a camper van to East Berlin and then Moscow. So perhaps the police were on to something. Blake himself settled in the Soviet Union and always maintained similar thoughts on Communism to Sofka – that he had given his life to a noble ideal and a worthwhile experiment which hadn't succeeded. However, the whole story left an unpleasant taste for Sofka, especially after tabloid journalists turned up on her doorstep wanting details. In a letter to a friend in London, Sofka expressed her disgust with British hypocrisy: 'We talk of personal freedom – but what of "surveillance" and phone tapping? What sort of dossier do they have on me too with police here looking for George Blake? Privacy my foot. And this country is by far the most "free" of any. What an unpleasant creature is the human animal!'

On her sporadic expeditions to London Sofka would 'hold court', as one witness put it, at friends' houses. Dressed in her best black dress, feet used to boots and slippers squeezed into ladylike heels, she would smoke Gitanes and drink as much as she ever had. She visited favourite friends like Olivier's first wife, Jill Esmond, went to the theatre (Shakespeare if possible) and bought books. Occasionally she saw her sons and their families: by the end of the 1960s, Peter had three children and ran an electronic music studio from a garden shed by the river in Putney; Ian had three daughters and had become a bank manager; Patrick had two young children and was soon to be divorced and go to Saudi Arabia as a geologist. It was already obvious that Peter and Patrick had taken after their mother: their countless love affairs, their complicated routes through several marriages, their various careers and a phoenix-like ability to start all over again were familiar ground to her. She was far more taken aback that she of all people could have produced a son who ended up a bank manager. And it was certainly out of keeping with family tradition that Ian remained married to his first wife.

The sons helped Sofka financially and she sent letters, books and even hand-knitted toys for grandchildren at Christmas. But the truth was that she would far rather be talking about books or the past with her old friends than dandling noisy infants on her knee. Jack, in turn, would refer to 'the bloody family', and told friends that he was not invited up to London to stay when Sofka went. He had the impression that he was not accepted by the three sons and their offspring, and it wasn't really until Sofka died that their affection for him made him realize how significant a member of the wider family he had become. Perhaps in the early days there *was* some resistance to Sofka's 'devoted prole'; she herself made little effort to bridge the gap between her already distant sons and Jack's stand-offish, self-contained nature. Few outsiders understood the bonds that formed the basis of their relationship.

* * *

In 1967, aged sixty, Sofka began writing her memoirs, using notes she'd jotted down during her first visits to Leningrad a decade or so before. 'The writing itself was cathartic,' she wrote later. 'It somehow smoothed, if not erased, the cruel edges of the war years, as though letting some of the poison of bitterness escape.' The book, *Sofka: The Autobiography of a Princess*, described her life up to the age of forty and was published by Rupert Hart-Davis. The cover featured an Easter-egg pendant that the Dowager Empress had given her during their flight from Russia, and which against all odds had survived and still remains in the family. The glamorous London launch party in 1968 was attended by old theatre friends like Sybil Thorndike, Edith Evans and Jill Esmond; Olivier sent a congratulatory telegram regretting his absence due to rehearsals; even Dog managed to come from the chaotic violence of Soviet-occupied Prague. Favourable reviews followed, Sofka appeared on radio and television, and she received a flurry of letters: a midshipman from HMS *Marlborough*; acquaintances from 1930s cocktail parties; women who knew her in Vittel; and even an anonymous note from a forgotten flirtation ('What a marvellous surprise to see you and hear you ... Lovely memories of Hamburg 1945. Officers Mess. I wonder if you remember. Bless you darling').

Having spent a lifetime facing instability, change, loss and fear, Sofka now rooted herself firmly into her Bodmin refuge. She had routines, around which everyone had to fit; visitors were welcomed warmly, and left with books and freshly picked vegetables, but if they were even ten minutes late they were scolded; invitations to lunch or drinks were frequently given with a departure time. When cut flowers were brought as a present, she was not diplomatic: 'corpses of flowers', she'd remark caustically. Some observers thought she treated Jack with a lack of respect, ordering him around and dominating conversations from her armchair, as if from a throne, while he sat quietly in his chair in the corner, providing precise dates when called upon. There were even people who were so thrown by the surprising match that they questioned whether the two were actually a couple. 'Perhaps Jack was her gardener?' someone suggested. But there were close friends who grasped the balanced strength of their quiet bond, and there on a shelf looking down at everything was a large collection of owls – a testament to the couple's early years together and the depth of Owl's love for Mongoose.

The eccentric Russian princess in old gumboots and scruffy clothes was quickly known on the moor: she was kind to local people, handing out books, help, food and even lessons to children. But woe betide them if they visited her between two and four, when she napped, or when she was watching tennis on television – a great passion. A retired colonel who lived close by once came around to apologize as his dogs had just killed her old goose in the field. Unfortunately it was during the middle of a match at Wimbledon. Rather than requesting that they speak later, Sofka roared, 'Go 'way!' rather as she had in her garret at Vittel when suffering from neuralgia. The colonel was so offended that he never spoke to her again. Perhaps this finicky quibbling and tendency to lash out was a sign of Sofka's lingering insecurity, but it is equally possible that she was merely taking on some of the autocratic ways of her grandmother.

Friends and relations came to stay in greater numbers, especially after a bathroom was installed in the old dairy and the cottage became increasingly snug. Apart from some privileged favourites – Rabbit, in particular – guests were given a strict programme, which allowed Sofka and Jack's lives to continue as undisturbed as possible. Breakfast in bed was obligatory – a tray with boiled eggs, buttered toast, marmalade and a pot of strong tea (Earl Grey mixed with Indian for the perfect blend). This was followed, irrespective of weather, by an obligatory day out.

Nobody was allowed back until late afternoon, when there would be hours of talk by the fire, with Jack's home-made wine. Provocation was still her speciality. Once, a nineteen-year-old relation arrived and was dumbfounded when Great-Aunt Sofka asked her whether she'd ever had sex. Ignoring the young woman's embarrassment, she said, 'It's the greatest thing there is,' and described the numerous lovers she had enjoyed on trips to Russia. She recommended her tested method of contraception: 'Use the cap, darling! It's something you can take in and out.' But visitors were also told about her extraordinary childhood and shown photographs of pre-Revolutionary Russian splendour, and one friend was surprised that a Communist so evidently enjoyed getting out *Debrett's* to exhibit the Skipwith entry, complete with Sir Patrick and her own name nestled close to Grey's.

Sofka produced predominantly Russian food for her visitors: salmon *koulibiac*, as she had eaten in the 1930s at the Hungaria; *bitki* (rissoles) with soured cream and mushrooms, as she'd cooked during the Depression, when married to Leo; ham in Madeira, which had been the celebratory dish served after Laurence Olivier's first night as Hamlet; borscht, based on her post-war Chelsea soup days; little *pirozhki* pies (her neighbours called them 'perishing skis') using cabbage from the garden; and sweet, fruity *kissel*, which reminded her of the nursery and her old *niania* in Petersburg. The kitchen was kept in an increasingly spectacular state of squalor, and although the food which emerged was usually richly delicious, certain squeamish guests wondered whether food poisoning might not be the inevitable price to pay. One friend believed that this unashamed dirt and disorder was a reflection of Sofka's instinctive grandeur: 'It was an aristocratic thing – you don't bother about little things like hygiene.'

Sofka and Jack's lack of money never prevented food being a priority, to be provided for guests in generous quantities. It seemed a natural development when Sofka decided to write a cookery book, *Eat Russian*, which was published in 1973, dedicated 'To Jack, who tasted'. All her favourite recipes were included, but there were many that sounded like distant memories of childhood feasts, or something plucked from aged books, rather than practical food. Did she really give Jack sweetbreads with crayfish and roast veal with caviare sauce? And what about bear, which must be marinated for at least four days, then braised for five to six hours?

This was the era that I remember – the 1970s, when I started to visit my grandmother, something which evidently did not fill her with enthusiasm when it involved family hordes, as she admitted to a London friend, Barbara Oliver: 'Gradual recovery from earlier invasion – Ian and his friends . . . Now quiet for a fortnight until son Peter arrives with his brood. I enjoy sons but it's their wives and children that fill the air space!'

It sometimes seemed as though Sofka disapproved of even discussing children; one woman friend (who had a young son and daughter) recalled how 'You didn't talk about children, just as you didn't talk about money – she'd look at you as if you'd said something vulgar.' Still, Sofka could grant grudging approval: 'That horrible man Evelyn Waugh says in one of his letters: "The oftener I see other people's children, the less I dislike my own." Surprising thing about Peter is how nice the children are!'

Later on, she established real friendships with some of her grandchildren, including me, but we had to earn it. When we did, the rewards were great: memorable visits to Bodmin on our own, marvellous letters and inspirational reading-lists. Sofka was delighted when Ian's oldest daughter, Fiona, emerged as a rebellious young woman, who rejected her father's 'safe' ways. It appeared that she was following in her grandmother's footsteps, as she went on CND marches, set off for long travels and had a baby without marrying. 'What's the point of getting married?' Sofka would say challengingly, proud that she and Jack had not followed convention.

Like her grandchildren, Sofka's sons could never be certain of their mother's appreciation, though occasionally she revealed her pride, almost in spite of herself. This was particularly true when she believed they had adopted her values, and her comments to Barbara about her oldest son could almost have been applied to herself and Jack: 'How nice that you both like Peter and their type of life. Really they demand little – books and music – growing things – friends, but not bothered about cars and clothes and other "moneyed" things in any way. Far less than Patrick who likes to spend or Ian who seeks "bargains" and tells you how he gets boxes of stuff on the cheap. How utterly different siblings can be.'

> Who was it – some wise biblical prophet – who set life's span at 3 score and ten? Well he was right because however long you live it is at that age that you feel things really give – memory . . . knees . . . eyes . . . etc etc. It really is quite definite and like the village ancient 'sometimes I sits and thinks and sometimes I just sits' – well I have now understood the 'just sits' part of it.

By the 1980s, Sofka began to suffer the physical punishments of age, confessing it in letters to friends like Barbara: 'Stiff, gout, aching, but think if it was brain rather than leg – one can but thank the gods!' Her seventieth and eightieth birthdays were celebrated in brave attempts at family get-togethers at her sons' houses: at the first, too much was drunk; the three sons sparred, wrestled and bickered as they had as children; and screaming teenage granddaughters were chased by their unsuitably enthusiastic uncles. At the second, there were too many current and ex-daughters-in-law for comfort but Sofka put on a brave face. After all, she'd seen a lot in her life, hadn't held back on the drink herself and would soon be going back to Cornwall. Increasingly, she preferred to stay at home, where she read constantly and (after the dogs died) took to adopting whatever wild animal or bird accepted her hospitality. In a typical early-morning letter to Barbara she wrote, 'Time to get up and feed Ediepuss (uneducated wild cat, he can't spell) who has hurt his front paw . . . No question of being tamed. It shelters in the coal shed snug on the sacks and yells for food and milk to be brought to it in bed . . . '

Of all the elements in Sofka's life which gained in stature as she aged, it was the war that loomed largest. Like many old people she was increasingly preoccupied by memories of her younger self, but her experiences from 1939 to 1945 encapsulated most of the elements that came to define her: her love for Grey; his death; her burgeoning faith in Communism; and her horror at the Holocaust. It was only Rabbit who still shared this catalytic period with her and they both kept it alive in their weekly letters and regular meetings. Rabbit often stayed at Bradford Cottage for several days and the two old friends would sit reading English and Russian poetry as they had in Vittel. The younger woman had remained remarkably unchanged in forty years; only her tidy bob was now grey and the profile of her round cheeks somewhat softer. It was Sofka who had changed physically, with her unkempt grey hair pinned loosely in a bun and her nonchalantly large, bra-less figure in clothes which were now merely functional. But none of that counted for either woman.

By the time Sofka was eighty, memories of the past had become increasingly significant. In particular, the war and the Holocaust represented pivotal experiences in shaping her character and values and anyone who visited would leave with books, papers or poems connected to this era.

At the core of the two ageing women's long intimacy was their continuing preoccupation, even obsession, with the Holocaust. Sofka had amassed a huge collection of Holocaust-related publications and nurtured a torturing sense of guilt that she had not been able to avert the tragedy she witnessed at Vittel.

This pain was central to Sofka's sense of herself and the life she now looked back on. And if Darling had inspired her to a greater emotional understanding, it was the broader picture that mattered; she never revealed her private loss. 'Now we are the ones who read all the books about the camps, about the ghettoes,' she wrote. 'We, who did not actually endure it, feel the burden more than those who did. They suffered and shared. We failed either to suffer or to prevent suffering.' This, she said, was the heaviest aftermath of the war. But, she argued, 'One owes it to them never to let oneself forget.' And she didn't let others forget either. If the horrors of the concentration camps are said to affect the generations that follow the victims, then the descendants of witnesses also carry a small portion of that burden. Visitors of all ages left the cottage laden with books and photocopied articles from Sofka's archives and her letters were full of references to Holocaust research and literature.

It was in 1980 that Rabbit discovered the fate of Vittel's Poles, while looking through the official records for transportations. Their names were there in a 1944 convoy for Auschwitz from the Drancy transit camp outside Paris. Rabbit told Sofka that the Poles had all been shot on arrival, after a woman bit the hand of a Nazi officer – 'surely a death more merciful than the march to the gas chambers, the suffocation by Cyklon B', wrote Sofka. Perhaps Rabbit had been protecting Sofka, however, as I came across another, more detailed version, by Filip Müller in *Eyewitness in Auschwitz*. He was a *Sonderkommando* – an inmate working on crematorium duty – when the Vittel prisoners were taken to the changing rooms. As they were undressing, a strikingly glamorous woman (Franciszka Mann, a former dancer) distracted the guards by launching into a striptease. Standing half-naked, she lifted her foot to remove her shoe, and slammed its heel into an SS officer's forehead. She then grabbed his pistol, and as panic took hold amongst the guards, fired the gun and escaped into the crowd. The lights were switched off, most of the guards somehow escaped through the door and panic set in amongst the bewildered people, who couldn't understand what was happening. 'We have valid entry visas for Paraguay,' shouted one terrified man. 'And we paid the Gestapo a great deal of money to get our exit permits.' The door eventually opened, to the glare of spotlights, the crematorium workers were called out and 'steel-helmeted SS men were lying ready to operate the machine guns'. Those who weren't mown down immediately were seized afterwards and shot. I'm glad Sofka never learned these details of what were almost certainly Darling's final moments.

In 1985 Sofka received a letter from Dr Abraham Oppenheim, an academic at the London School of Economics, who was writing a book. 'My research concerns a remarkable and unique exchange which took place during World War II, of a group of over 200 Jewish concentration camp victims ... against a similar number of German internees from Palestine ... The evidence seems to suggest that your efforts were instrumental in causing official pressure to be brought to bear on the Germans ...' He explained how during his research in Foreign Office archives he kept coming across a mysterious Mrs Skipwith, who seemed to have contributed significantly to the fact that over fifty of the Vittel deportees had been serendipitously plucked out of the system and joined the group of 222 European Jews who went to Palestine.

'For a long time I had wondered what might have become of Mrs Skipwith,' Oppenheim wrote in his book *The Chosen People: The Story of the '222 Transport' from Bergen-Belsen to Palestine*, published after Sofka's death. Having traced so many threads in the bizarre story of his Dutch-Jewish mother's family and their improbable release from Bergen-Belsen, he was determined to find Mrs Skipwith. His initial assumptions were that this campaigner with contacts in surprisingly high places must have been Jewish. Why else would she have taken such an interest? This theory collapsed when he located some Skipwiths in the phone directory and someone suggested *Debrett's*. It wasn't long before an increasingly intrigued Oppenheim was travelling down to Bodmin Moor to see Sofka.

Bram, as Oppenheim was henceforth known throughout a lasting friendship, told Sofka the strange story of the exchange in which his mother's family had been saved. It had occurred just as Sofka was making her own winding train journey across Europe, returning home from Vittel, in July 1944. What she had never known was how her desperate requests to prominent people in the Foreign Office, the Home Office and the Red Cross *had* actually made a difference. Bram brought photocopies of Sofka's letters and the subsequent official comments and explained how everything had ultimately been down to the German insistence on lists; Sofka had been absolutely correct to believe that naming everyone had been the best chance. It was lists that determined why a few with Palestinian papers lived while most had died. And when certain authorities (such as the Swiss, the British Foreign Office and the High Commissioner for Palestine) managed to pressurize the Germans into releasing a few terrorized people out of concentration camps, it was all on the basis of lists. Among the photocopies was one of the cigarette papers which Sofka had used in Vittel to write the names of every Polish Jew in the camp and which had been smuggled across Europe in capsules and toothpaste tubes by the Resistance. There, in microscopic letters, were all the names, listed under the South American countries whose visas they held. Under Honduras was Izidor Skossowski – Darling – and his family, filed in the Public Record Office in Kew, ref. FO 371/42871.

At a time when Sofka was feeling her age increasingly and her life was becoming much quieter than before, it was overwhelming to be confronted so tangibly with her painful past in Vittel. Oppenheim's research reopened wounds, but it also affirmed this intense part of her life. Later that year, she received an unexpected letter from Israel and turned to Bram for an explanation.

'Well now,' he replied, 'about that letter from Jerusalem. Yes I confess it is in a sense my doing, but I had no idea they would write to you. Yad Vashem, the Holocaust Remembrance institute, over the years had done its best to honour those who stood up for the Jews during the war. They use an unfortunate term, calling them "the righteous" but the intention is good . . . ' He explained how 'even at this late date', he wanted her and Rabbit's good works to be acknowledged. Sofka herself replied to Yad Vashem's enquiries saying, 'Sadly, my efforts in the Internment Camp of Vittel did not succeed in saving Jewish lives, but I feel proud to be among those who attempted.'

Yad Vashem's decision came too late for Sofka; she had been dead for several years when they finally decided to carve her name on the lists of those who risked their lives to help Jews during the Holocaust. Rabbit had campaigned with Oppenheim to make it happen, and but for her modesty and certain awkward bureaucratic rules (Yad Vashem insists on eye-witness accounts), she would certainly have been rewarded too. Jack and Rabbit appointed me as Sofka's representative, even though I was living in Rome at the time. An official from the Israeli Embassy came to my apartment with Sofka's medal in an olive-wood case and I invited a few close friends, laid on some Russian *zakusky* and iced vodka, and arranged some photographs and memorabilia from Sofka's life. It was a strange little ceremony. There was a sense of it having come too late – that Sofka had been cheated of seeing her medal by red tape – but I suspect it would not really have changed much for her. As for me, I was only too aware of the irony of being given a humanitarian award by a country that was behaving so brutally and inhumanly to the Palestinians. But despite all this, and even though I still had no idea about Darling, it was a terribly touching moment. Over half a century after the dreadful events that wrenched Sofka's life apart, something had been completed.

* * *

By the late 1980s, Sofka was a great-grandmother, and what she called 'the ravages of age' meant that life wasn't always easy. 'I try to believe that age is mostly a matter of mind,' she wrote. 'If you don't mind, it doesn't matter. But . . . ' She was always able to poke fun at herself, as she proved in a chirpy poem, 'Life at Eighty-one':

The legs that once strode over Byron's Albania
Now quiver and ache at two metres from home!
My mind sinks deep into fumbling senilia
As I hunt for my glasses through room after room.

Fingers drop cups and my eyes are weakening –
Arthritis, sciatica pains are severe –
Effort exhausts. I drowse morning and evening –
What's happened today is already unclear.

All of no matter! Life is still glorious –
Book-laden shelves offer treasure in store!
The garden is bird-filled; friends come to visit us.
Stillness. Content. And the winds of the moor.

The remarks about life still being glorious were quite true. She and Jack were happy with the existence they had created, whatever the inconveniences of old age. She had proved to him that she would stick around if she was given the opportunity, and the couple basked in their quiet equilibrium.

Jack was with Sofka when she died of heart failure in February 1994, aged eighty-six. Her sons celebrated one of her favourite Chinese aphorisms ('If you have money for two loaves, buy one and flowers') and placed a loaf of bread and a bunch of flowers on her coffin. She was cremated and the ashes spread in her garden.

Sofka had ended up with a life that was impossible to imagine when she was a child. Time and again what appeared an inevitable future was shattered and she had to move on, grasping at whatever she could. Although she rejected the values with which she had been brought up, she always recognized where she had come from.

Some years after she gave me her Parisian diary, my grandmother related a dream she'd had. It concerned me, she explained. She had promised me to write down the lives of Sophy, her mother, and Olga, her paternal grandmother, and to continue her own memoirs. She proceeded to work on these three lives, calling them *Prelude to Revolution*, *Victim of Revolution* and *Sequel to Revolution*, and even entered into ultimately unsuccessful negotiations with a publisher.

Sofka's narrowing horizons sent her attention back into the past and her late writing transported her to her own childhood, but also far beyond, to her mother's youth at the turn of the twentieth century and further back to the mid-nineteenth century, when her grandmothers were born. Sitting at her typewriter in the small Cornish house, memories rose to the surface as though time had compressed. It became strangely easier to conjure up what Olga had told her of a childhood in the dazzling Shuvaloff Mansion on the Fontanka canal than it was to remember to pay the gas bill or who was coming to lunch. Her grandmother's words returned with clarity: images of her first balls in the Winter Palace, aged only sixteen; rooms decorated with orchids from the imperial hothouses; and ceilings so high that they seemed to vanish in gloom above the candles. It was as effortless to picture herself lying on her mother's rose-coloured bedcover, hearing about the battles in 1915, as it was to recall the desolation of being parted from Grey in 1940. On the cusp of infinity it only required a small step to envisage her great-great-grandmother La Belle Greque, the Constantinople slave-girl, and her conquest of Europe's male hearts.

The world to which these women had belonged was barely any stranger than that into which Sofka herself was born. But she had more in common with them than just the lacy dresses, velvet-coated diaries and carriage rides by the Neva; they were also courageous and resolute, each in her own way. It was this legacy that counted most to Sofka – far more than what she saw as the absurd privilege. Above all, it was the sense of searching and seeking, which she always believed should be the most important thing in life. 'It doesn't matter what you seek,' she said, 'or how hard the disappointment is.' There was a Kipling poem she liked to quote, which she said had inspired her since her youth:

> *Because I sought, I sought it so*
> *And spent my days to find –*
> *It blazed one moment e'er it left*
> *The blacker night behind.*

ACKNOWLEDGEMENTS

Agreat number of people helped me with this book. Some of them are mentioned in the text, but many are not and I have changed a few names to protect privacy. I am deeply indebted to Kyril Zinovieff for his generosity, wisdom and love, even when it was difficult. Madeleine Steinberg was also a wonderful source of information and support from beginning to end.

Some of my relations made invaluable contributions to my search. In particular, I thank Peter Zinovieff; Ian Fitzlyon; Patrick Skipwith; Elena de Villaine; Egerton and Deirdre Skipwith; Victoria Zinovieff; Fiona Zinovieff; Jenny Hughes and Jenny Zinovieff.

For catching up with Sofka's trail in France, I am deeply grateful to Shula Troman; David and Marjorie Rocheman; and Raymonde Dubois. In Russia, the following people were especially helpful: Valeria Kobets; Olga Pishenkova; Andrei and Tatyana Gagarin; Ekaterina Gerasimova; Marina Vershevskaya; Anna Abramovna; Galina Filatova; Natalya Kushmelyova; Lev Baron; Tanya Illingworth; Prodromos Teknopoulos and Sebastian Zinovieff.

Many thanks to Annelise Freisenbruch, for her wonderful archive work and to the following for all their help: Lou and Rafa Kenton; Anne Hendrie; Margaret Jarvis; Barbara Oliver; Jean Cardy; Peter Rosenfield; Sonia Goodman; Tarquin Olivier;

Tina Tarling; Phyllis Birchall; Angela Thompson; Ann Wilson; Dot and Ray Hunt; Terry Coleman; Jane Whitely; Sheena Hilleary; Marina Lermontov; H. N. Mottershead; Rosemary Wells; Alexandre Dolgorouky; Nikita Dolgorouky; Anna Greening; Prunella Power; Peyton Skipwith; the late Audrey Negretti; David Suckling; Shura Shivarg; Alessandra Stanley and Peter Carson.

I am enormously grateful to Adam Nicolson, for his help with the manuscript, and to Fiammetta Rocco, Fani Papageorgiou and Cressida Connolly. Many, many thanks to my agent, Caroline Dawney, and her assistant, Jean Edelstein. Also to Sajidah Ahmad, Bella Shand and everyone at Granta.

I am especially grateful to George Miller – a marvellous editor. I have been particularly lucky to work with him.

Love and gratitude to my husband, Vassilis, and our daughters, Anna and Lara, for everything.

A Note on Sources

This is not a scholarly book and I will not give a full bibliography. However, I would like to provide a short list of books which were particularly useful in my research:

Anna Akhmatova, *The Complete Poems of Anna Akhmatova*, trans. by Judith Hemschemeyer, ed. by Roberta Reeder (Edinburgh, 1997)

Miss M. Bayliss, *Unpublished memoir 1940–44*, Archives of the Imperial War Museum

Nina Berberova, *The Italics Are Mine* (New York, 1992)

Nina Berberova, *Moura: The Dangerous Life of Baroness Budberg* (New York, 2005)

Varvara Dolgorouky, *Gone Forever* (Unpublished memoir)

A. P. Herbert, *Holy Deadlock* (London, 1934)

Richard Holmes, *Footsteps: Adventures of a Romantic Biographer* (London, 1995)

Alan Moorehead, *The Russian Revolution* (London, 1958)

Dimitri Obolensky, *Bread of Exile* (London, 1999)

Vice-Admiral Sir Francis Pridham, *Close of a Dynasty* (London, 1958)

Simon Sebag Montefiore, *Prince of Princes: The Life of Potemkin* (London, 2000)

Abraham Shulman, *The Case of Hotel Polski* (New York, 1982)

Sofka Skipwith, *Sofka: The Autobiography of a Princess* (London, 1968)

Norman Stone and Michael Glenny, *The Other Russia* (London, 1990)

Tibor Szamuely, *The Russian Tradition* (London, 1974)

John Van der Kiste and Coryne Hall, *Once a Grand Duchess: Xenia, Sister of Nicholas II* (London, 2002)

Joseph Vecchi, *The Tavern Is my Drum* (London, 1948)

Solomon Volkov, *St Petersburg: A Cultural History* (London, 1996)

William Wiser, *The Crazy Years: Paris in the Twenties* (London, 1983)

Princess Peter Wolkonsky, *The Way of Bitterness* (London, 1931)

Felix Youssoupoff, *Lost Splendour* (New York, 1953)

Elizabeth Zinovieff, *A Princess Remembers: A Russian Life* (London, 2001)

Kyril Zinovieff and Jenny Hughes, *The Companion Guide to St Petersburg* (Woodbridge, 2003)